W9-DBN-017

ANTHROPOLOGY TOWARD HISTORY

Anthropology

CULTURE AND WORK IN A 19TH-CENTURY

WESLEYAN UNIVERSITY PRESS

toward History

MAINE TOWN / BY RICHARD P. HORWITZ

MIDDLETOWN, CONNECTICUT

The publisher gratefully acknowledges the support of the publication of this book by the John Anson Kittredge Educational Fund and by the Andrew W. Mellon Foundation.

Library of Congress Cataloging in Publication Data

Horwitz, Richard, 1949–
Anthropology toward history.

Bibliography: p.
Includes index.
1. Winthrop, Me.—Civilization. 2. Winthrop, Me. —Occupation. I. Title.
F29.W9H67 974.1'6 77-74560
ISBN 0-8195-5014-0

Manufactured in the United States of America
First edition

It is often an object of wonder to me to behold the differences among mankind, and the versatility of characters with which we are surrounded. Any one who is fond of observation, may find a variety of wit, humor, propensities and inclinations to amuse his imagination his whole "life long" within the confines of a single country town. He will ever find something to admire, and certainly enough to abhor. Indeed within a little atmosphere consisting of only a few thousand inhabitants, and with those favors of Nature incident to the picturesque scenery of Maine, one might study the WORLD in miniature. . . . The little COMMUNITY AROUND US with its varied and ever changing appearances gives UBIQUITY to the mind.

— Letter from Ralph of Winthrop, *Maine Farmer,* November 21, 1834

Winthrop is a fine town. Oh!, of course, but it isn't the world.

— Letter from Samuel L. Clark in Bangor to the Clark family in Winthrop, November 11, 1849

Contents

Figures & Maps

Preface

The history of this book, like that of so many books with academic authors, begins with university experiences, influential teachers, students, and texts. It begins, too, with dissatisfaction. I have been a student in American studies, a field whose foundations, laid in the early 1950s, crumbled in the late 1960s. Classic pieces on American "myths and symbols" lost credibility, and American studies lost its center.

I was fortunate to have teachers who encouraged me and others of my generation to develop a better approach to the description of American cultures. My friends turned to popular or mass culture materials, cliometrics, new journalism, various forms of structuralism, cultural ecology and geography, psychohistory, folklore, and so on. I wish I could say that my approach was systematically culled from the alternatives. But a more likely source is the particular sequence of ideas and advocates that I encountered during my graduate days at the University of Pennsylvania.

I was early impressed with what were known as the *new ethnography* and the *new social history*. The first tended to be crudely idealistic and synchronic, and the second naively realistic and diachronic, but both, I felt, held promise. In fashioning a synthesis I sought new friends among the historians in College Hall and the anthropologists at the University Museum.

I am particularly indebted to University of Pennsylvania Professors John Caughey, Gordon Kelley, Melvyn Hammarberg, Patrick Malone, and Robert Zemsky in American civilization, Richard Beeman in history, and Ward Goodenough, Igor Kopytoff, and Anthony

Wallace in anthropology. It was Tony Wallace who directed most of my graduate research. Help also came from Maine historian Ronald Banks of the University of Maine, James Spradley of Macalester College, and Professors Harvey Sarles and Mischa Penn of the University of Minnesota. My wife, Noni, helped in ways that I cannot begin to detail. I also want to acknowledge the generous financial assistance of the University of Pennsylvania and the John Anson Kittredge Educational Fund. These and many other teachers and friends are owed my thanks (and apologies in so far as I have misapplied their help). I hope that I have not just borrowed from but contributed to all the fields concerned.

I still have difficulty locating this work in a particular discipline. This is in part because I have tried to make a wholly positive statement—no surveys of the literature or harangues about "where we've gone wrong." "We," then, remains rather loosely defined.

Most of all, I wanted to put together a descriptive theory, method, and application. Too often, I believe, all these levels of analysis fall victim to the academic division of labor. Accomplishments at one level pass but slowly to the next. People who are more empirically inclined may rightly ask, "Sure, it's sensible, but will it work?" I have tried to keep the skeptics in mind. Chapters 1–3 are intended to argue for the approach, to explain that it should work, while chapters 4–10 are to show that, in fact, it does. Nonetheless, each section should stand on its own. At the very least, for example, I hope that readers can learn something of workaday life in a nineteenth-century town.

But there is more than an academic story to be told. I spent nearly three years in the Winthrop area preparing this book and falling in love with Maine. "Home" for Noni and me is still our place in Wayne, on Winthrop's northwest border. As I reread these pages, I recall the joys of the hunt: hitchhiking to assorted libraries and archives, poring over old diaries and photos, and rummaging through basements, attics, and closets wherever "old Stuff" was rumored to lie.

The most fun, I suppose, was tracing the rumors themselves. At least part of each working day was dedicated to chats in the kitchen, parlor, or barnyard over innumerable doses of coffee, tea, and beer. I am ever grateful to the people of Winthrop for trusting me with their heritage, but I am even more grateful for their friendship. I want in particular to thank Mary Oatway and Dorothy Irish, who shared their life's work in Winthrop history; Sue Thomas and the town officers, who helped me scour the town records; the Foster and Cobb families, who allowed me to borrow their remarkable collection of old papers; Carleton Woolen and Engineer Shepard, who despite insurance regulations showed me about the old mill; and the Reverend Messrs. Misner, Estes, Tuttle, and Palmer, who guided me through local religious history. I was blessed with the recollections of Mrs. and Mr. H. Clair Miller, Alice Whiting, Eleanor Bailey, Arline Lovejoy, Harriet McCroary, and many others. Credit for initiating many of these friendships belongs to Doris Dow, librarian for Winthrop's Charles M. Bailey Public Library. She eased every phase of my work in the community, a warm and trusting companion through the best and worst of times. A special word is due Mom and Charles Foster, who first welcomed me to Maine. I remember their words of encouragement that first winter, by the fieldstone fireplace in their log house on Lovejoy Pond. I only wish they had lived to see this work complete and the lovely autumn Maine enjoys almost every year.

In short, despite the admonitions of my colleagues about wandering from the major collections or entering Yankee-dom as an outsider, I found plenty of help and damn-near too much material. Noni and I learned how to find fiddleheads, handle a splitting mall, dance a "Lady of the Lake," prune tomatoes, catch sheep, and jig for salmon. We learned the true meaning of "cold" and how to "get by." But most of all we made friends that we will not soon forget. They more than anyone have taught us about living in America.

ANTHROPOLOGY TOWARD HISTORY

CHAPTER I

A Theory of Description

Let us begin with a simple question: What were Americans like in the early nineteenth century? Surely there is something about their tracts, sermons, and political speeches that sounds typically nineteenth century. But what is that something? Who, indeed, were the people that historians have come to know as "common folk" in "the age of Jackson"?[1]

My answer should comprise a thorough, accurate description of Americans, here the members of a New England community, living between 1820 and 1850. It should, in particular, be a humane and credible account. My methods should be those that most systematically avoid bias in fact or interpretation. Yet the pursuit of veracity should go far beyond checking the reliability of evidence. One must, of course, begin any research with a verification of the origin, form, purpose, and context of each source, but this hardly guarantees a singular interpretation of its content. Though the Constitution is a "reliable" piece of legal evidence, we have been disagreeing about what it says for two hundred years. Individuals at various times have found contradictory "facts" in what is ostensibly the same source. Who is right? Which is the more credible account?

This is a problem for historians as well as the Supreme Court; it is a problem for social scientist and humanist, alike.[2] No version of what "really" occurred can be defended without an explication of what the word "really" means, how to distinguish fact from fiction.

My position is that, insofar as there is a singular truth, it belongs only to an omniscient observer. The only "facts" apparent to the mortal are those referenced to an implicit or explicit theory of truth. Since most learning takes place in social interaction and since group members tend to agree on what constitutes fact, I assume a social construction of reality.[3] People faced with (what is to the omniscient observer) a single object or event may with equal rigor and "objectivity" disagree on what it is.[4]

I have neither the space nor the expertise to defend this position on philosophical grounds, but the cross-cultural experience seems sufficient basis for its assumption. Note, for instance, Irving A. Hallowell's observation in the mid-1950s that the Northern Ojibwa do not distinguish animate and inanimate objects, at least not as we do. "Persons," they say, may include what we call animals or stones as well as human beings. Would, then, a "factual" sociology of the Ojibwa include stones and animals?[5] Historians face the same difficult question. They are, after all, also studying foreign societies, less exotic, but nonetheless different from their own. To posit historical fact is to specify a perspective.

Among the many perspectives available to the social analyst, there are two sets that offer the clearest alternatives, one's own and the subject's. In the Ojibwa example, "real persons" are humans for the sociologist, while they are humans and nonhumans for the Ojibwa.[6] The naive assertion that one definition is more "factual" than the other carries broad implications. A simple description of "what people do" will be most directly affected by whose definition of "people" is used.

The work of Kenneth Pike greatly clarifies the issues involved in choosing a perspective. He begins with the familiar distinction between phonetics and phonemics in linguistics. (Phon*emics* refers to the sounds recognized and used by a particular language group, while phon*etics* refers to the sounds used by all the world's groups.) By analogy Pike outlines what he calls "etic and emic standpoints for the description of behavior." Put too simply, etics are facts for the analyst, while emics are facts for the subjects.[7] In this sense an etic sociology of the Ojibwa would be a study of "persons" as we, a society of Western scholars, define them, and an emic sociology would be a study of "persons" as the Ojibwa define them.

Though the two forms are not dichotomous, Pike explains, an etic description, be it linguistic, sociological, or historical, differs profoundly from an emic one. He outlines the following principal differences between an etic and an emic approach:

1. CROSS-CULTURAL VERSUS SPECIFIC. An etic approach is comparative in that similar phenomena are recognized in different societies. An emic approach is subject-specific in that different phenomena are discovered in different societies.
2. UNITS AVAILABLE IN ADVANCE VERSUS DETERMINED DURING ANALYSIS. An etic approach defines phenomena before beginning research. An emic approach discovers phenomena through research.
3. CREATION VERSUS DISCOVERY OF A SYSTEM. An etic approach organizes phenomena a priori. An emic approach organizes phenomena a posteriori.
4. EXTERNAL VERSUS INTERNAL VIEW. An etic approach introduces phenomena of interest to the subject matter. An emic approach learns phenomena of interest from the subjects.
5. EXTERNAL VERSUS INTERNAL PLAN. An etic approach organizes phenomena according to a logic of inquiry. An emic approach discovers the organization of phenomena that is relevant to the subjects.
6. ABSOLUTE VERSUS RELATIVE CRITERIA. An etic approach isolates phenomena through definition. An emic approach recognizes phenomena by their interrelationships.
7. NONINTEGRATION VERSUS INTEGRATION. An etic approach may not place every phenomenon in a larger setting. An emic approach must relate phenomena to their overall structure.
8. SAMENESS AND DIFFERENCE AS MEASURED VERSUS SYSTEMATIC. An etic approach compares phenomena by their effect or score on a research instrument. An emic approach compares phenomena by the responses they elicit in the subjects.
9. PARTIAL VERSUS TOTAL DATA. An etic approach may be based upon an aspect of a society. An emic approach should be based upon a knowledge of the whole society.
10. PRELIMINARY VERSUS FINAL PRESENTATION. An etic approach is the tentative access to a social system. An emic approach replaces the initial etic units with as many emic units as possible.[8]

Generally, an emic approach "is an attempt to discover and to describe the pattern of the particular language or culture in reference to the way in which the various elements of that culture are related to each other in the functioning of the particular pattern, rather than an attempt to describe them in reference to a generalized classification derived in advance of the study of that particular culture."[9]

Each standpoint has its value for social studies. An etic approach offers the scholar (a) an exposure to some of the variety of experiences that must be distinguished, (b) a terminology in which to communicate findings to other scholars, (c) an access into a foreign "reality," and (d) a standard language for comparing societies. An emic approach, on the other hand, offers the scholar (a) a view of social behavior as an operating whole, (b) an understanding of how the individual relates to the whole, and (c) possibly the most promising avenue for a predictive science of behavior.[10]

Patterns of many phenomena in a society are more efficiently exposed through an emic approach than through an etic one. As William Sturtevant puts it, "regularities will appear if one measures continental European manufactured goods with an American or British yardstick [eticly], but measuring with a meter stick [emicly] will much more readily reveal the principles of the system relevant in European culture."[11] Clearly, the emic approach offers the more direct route to thorough, accurate description.

It must be emphasized, however, that the emic approach is not anti-etic, for the two are dynamically related. In the above example, only by initially analogizing from a yardstick (etic) to a meter stick (emic) can we begin to understand the Continental principles, and only by translating yards (etic) to meters (emic) can we compare American and Continental production. Once we understand the meter (emic), furthermore, we may adopt it as an absolute, analytic measure (etic), which may then be used to initially approach another society's principles (emics). Etics and emics can thus play complementary roles: our training in etics helps us to begin to understand a foreign "reality" and hence to develop an emic representation. This emic representation informs our set of etic discriminators, our "etic kit," and allows us to contrast or generalize about different societies; this expanded set of etics, in turn, broadens our potential access into other societies, which promotes more emic representations, and so on.[12]

This is not, again, to deny the benefits of a purely etic approach. Questions about population or wealth distribution, geography, or the like might well be addressed through a standard language science. Yet, if the questions relate to human being, to such matters as values, communication, thought, or personality, an emic approach is in order. Whether the aim is description or comparison, an analyst with these interests should begin by discovering the elemental forms of experience recognized in each subject society.

The key to such an approach, as I have presented it, is *perspective*. My description will be objective and factual if nineteenth-century Americans would have said, "That's right — you've got it!" But how does one capture another's perspective? Is there a methodology to empathy?

Here, I think is the heart of the problem. Though essential for humane and credible description, perspectives cannot be simply observed. One might explain that they are actions patterned by a material substructure (e.g., biological, ecological, or economic) of which we are only partly aware. Alternatively, one might explain that they are more ideational than phenomenal, more like an ideal or form in the mind than a tangible part of people, their behavior, or the environment. Social and behavioral scientists and humanists often justify their work by standing on one side or the other of this mind-world dualism. Though I doubt either stance is in any sense valid or logically necessary, I trust both correctly suggest that the foundations of observation are more complicated than notions like "objectivity" or "bias" would allow.[13]

Fortunately, some formal techniques are available for addressing this problem. When most broadly defined, perspective is what some social scientists call *culture*. It is "what makes you a stranger when you are away from home. It includes all those beliefs and expectations about how people should speak and act which have become a kind of second nature to you."[14]

Culture will here be used more specifically as it has been defined in a field varyingly termed *ethnoscience, ethnosemantics, ethno-*

graphic linguistics, semantic analysis, cognitive anthropology, or, more generally, *the analysis of world view.* As Ward H. Goodenough puts it: "A society's culture consists of whatever it is one has to know or believe to operate in a manner acceptable to its members and to do so in any role they accept for any of themselves." It includes a knowledge of the form and organization of phenomena, what to expect in life and what to do about it. "Culture, then, consists of standards for deciding what is, standards for deciding what can be, standards for deciding how one feels about it, standards for deciding what to do about it, and standards for deciding how to go about doing it." Culture, in short, consists of "standards for perceiving, believing, evaluating, and acting."[15]

Accordingly, to describe who nineteenth-century Americans were is to describe a facet of their culture, to present an "emic ethnography."[16] The desired end is not so much a modern catalogue of the past as a grasp of the rules by which nineteenth-century Americans may have "catalogued" themselves. What kinds of people did they see? How did they recognize similarities and differences in one another? What standards must we learn to know, as they, the "insiders," knew, the composition and organization of a nineteenth-century social world?[17]

These are cultural questions requiring ethnographic answers. The logic of inquiry taken here is probably best summarized by Goodenough:

> The human approach to experience is categorical. Fundamental to every individual's organization of experience, therefore, is a catalogue of forms or form categories that he has learned to discern directly with his senses. . . . A systematic description of a culture would properly begin with these primitive forms and then use them as the points of reference for describing the more complex forms derived from their various combinations. This approach is what anthropologists have in mind when they speak of describing a culture "in its own terms" and of emic ethnography.[18]

The discovery of these forms is no simple task, for they appear in subtle and complicated ways. Although, for instance, recognizing that two people are quite different individuals, we may also recognize that they are similar "forms" of people, say, "men" or "farmers." This recognition is a function of our knowledge of the qualities that in our society allow people to be treated similarly in a given context. We learn to have special expectations of forms of people and to respond to their defining qualities. This is the meaning of our "categorical approach to experience," our tendency "to render discriminably different things equivalent, to group objects and events and people around us into classes, and to respond to them in terms of their class membership rather than their uniqueness."[19] "Forms" or "classes," "knowledge," "expectations," and the like cannot be directly observed. They must be inferred from human action, its context and effects. The essential task is thus to learn the fundamental categorizing processes that are implied by social action.

Some say this approach can only yield impressionistic and, hence, near-worthless results; one cannot empirically "read minds," so why speculate?[20] This condemnation fails for several reasons. Even if the problem were simply impression versus empirical fact (which it is not), the conclusion would hardly be merited. It bespeaks intellectual cowardice. Surely important questions should guide research at least as much as certain answers. The naive insistence upon "nonintuitive" procedures can only produce gross or trivial results. The victim is precisely those insights that motivate scientific as well as humanistic discovery.[21]

Second, and more important, the skeptics unnecessarily assume a conflict between the "two cultures." Their phrasing of the problem points to an inevitable dilemma. "How," as Gerald D. Berreman puts it, "to be scientific and at the same time retain the humanistic insights — the human relevance — without which no account of human beings makes sense. . . . I believe that the dilemma can be resolved if we take as the relevant question not *whether* to be rigorous or insightful, scientific or humanistic, but rather how to be *both* — how to develop a methodology which is at once subject to verification and conducive to perceptive insights in the study of men."[22]

Cultural study may begin with "mere intuition," but this does not exclude the possibility of scientific inference. The two are not dichotomous. I must agree, again, with Berreman, "that intuition is nothing more or less than inference that is unanalyzed because it is based on complex cues, subliminal cues, or subtle reasoning. In the last analysis, intuition is inference and as such is the basis for all science.'' By systematizing insight, by explicating the intuitive process, much of the distance between impression and empiricism disappears.[23] The forms of nineteenth-century experience are as appropriate a subject as any in working toward this end.

Ethnoscience, the model of cultural description to be used here, was in part created for this very purpose, to portray in a rigorous manner complicated relationships for which otherwise we have only a vague sort of ''feel.''[24] Such a portrayal can be achieved by exploiting a relationship between language (the standards that order speech behavior) and culture. Language can be considered both a product and a vehicle of our categorical approach to experience. The principles people apply in assigning expressions to phenomena in their world, the *semantic system,* is the key to emic ethnography. [25] By capturing the way a people symbolically represent their world, one begins to learn how they know that world and hence their culture.

For instance, to say ''Apple-growers are a type of farmer'' is to reveal two categories and a relationship between them that exists for culture as well as language. We know not only that the class ''farmer'' may include the class ''apple-grower'' but also that the people we refer to as ''farmers'' may include those we could call ''apple-growers,'' that the expectations we have of farmers could apply to apple-growers, that farmers and apple-growers have something in common, and so on. By carefully analyzing the vocabulary and structure of a society's speech one learns a great deal about the content and organization of the referent of that speech, the universe as the speakers know it.

In so doing the analyst's experience is analogous to that of a newcomer or child in the society. Both develop a cultural competence. To describe a community's culture one must learn something like what its members have learned; that is, something of the categorization of phenomena and events by which people deal with one another and their surroundings. The categories are a major part of their culture and are represented largely, though far from completely, by the words and expressions in their language. Success for the analyst, as for a native child, is to come to know and communicate experience in those terms.[26]

The relationship between language and experience is so close that we frequently even "think in words." Deliberation is often, quite literally, a sort of dialogue. As one learns to use words in identifying and organizing experience, the experience and its representation become almost inseparable, for the semantic system is in large measure a medium for making sense of the world.[27] Linguistic behavior is thus one of the major manifestations of culture and, as such, a particularly rich source for the ethnographer.

The terms that members of a society assign to phenomena are clear indicators of cultural categories relevant in that society. As Charles Frake suggests, we should "look upon the task of getting names for things not as an exercise in linguistic recording, but as a way of finding out what are in fact the 'things' in the environment of the people being studied."[28] *Semantic analysis,* the study of meaning in expression, is consequently the central method in emic ethnography and thus, too, the method best suited to studying culture in a nineteenth-century American society.

But how can ethnographers be assured that their inferences are right, that the categorizing processes they abstract are the ones that their subjects actually use? In short, how can an emic ethnography be verified? This question has engendered considerable controversy among anthropologists.[29] I do not propose to settle that controversy here but merely to state my position on some of the key issues.

As Anthony Wallace and John Atkins point out, the verification question is probably best considered from two standpoints, those of *structural* and *psychological validity*. Though one might quarrel with their terminology (e.g., I prefer *experiential* or *existential* to *psychological*), I think that the distinction is useful. A structurally valid description may be defined as a statement of a logically complete set of standards that, when followed, produces socially acceptable behavior. A psychologically valid description is a statement of a set of standards that approximates the set that subjects may actually use.[30]

There are a number of subtle yet important differences between the two standpoints.

1. REFERENCE OF REALITY. The standards in a structurally valid model are *real,* that is, actual cognitive operators, for the ethnographer in accounting for or simulating subject behavior, but they are not necessarily real for the subjects. The standards in a psychologically valid model, on the other hand, may be real for the ethnographer and for the subjects. The distinction is significant because there are an indeterminate number of different models that can account for the same behavior. For example, an observer might model the categorizing process represented in the statement "Mr. Smith is a doctor" by defining a doctor as a person who has received a medical degree, or a person who provides professional care for the sick, or a person who can sign official health assessments, or a person who has X-score on some sociometric index, and so on. Using any of these definitions one might properly conclude that an individual is a doctor; thus all of the definitions are structurally valid. Presumably, however, the subjects generally use only some subset of these definitions. (Nineteenth-century Americans could not, for instance, literally respond to one another on the basis of their SES [socioeconomic status], a measurement developed in the next century.) Members of this subset are psychologically valid.
2. POOL OF VALID STATEMENTS. Thus, the two standpoints imply a different number of valid models. There are a virtually limitless number of structurally valid models of the same action. The set would include every calculus that has been or will be designed by human or computer that produces the same result. The number of psychologically valid models, however, is limited by the *public culture* of the subject society, that is, "all the individual versions of the system or systems of standards that a group's members expect one another to use as their operating cultures in the various activities in which they have mutual dealings."[31]
3. PREDICTION. Statements that have either type of validity are predictive in the very special sense dictated by the culture concept. Since culture is whatever one has to know or believe to operate in a socially acceptable manner, "the model of an ethnographic statement is not: 'if a person is confronted with stimulus X, he will do Y,' but: 'if a person is in situation X, performance Y will be judged appropriate by native actors.' "[32] From both standpoints valid

models predict not what *will* happen, but what *may* happen. To use the previous example, one would not predict that, when asked "Who is Mr. Smith?" people will respond, "Mr. Smith is a doctor," but only that this is an acceptable response. Yet the breadth to which this principle is applied does vary. A structurally valid model need only predict that the behavior it implies will be accepted by the subjects. A psychologically valid model predicts that the subjects will accept both the implied behavior and the model itself, i.e., not only the action but the standards that guide it. One model tells us how to do the right thing; the other tells us how to do the right thing for the right reasons.

4. EVIDENCE. Because the two standpoints differ in purpose, they differ in the evidence they must use. A structurally valid description must be constructed from all available examples of appropriate behavior (and, of course, enough examples of inappropriate behavior to establish the difference) and, if possible, from successful simulations. A psychologically valid description requires this much in addition to native descriptions of the principles guiding appropriate behavior. It is important to know both (a) that people may consider Mr. Smith a doctor and (b) what attributes of Mr. Smith they may say make him a doctor. Yet the purpose and competence of the source of any explanation must be taken into account. Metaphor, a slip of the pen, leg-pulling, misunderstanding, and plain ignorance on the part of the informant must be distinguished from more direct statements of the rules that are most generally applicable.[33] The validity thereby attained is "psychological" in a very narrow sense of the term. A psychologically valid statement contains only the minimal set of rules necessary to appropriately discriminate and classify phenomena. It alone does not account for metaphor, extensional meaning, connotation, or any of the vast array of emotions or memories people may consciously or unconsciously associate with a phenomenon, unless the phenomenon cannot be discriminated apart from those associations.[34] Psychologically valid conclusions are thus restricted to the more overtly cognitive and conscious aspects of being.

5. SELECTION CRITERIA. Given two sets of "true" statements, one structurally and the other psychologically valid, there are slightly

different ways to select the "best" (i.e., the most desirable for use in description) from each set. Members of both sets should, of course, be judged first by their sufficiency, their ability to account for all available evidence. One would also choose from either set the most parsimonious statements, those "specifying only the absolute minimum of assumptions that are necessary to account for the data of the empirical collection or to generate an exact replica thereof."[35] Yet since the evidence, the empirical collection, for a structurally valid statement differs from that for a psychologically valid one, parsimony assumes a slightly different meaning from each standpoint. A psychologically valid model is unique in that it must conform to actual cognitive operations appropriate in the subject society. The best psychologically valid statement must therefore be parsimonious in the context of the inconsistencies and asymmetries of cognition.[36] A structurally valid model, on the other hand, does not reflect these properties. In this case parsimony is a matter of elegance; the best structurally valid model is the most simple, symmetrical, and unitary by contemporary standards.

6. RELEVANCE. In sum, structurally and psychologically valid accounts make quite different contributions to social studies. In the five areas I have discussed, the key difference is in their attention to the subject's "standards for perceiving, believing, evaluating, and acting." Accounts valid from either perspective are productive statements about society. They can make behavior that is accepted in another society, even if bizarre in our own, "understandable" by offering principles that make that behavior lawful and expectable.[37] Yet, since only a psychologically valid account approximates the principles recognized by the subjects, only a psychologically valid account is a productive statement about both society and culture.[38] To be truly ethnographic, then, a description must aim for the reality, limits, predictions, evidence, and selection procedures of psychological validity.

In view of all the foregoing, the desired thorough, accurate description may be called (with apologies for the jargon) a *psychologically valid emic ethnography*. Most of the previous work that may be so named deals with contemporary societies and is based on research in the field.[39] But there is little reason this approach should not be extended to the study of historic societies.

In combining anthropology and history there is no blasphemy intended. The adage "Anthropologists work in the field and historians work in the past" has lost most of its persuasiveness. As Wilcomb Washburn notes, "Squabbles about the boundaries and prerogatives of each discipline seem to me more often than not to be concerned with establishing institutional prerogatives than with increasing or defining knowledge." Of ethnohistory, an explicit melding of anthropology and history, he concludes, "To the historian, it will provide a method of adding the dimension of culture theory to strict chronology. To the ethnologist, it will continue to caution against too easy identification of present cultural traits with past events. In its own right . . . it will provide a discipline combining the cautious accuracy of the historian with the imaginative theorization of the social scientist." I heartily agree, and with Robert Anderson recommend "the application of specific anthropological concepts to limited historical problems."[40] This study is one response to that call.

Such an interdisciplinary effort is but a logical consequent of the theory of description I have proposed. An explicitly emic approach to the past makes good sense not only in terms of the theory, but also in terms of the effective exploitation of historical sources. Traditional historical writing is largely devoted to drawing an accurate picture of what happened, that is, reconstructing events and generalizing about behavior in the past. Besides struggling with a vague and often ethnocentric conception of accuracy, historians have had difficulty with the inherent weaknesses of their sources. In particular, scholars note that historical evidence is disproportionately:

1. LINGUISTIC. Unable to observe, historians must greatly rely on written statements by or about their subjects.
2. IDEAL. Documents generally reveal what the subjects say they do, say they ought to do, or expect each other to do. There is little way to check these statements against the actions that historians would have observed were they present.
3. NONRANDOM. In generalizing about behavior, historians are constantly handicapped by the selective processes operating in the

creation and survival of documents. Their conclusions about "what people usually did" suffer from a sample bias that may be quite severe.[41]

By reorienting analysis from behavior to culture, as I have suggested, at least these difficulties are alleviated:

1. Semantic analysis only benefits from a rich linguistic record.
2. Evidence of "ideal" or "expected" behavior is a most appropriate source for emic ethnography, and
3. The randomness of the data sample is of less consequence in specifying what may have occurred (versus what necessarily did occur).

Emic ethnography thus turns to advantage some of the pitfalls of traditional history.

Just as history need not suffer in an ethnoscience approach, I think ethnoscience need not suffer in a historical application. Although the methodology is oriented toward *elicitive frames* (question-response forms for use in the field), this is not an inherent limitation. Indeed, as Sturtevant observes, "In practice much of the best data comes from observing linguistic behavior outside the formal eliciting situation with an informant."[42]

Since ethnography, as here defined, depends upon inference, the ethnographer studying a contemporary group can no more observe culture than can the historian whose subjects are dead. All either can do to verify an abstracted model is to test it against the available evidence. Of course, the field researcher can conduct additional interviews, but the historian can also check conclusions by assuring that they account for the full documentary assemblage.[43]

Furthermore, the absence of interview data in history may be compensated by the greater purity of documentary evidence. Since standard eliciting procedures require rather rigorous introspection by the informant, ethnoscientists are frequently accused of overtraining their subjects, of making ethnographers out of their informants, thereby altering the very perceptions that are the object of analysis. Surely this charge cannot be leveled against the historical use of ethnoscience.

What I propose, then, is an approach to description that belongs at once to history and anthropology, while doing injustice to neither. Through such concepts as the emic-etic distinction, culture, language, category, and structural and psychological validity, I have provided a theoretical referent for a humane and credible description. The composition and organization of a historic social world will be portrayed in a psychologically valid emic ethnography. The required methodology of empathy is semantic analysis, and it is this methodology that guides my description of society and culture in a nineteenth-century community.

CHAPTER 2

Methodology

Semantic analysis is one way to determine what types of people live in a community. The rules of social organization in culture are largely manifest in the meaning and organization of social terms in language. Social structure is thus understood by learning the terminology of community membership. But fundamental to this approach is a rigorous conception of meaning and definition in language.

Clearly, meaning involves communicating the relationship between an expression and some phenomenon.[1] A word is *meaningful* when it refers us to some idea or thing. But meaning, and hence definition, can be conceived on a variety of reference levels ranging from the most limited and concrete to the most general and abstract. Semantic analysis generally proceeds through the typology coined by Charles W. Morris.

1. DENOTATUM. A denotatum is the specific referent of a term on a single occasion. For example, in the statement "Mr. Jones is a weaver," the term "weaver" *denotes* the individual Mr. Jones. Hence one may begin to define a term by stating its denotatum. This definition would, of course, hardly help to explain any other instance of usage.
2. DESIGNATUM. A designatum is the set of all possible denotata, the range of reference of a term. Here "weaver" *designates* the class of individuals who may be called "weavers." Hence one may build a more inclusive definition of a term by stating its designatum, an exhaustive list of the denotata. Yet such a definition is unwieldy, to

say the least. From this standpoint "telephone number" would be defined by listing every entry in the directory.

3. SIGNIFICATUM. A significatum is a distinctive feature of the designatum; it is an attribute of a phenomenon that makes it an acceptable denotatum of a term. Here "weaver" *signifies* what there is about Mr. Jones — for example, his occupation or skill — that makes him a "weaver." Significatum is the desired inclusive yet economical sense of meaning. One may define a term by isolating the necessary and sufficient conditions for inclusion in (or exclusion from) the designatum.[2]

The relationship between cultural and semantic description is focused when meaning is considered from this standpoint. While culture is in part the principles one must know to appropriately categorize one's fellows, significata are the principles one must know to appropriately categorize them in words. A primary goal of semantic analysis is therefore to represent the significata of a terminology. "We proceed from extensional definitions (definitions by listing of denotata) to intensional definitions (definitions by specification of distinctive features)."[3] In this case, the goal is to represent principles organizing the terminology of membership in a nineteenth-century community. When psychologically valid, these principles are a direct reflection of principles of social organization in the community's culture.

Of course, before analyzing a terminology, the analyst must be able to recognize meaningful terms. Fortunately here, the documentary sources are written in the familiar expression system of English. I can, for instance, note that "go fish" contains two terms (or one, if you are playing the card game). Assuming some continuity of syntax and grammar over the past couple of centuries, it is easy to recognize terms. The danger, however, is making assumptions about the continuity of their meanings. The methodology is intended to explicate and minimize such assumptions, to assure that knowledge of meaning is a product rather than a presumption of research.[4]

But one could not formally analyze every term appearing in the sources. Inquiry must be limited on some criteria of relevance. In emic ethnography, as I have explained, relevance must be defined as much as possible in the subjects' own terms. With this intent, an ethnoscientist isolates relevant terms by their structural status in the terminological system itself.

Semantic structure can be represented in many ways, but probably most conventional in ethnoscience is the *taxonomy,* a composite of *segregates* and *contrast sets*. A segregate is a "terminologically distinguished (i.e., conventionally named) grouping of objects." In other words, a segregate is a category with a name. A contrast set is a class of all contrastive segregates that "in a given, culturally relevant context share exclusively at least one defining feature." In other words, a contrast set is a collection of all the different named categories that "have something to do with each other."[5] That "something" is the situation or context in which a category is named. For instance, "accountant" and "salesman" appear in such similar contexts that the use of one helps to indicate the use of the other. People say, "Accountants and salesmen are types of businessmen," or, "The company has openings for accountants and salesmen," or, "Bill works in the store but he's an accountant rather than a salesman." The terms stand in direct contrast because they tend to appear in the same frame of reference. On the other hand, the categories labeled "accountant" and "bullfinch" appear in such disparate contexts that the use of one reveals nothing about the use of the other. People hardly refer to an accountant as in any way like or unlike a bullfinch or wonder, "Should I call that an 'accountant' or a 'bullfinch'?" Only segregates related as those termed "accountant" and "salesman" belong to a contrast set.[6]

A taxonomy is a hierarchy of contrast sets related by inclusion. Contrast sets are arranged in "hierarchical levels, with each segregate at one level included in (only) one segregate at the next higher level."[7] But "inclusion" here carries more than a structural meaning. A taxonomy should reflect not only that the designatum of a lower level term is a proper subset of the designatum of a higher level term, but also that the subjects recognize this relationship. They should, for instance, regularly speak of one as a "type of" the other. An analyst would want to record all such "type of" statements, noting the particular semantic relationship each statement contains. As James Spradley and David McCurdy note, these relationships — x (f) y — may vary, but a taxonomy should be constructed about a single reference frame, that is, about a single semantic relationship, for example: strict inclusion ("puppy love *is a kind of* affection"), part-whole ("my elbow *is a part of* my arm"), cause-effect ("he was arrested *as a result of* a complaint"), rationale ("deterrence *is a reason for* armament"), location-for-action ("the bedroom *is a place for* having sex"), purpose ("the car *is used for* commuting"), means-end ("hard work *is a way to* get money"), sequence ("the first date *is a step or stage in* courtship"), or any other relationship that people regularly use to signify inclusion. Taxonomy is thus intended to represent a psychologically valid, species-genus arrangement of named categories.[8]

Take, for example, the terms for football players.[9] Figure I is a two-dimensional model of semantic structure. The vertical lines join terms designating segregates in a contrast set; thus, the vertical represents contrast. The horizontal lines join terms designating segregates in a species-genus relationship; thus, the horizontal represents inclusion, here, strict inclusion. One result is a *taxonomic definition* of each term; for instance, "guard" signifies a type of "lineman" to be distinguished from a "center," "tackle," or "end." More important for this discussion, however, the result is a collection of terms that are related in meaning. The semantic structure of the terms themselves indicates their relevance in a discussion of football players.[10]

Clearly a much more general taxonomy could be constructed;

FIGURE I

A Taxonomy of the "Football Player" Domain

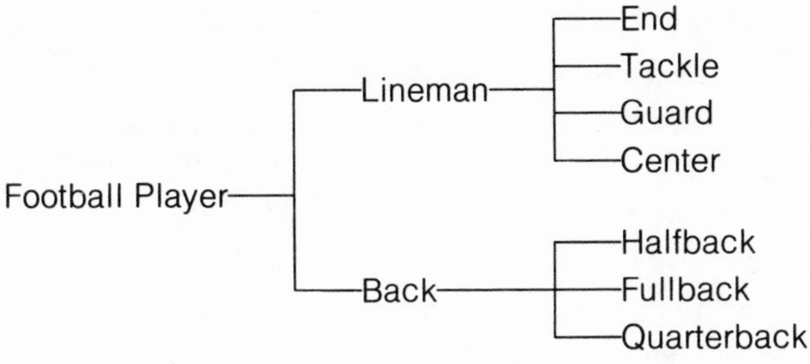

''football players'' are types of ''athletes,'' who are types of ''persons,'' who are types of ''living things,'' and so on. Theoretically one could map all the named categories in a culture in one massive taxonomy. It would represent almost the entire universe spoken of in a society. Some ethnoscientists have gone so far as to say that culture is such a supertaxonomy, that culture is only the sum total of a society's folk classifications. Yet without going this far it may be asserted that taxonomy outlines real aspects of culture. The use of taxonomic systems is apparently not confined to botanists or librarians; it can be considered a fundamental principle of human experience.[11] A taxonomy may therefore be used to limit an emic ethnography. An ethnographic universe is not so much defined by the analyst as discovered in the subjects' use of related meanings. One simply begins at a node in the taxonomy and works outward.

Ethnoscientists refer to the term at such a node as, naturally enough, a *cover term.* A cover term designates the most inclusive segregate in a taxonomy (e.g., ''football player''). The range of meaning of a taxonomy or contrast set is called a *domain.* Hence, the illustration is a taxonomy of the ''football player'' domain. I could, of course, use a more or less inclusive cover term (e.g., ''athlete'' or ''lineman'') and have a correspondingly wider or narrower domain. But, however limited, a domain represents a segment of folk classification, that is, a portion of the system in terms of which people may act and interpret events. If a topic constitutes a domain in the subject culture, it is a proper topic of emic ethnography.[12]

The existence of a ''person'' domain in the cultures of nineteenth-century America hardly requires demonstration. Unlike the Ojibwa whom Hallowell describes, most Western peoples have steadfastly partitioned the universe into human and nonhuman categories. Such ambiguous entities as ghosts or demons can be dismissed as ''unnatural,'' as parties of some ''other world'' or just ''superstition.'' In the community studied here, abolitionists could appeal to ''the fundamental and eternal distinction, which God has established between persons and things.''[13] The ''person'' domain is therefore a proper frame for this emic account. The terms in a taxonomy of this domain constitute the relevant terminology of community membership. In the meaning of these terms are the principles some Americans deemed appropriate in organizing their social experience.

As already mentioned, one representation of meaning is the taxonomic status of a term. A taxonomy indicates the segregates that in generality stand above, beside, and below the designatum of a term (e.g., a "lineman" is a type of "football player" who is to be distinguished from a "back" and who may be an "end," "tackle," "guard," or "center"). Yet taxonomic definitions state only the significata of a term that are a function of inclusion. They do not relate nonhierarchic elements of meaning, namely, how to distinguish categories *within* a contrast set (e.g., how to know that a "lineman" is a "guard" rather than a "tackle"). At each taxonomic level the question remains: To what specific things may the subjects attend as they verbally recognize a certain type of person? What features make people in the society essentially the same or different? What, again, are the real, defining attributes of named social categories?

One route to discovery is to return to the notion of meaning as significata. A term signifies a kind of class product, a unique combination of semantic features or components. These features are patterned in a domain. Since the terms in a domain designate segregates that are included in a superior segregate, they share a semantic feature; that is, they have a common *root meaning* (e.g., "lineman" and "back" share the significata of "football player"). Even their distinctive features may be seen as different values of the same semantic variables.[14] This is simply to say that related categories differ in kind. One way to approach definition, then, is to isolate the semantic variables that structure a set of terms. The values of these variables that a term signifies are its semantic components, its significata.

Take, for instance, the lineman-back distinction. As a spectator, I usually recognize the difference by a player's position on the field. If a player stands at the line of scrimmage, I know he is a "lineman"; if he stands in the backfield, I know he is a "back." One variable ("position on the field") partitions football players into their two types. A value of this variable ("at the line" or "in the backfield") in conjunction with the root meaning ("football player") comprises a sufficient, parsimonious, and psychologically valid definition of either term.

Often, of course, the relationship between terms is more complex. Any two categories may differ by the value of only one variable, but the distinction of several categories in a domain may be expected to involve several variables. One may approach a domain as a kind of logical space, the dimensions of which are the semantic variables, like "position on the field," that people may use to appropriately assign terms to phenomena. Ethnoscientists generally call this arrangement a *paradigm*.[15] There are as many dimensions as are necessary and sufficient to discriminate related categories. From this perspective the meaning of a term is simply its position in the paradigm. A *componential definition* represents term meaning as a set of coordinates, a bundle of components, along each dimension of the logical space.[16]

My own understanding of the "ancestor" domain may serve to exemplify an approach from this perspective, *componential analysis*.[17] (For simplicity, discussion is limited to "direct ancestors," i.e., lineal ascendants — "parents" — within three generations of ego.) Each category may be constituted through simple principles rather than complex genealogy.[18] I do not, for instance, usually think about whether my great-grandmother is my father's father's mother or my mother's father's mother. It is often strictly a matter of generation. My great-grandmother is one generation older than my grandparents or, more directly, three generations older than I. Similarly, one criterion — the sex of the ancestor — may account for the "mother" or "father" root of each term.

Therefore, in this case, the "ancestor" domain has two dimensions — sex and generation. Values on the sex dimension are male (m) and female (f). Values on the generation dimension are one, two, or three generations above ego. The terms thus signify the following coordinates:

"father"	m, 1
"mother"	f, 1
"grandfather"	m, 2
"grandmother"	f, 2
"great-grandfather"	m, 3
"great-grandmother"	f, 3

These coordinates represent componential definitions of terms in the "ancestor" domain. They are logically mapped in the paradigm shown in Figure 2.[19]

FIGURE 2

A Paradigm of the "Ancestor" Domain: Sex and Generation

Generation		Sex: m	Sex: f
↑	1	father	mother
	2	grandfather	grandmother
↓	3	great-grandfather	great-grandmother

Note that here, as elsewhere, semantic variables may be nominal, ordinal, interval, or even ratio scales. The order of the segregates, then, left to right or top to bottom in the paradigm, may or may not be significant. If the level of measurement for the variable is nominal (e.g., sex), clearly the order is meaningless. But if the level is ordinal or higher (e.g., generation), to be indicated by arrows, then the order represents a true scale.

To no one's surprise, the substantive implication of this model is the operation of sex and generation as principles of social organization. In terms of method, however, the implications are more significant. Here is a way to systematically identify social categories and the principles that order them.

The principles are structurally valid insofar as they outline necessary and sufficient conditions for an individual to be a denotatum of a social term. In historical application this can be assured by checking every available use of the terms. In the "ancestor" example, no competent individual should label a woman "father" outside of special contexts such as mistakes, jokes, or metaphors.

An exhaustive search of the documented denotata for systematic similarities and differences would suffice if only structural validity were desired. But to be psychologically valid these similarities and differences must be systematic in a special sense, that is, systematic in the subject's terms. In assuring the cognitive relevance of their conclusions historians must rely far more on inference than do fieldworkers. Historians can neither directly question nor experiment with their subjects' choice of social terms. But as Wallace suggests, "In question is *how* the native speaker, confronted by a reference object, reckons to choose the appropriate reference term." This information can be garnered from documented, native explanations of term choice.[20]

Historical evidence of features (F_i) that subjects actually use to verbally assign an individual (I) to a social category (C_i) seem to appear in the following forms:

1. FOLK DEFINITION ($F_1 \rightarrow C_1$). These are statements that paraphrase in the abstract the meaning of a term (e.g., "A carpenter is a person who works with wood"). Clearly, as psychological evidence folk definitions do not carry the weight of more empirical forms.
2. POSITIVE RECKONING ($I \rightarrow F_1 \rightarrow C_1$).[21] These are statements of the features used to affirm a particular label assignment. These statements, like other forms of reckoning, may be direct (e.g., "Since Ann works with wood, I know she's a carpenter") or implied (e.g., "I wanted to hire Ann to do some woodwork, but she's an expensive carpenter").
3. NEGATIVE RECKONING (where $F_2 \nrightarrow F_1$, $I \rightarrow F_2 \nrightarrow C_1$). These are statements of features used to deny a particular label assignment (e.g., "Bill can't be a carpenter — he works with stone, not wood").
4. CHANGED RECKONING (at different times and in similar contexts, both $I \rightarrow F_1 \rightarrow C_1$ and $I \rightarrow F_2 \nrightarrow C_1$). These are statements of features used at one point to affirm and at another to deny the label given to a single individual or group (e.g., "Jim was a carpenter, but, since he gave up wood for stone work, now he's a mason"). Evidence in this form is most productive, since it indicates both the presence and dynamic interrelations of semantic components.[22]

The more examples of different forms of evidence the documents contain, the more support there is for a claim of psychological validity. All primary sources are in this way historically significant. Folk definitions of social categories are likely to appear in dictionaries, census instructions, contracts, schoolbooks, charters, and the like, while examples of reckoning are likely to appear in more freewheeling letters, diaries, speeches, and other commentary. The values of variables that best correspond to native explanations in definition and reckoning and that best account for all documented denotata are real, defining attributes of named social categories.

They are *values* in a cultural as well as a mathematical sense. In recognizing that an individual is a certain type of person, people assume that she or he should have the qualities that define that type. For instance, if a man represents himself as a "carpenter," his employer will surely think he should work with wood on the job (and may fire him if he does not). The very act of categorizing implies the recognition of some most important features, features that render people "essentially" the same or different. Such explicit or implicit notions of what should be, conceptions of the important or desirable, are values in the subject culture.[23]

Clearly there are many values associated with a social category that are not necessarily part of the definition of the category. A whole array of values, for example, may be invoked in distinguishing a "good" from a "bad" carpenter, without challenging the fact that the individual is, after all, a carpenter. Nonetheless, the components of social categories are values that play a defining role in social relations. As evidenced by the frequency, breadth, and consistency with which they are invoked, they represent fundamental social values.[24] When they are considered along with matters of context and connotation, a great deal is learned about social identity.

In sum, I have presented a methodology for the description of a historical society in its own terms. The methodology is applied here to discover the cultural context of social relations in a nineteenth-century community. It seems a most promising avenue to the thorough, accurate description I have proposed. The account can be thorough because it is a systematic analysis of all available sources; it can be accurate because it is referenced to an explicit theory of description. It is my best answer to what Americans were like in the early nineteenth century.

CHAPTER 3

Application

For those interested in describing Americans or any other large group, there seems to be an inevitable problem of time. How, in less than a lifetime, can one deal with the incredible number of people, the variety of groups and subgroups in a complex society?[1] One ready solution, particularly when studying quantities, is the sociological survey. Inquiry can be limited to a population sample of manageable size that relates predictably to, that is, "represents," the whole.

An alternative is the case or community study. Although sacrificing the representativeness of a survey, such an approach has ample benefits, particularly here where questions relate to cultural and historical matters. Among its familiar advantages are: (1) a definition of the research unit that is learned from the subjects rather than imposed by the analyst; (2) a representation of social life as an integrated, operating whole; (3) an understanding of the individual's relationship to his or her immediate milieu; and (4) an opportunity to study the full documentary assemblage in the context in which it was created.[2] Community study, then, is a suitable format for ethnoscience in history.

Unfortunately, there is a bewildering array of definitions of *community*. Clearly, as Robert Redfield explains, it is "one kind of human whole," but the particular kind may depend upon the organization of the subject society and the interests of the analyst.[3] In ethnoscience a community is usually indicated by a pattern of communication. Michael Agar explains that the ethnographer can begin with any group where members communicate with each other in a manner not understandable to an outsider. Such a group has been called a "speech community," although "communicative community" might be a broader term to suggest the nonlinguistic modes as well. Following Goodenough's lead, then, the ethnographer can work to learn the knowledge necessary to understand the communicated messages in that community. The description of that knowledge is a description of a culture.[4]

One indicator of such a *communicative community* is the terms that members of a society apply to themselves. "Football players," "Baptists," or "congressmen" may all in this sense be communities. The membership may vary in size or geographic distribution and one may overlap with others, but in speaking of "we" as opposed to "they" or "some of us" a community is implied. By definition, then, a communicative community is a culturally relevant social unit.

There are a near infinite number of such units that could be used in studying culture in America's early nineteenth century. For this study, I selected the citizens of the town of Winthrop in Kennebec County, Maine, 1820 to 1850. According to the given definition they surely constitute a community; in fact, they referred to themselves as such. So-called "residents" regularly deemed their activities a property of the town and could distinguish "native" from "foreign" ways. The town line was thus a significant social and cultural as well as geographic boundary.

I could, of course, have chosen a smaller or larger unit. Winthrop contained recognizably distinct "neighborhoods" and was identified with a series of more inclusive bodies, ranging from the county to the human race. Similarly, there were many groups that cut across geographic boundaries: "children," "abolitionists," "Whigs," and the like. All of these at times constituted communication networks. Yet the town was the dominant social scene. It was apparently the most common referent of social action in the widest variety of contexts.

There are, too, more purely historical reasons for the selection of Winthrop. Maine has been sorely neglected in scholarly research, an omission which suggests that Down Easters were somehow out of the

American mainstream. Nevertheless, at least in Winthrop, residents participated in some of the most interesting, if not characteristic, developments associated with the early 1800s: industrialization, religious revivals, heavy sectarian and political disputes, and the more general extension and centralization of a broad range of social institutions. Movements for "benevolence" or "moral reform" were dedicated to temperance, sabbath schools, abolitionism, missionary and Bible circulation, vegetarianism, female education, scientific agriculture, and common school reform. There were likewise the predictable changes in day-to-day life ranging from the introduction of the friction match to the rise of "fashion."

This is not, however, to argue that the period marks a revolutionary change. In many respects, Winthrop remained the same. At the end of the period, for example, residents were almost as purely of British Protestant descent as they were in 1771, when the town was incorporated. There was an orderly growth in the population from 1,619 in 1820 to 2,154 in 1850, a modest 33 percent. New arrivals still came from Massachusetts and New Hampshire, but the Canadian and the Irish Catholic migrations were yet to come. Generally, in 1850 as in 1820, kin still lived and worked together, gathered for town meeting, attended Protestant churches, and recognized the same prominent families. Many of them were disappointed, but nearly all could admit, that social and political conservatism remained popular.[5]

Winthrop, then, cannot be said to represent any particular kind of community; it was neither typical nor remarkably atypical. Nevertheless, it is surely a town of interesting characteristics and well worthy of study. (The historical background will be discussed in more detail in introductions to chapters on related domains.)

The study of Winthrop is facilitated by the great wealth of source materials: census, government, church, and society records, newspapers, schoolbooks, sermons, diaries, and even highly personal correspondence. This analysis is based on a careful reading of every extant source identifiably written or read in Winthrop from 1820 to 1850. A host of varyingly more secondary materials are valuable, when treated skeptically, in gaining cultural insights and placing the primary data in context.

All of these materials were to be used in following as closely as

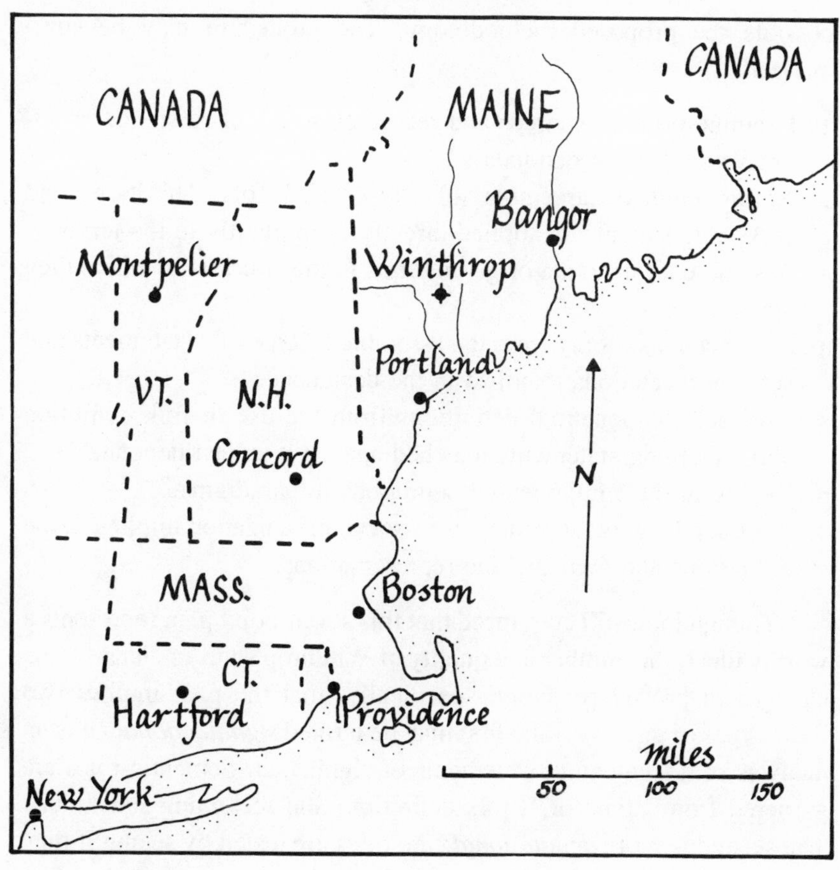
CANADA
MAINE
CANADA
Bangor
Montpelier
Winthrop
Portland
VT.
N.H.
Concord
N
MASS.
Boston
CT.
Hartford
Providence
miles
50
100
150
New York

possible the proposed methodology. The procedure may be summarized:

1. Examine primary sources and record all terms of reference or address with human denotata.
2. Noting context, assemble all "type of," folk definition, and reckoning statements applied directly or implicitly to the terms.
3. Assemble all denotata of given terms in the contexts in which they appear.
4. Abstract a taxonomy from the assembled "type of" statements and set-subset relations manifest in the designata.
5. Abstract componential definitions from the use of folk definition and reckoning statements matched against manifest denotata.
6. Represent the componential definitions in paradigms.
7. Abstract the general principles of social organization implied in the definitions and their graphic representations.

Though I am still convinced that this seven-point plan represents a worthy ideal, the number and quality of Winthrop sources dictate some changes in procedure. Note, specifically, that the plan implies two basic types of analysis. The first may be termed *significational;* it is an analysis of documentary statements of significata. Semantic rules are garnered from "type of," folk definition, and reckoning statements. The second is more *denotational;* the rules are tested by seeing if they account for denotata in evidence. The second type of analysis is thus a check on the first. If, for example, the significational analysis suggests the rule "A shepherd is a type of farmer," there should be no references (outside of mistakes, jokes, etc.) in which an individual is at once called a "shepherd" and excluded from the class of "farmers."[6]

On initial application, however, such a thorough denotational check proved both impractical and, I believe, unnecessary. This was most obviously the case with broad, collective nouns such as "the town" or "the destitute." To fully list every resident ever labeled "male," for example, by the local census-taker, would be theoretically sensible but in practice just a waste of time. There were also many cases in which significata were abundantly clear, but individual references were so vague or context specific as to be essentially useless. Evaluative labels like "villain" or "patriot," for instance, are clear in their general meaning, but usage can be expected to vary widely with the perceptions of the speaker. A collection of denotata would reveal more about contingent than necessary meaning.[7]

To remedy this situation the denotational side of the analysis was greatly relaxed. Rather than enumerating all manifest denotata, a simple grab sample was drawn. This more casual approach seems adequate when the significational analysis remains thorough and when there is abundant source material. This modification of the seven-point plan (particularly the third point) makes the operation far less tedious without, I believe, significantly altering the credibility of the results.

Such an explicit plan is not, however, a substitute for good judgment on the part of the analyst. A thorough understanding of the methodology is necessary if the application is to be theoretically sound. Much care, for instance, must be used in distinguishing metaphorical as opposed to more strict use of terms, that is, appeals to associated versus necessary meaning. The analyst should also be sensitive to the particular demands of the project. In documentary work, for example, it is often difficult to rate the relative importance of cultural phenomena. The simple frequency of reference may be quite misleading. Official records, for instance, may give undue attention to such terms as "officer" or "member" and their legal definitions. One should, then, carefully weigh the context, especially the salience and popular appeal, of each reference.

Yet, even with the best of sources and the most diligent application, the approach has certain inherent limitations. Obviously, for example, it is difficult to learn about *unlabeled taxa,* that is, cultural categories that do not have names. Nor is one likely to find native explanations of some of the most fundamental concepts. These may be thought so "obvious" that residents would explain them only to an infant and certainly not in written media. Yet such cases are apparently rare and may be handled through other available information.

A more serious drawback of the approach is its lack of attention to some of the pragmatic concerns of daily life. This study deals with ways to identify an individual of a recognized social type, not necessarily the intricate set of privileges and duties of his or her role. Ethnoscience can be used to study the latter issues, but the methodology outlined here is aimed primarily at naming or classificatory behavior.[8] It should be emphasized, then, that the following analysis relates to only a portion (though, I think, an important one) of the culture of Winthrop society.

The great wealth of source material necessitates one further restriction of my purpose. An overwhelming amount of data was collected on hundreds of categories in dozens of distinct domains. It would be nearly impossible to treat all of them adequately in a single volume. Unfortunately, too, the data, like the sources from which they came, are of varying quality. Much, for example, is learned about occupations, somewhat less about religion and moral reform, and very little about politics and the family.

In order to make the best use of the sources and to promote a detailed yet coherent account, this study is limited to occupational categories. Occupations may have been neither the most important nor the most inclusive social institutions in Winthrop. Both women and young children, despite their labors, were largely denied a vocational designation. Occupations were, nonetheless, of great cultural significance and the subject of much writing. In many contexts, a person's job could determine what type of "man" he was. Such terms as "merchant," "weaver," or "hand" could provide the most appropriate response to the query "Who are you?" Furthermore, it will be argued, these identities could greatly influence a man's overall "standing" in the community, his wealth and honor.

Occupational categories should be important to the society of historians, too. Here is an issue that concerns both elites and common folk. It is especially vital in understanding the human impact of the important economic and technological developments of the period. Many of these changes could be expected to strongly affect the lives of working people. An analysis of occupational categories, their structure, continuity, and change, is thus important to subject and analyst, alike.

SOME readers may have found the foregoing chapters disturbingly technical or abstract. But these pages cover only elementary concepts in ethnoscience, those necessary to explain how this analysis proceeded and, I hope, to promote similar studies in the future.

Readers may be further disturbed to find many of the substantive conclusions about Winthrop intuitively obvious; hence, why the elaborate methodology? First of all, remember how often allegedly obvious claims can conflict. At some times, for example, commentators argue that Americans are clearly idealistic, and at other times that they are clearly materialistic. The industrial revolution, some claim, surely signals an emphasis in the West on production, on laboring — or is it labor-saving? When such obvious yet opposing claims are possible, something is amiss.

The problem, I believe, is that the relationship between what is obvious and what should be believed is more complicated than it appears. Scholars who make judgments about people or just "data" are engaging in an interaction that is as much a part of their personal history as their wealth or childhood traumas. Hence, things may appear obvious for a very large number of reasons, and assumedly some of them are better than others. Historians, for example, may tend to respond to features of early cultures that are most obviously like or unlike their own. Yet to avoid ethnocentrism there should be equal attention to all areas of the subject culture, with minimal regard for their relationship to present understanding. Apparently, though we might trust our intuition to help provide alternative interpretations, we cannot trust it to choose among them. An explicit theory and method of description can provide some clear and uniform grounds for evaluating an account.

This is not to argue that methodology is a shortcut to truth. Clearly, we can be duped by methodological as well as substantive trickery; seductive quotations and slick rhetorical leaps appear in culture theory no less than in traditional history. But I trust, at the very least, I have raised issues that will help readers react not only to what is described but also to the credibility of the description itself.

A final word is due those who find that the substantive chapters read much like traditional history. This is largely intentional. Theoretical discussions to be precise may have to rely on scientific jargon, but the description of human beings is a wholly different matter. Unfortunately, many emic ethnographies in anthropology read with all the literary style of a tax return. The grander style of traditional history seems far more worthy of emulation.

Such a goal, however, requires some compromise in precision. In the interests of style, for example, phrases like "residents viewed" or "typically considered" are substituted for those more cumbersome yet correct, like "a resident might expect" or "it was socially acceptable to . . ." There is also a problem in documentation. Each conclusion is supported by dozens of references, each with its own contextual peculiarities. Again for stylistic purposes I choose the more traditional route of illustrating with evocative quotations and noting the best of others.

These compromises are merely in line with the dual nature of the work, its historical and anthropological scope. It has been theorized that ethnoscience can be valuable in history. The study of occupational categories in Winthrop from 1820 to 1850 demonstrates its value in practice.

CHAPTER 4

Farmers

PRACTICAL YEOMEN TURN SCIENTIFIC

In the first half of the nineteenth century agriculture occupied the largest and most outspoken group of Winthrop's working men. More than 80 percent of the workers reported in the 1820 census were "engaged in agriculture."[1] Among them were many of Maine's most prosperous and innovative farmers. Their successes lent the town a reputation for agricultural leadership recognized throughout the state.[2]

Yet it was during this same period that in many ways farming in Winthrop began its final decline. The agricultural part of the work force dropped in size slowly through the 1820s and 1830s and plummeted in the 1840s. Despite a growth of 33 percent in the population and more than 60 percent in the reported work force between 1820 and 1850, the number of farmers actually dropped from 366 to 300. By the end of that period only 40 percent of Winthrop workers were in farming; the majority were by then in some form of manufacturing.[3] Farmers estimated that the late 1820s marked the end of agricultural prosperity. For the next two decades they complained of "hard times" and chastised the young who migrated to southern mills or western fields, the victims of "Ohio fever." Sons were turning from the soil that their parents cultivated, turning to the shop and factory or simply leaving town.[4]

Winthrop farms were generally small, operated by a resident owner and his family with occasional hired help.[5] Only exceptional farms produced a surplus for market, reflecting the area's rugged terrain and short growing season. Farmers cultivated such traditional Maine items as apples, potatoes, rutabagas, and animal feeds (chiefly hay, corn, and oats) and raised milch cows, sheep, and horses in substantial number. Only apples and wool yielded significant profits. Yet this subsistence agricultural pattern also began to change in the early nineteenth century.

Farm production became increasingly oriented toward the marketplace. Success with apples and wool was, of course, important in this development, but most dramatic was the rise in dairy production, up nearly 500 percent from 1820 to 1850. By the 1860s Winthrop's dairy herd was known as the finest in Maine.[6] As commercial farming became more important, Winthrop seems to have given up some efforts to raise its own food. The value of orchard products and livestock came to vastly overshadow that of garden produce. But the change was most obvious in the case of breadstuff. The wheat crop in 1850 was only 14 percent of what it had been as recently as 1838. Rather than provide bread for their home tables, Winthrop farmers provided cash that they took "to New York to mill."[7]

Naturally, farmers expressed more frequent concern for the prospects of the season than of the decade. They recounted their latest success or failure, explaining it in terms of a number of factors. Some, they particularly lamented, could not be controlled; these were factors to be coped with rather than overcome.

Foremost among these was the weather. Winthrop was slow to recover from what became known as the standard of climatic disaster, the "cold season" of 1816. As late as June of that year the town received a hefty snowfall, and frost occurred throughout Kennebec County every month for more than a year.[8] This standard was recalled again and again as the cold took its toll. The bitter winter of 1831–32 devastated much of the town's orchards. The cold and drought of 1836 and 1837 aggravated an already severe grain and fuel shortage, only to be repeated in 1841 and 1849. Along with commodities the cold consumed cash for more high-priced essentials like bread, fuel, seedlings, and feed for starving stock.[9] Even normal winters were hard on barns, fences, and farm equipment. On the night of January 26, 1839, for example, rain and high winds leveled a barn and dozens of sheds in town.[10] Winthrop did, of course, enjoy some mild winters and promising springs, but farmers most often dealt with the weather as a problem.[11]

Disease and insect infestation were similarly viewed as elements of fortune. Only the "scientific farmers" considered ignorance a compounding factor, but they too suffered serious losses. Between 1828 and 1832 sheep diseases wiped out whole flocks. In the 1830s wheat succumbed to the midge and what was varyingly identified as "rust," "blast," or "mildew." And in the mid-1840s late blight destroyed young potatoes along with hopes for their commercial growth.[12]

Farmers were particularly subject to the ups and downs of the broader economic scene. From the early 1830s to the mid-1840s, they complained of heavy inflation and tight credit. Incredible rises in the price of "most of the necessaries of life" were reported. In just five years, 1831 to 1836, the cost of flour, butter, beans, hay, firewood, and other staples more than doubled. The bread situation grew more severe from 1835 on, as residents had to choose between switching to cornmeal or paying dearly for imported wheat.[13]

The problem was compounded by a simultaneous decline in the price paid for Winthrop's cash crops. The fleece market was particularly depressed, a situation residents blamed on high quality, inexpensive imported wool and "speculators."[14] In 1840 a Winthrop yeoman observed: "The great staple article with many farmers, viz., wool, is hardly called for. This used to be a sort of spring harvest . . . a cause of considerable influx of money among us." Wool prices did not take a sustained upward turn until about 1843, presumably because of the protective tariff enacted in 1842. Even Ezekiel Holmes, probably the most optimistic "agriculturalist" in Winthrop, if not the state, in 1840 complained: "Hard Times. There is no mistake now in this old expression. The times are truly hard enough. Business is dull — little money circulating, and little encouragement of any sort."[15]

It was, however, the farmers more than any other occupational group who rallied against ecological and economic hardship. They turned to state and county as well as local agencies to improve farm conditions. State governmental policy represented both a cause and a consequence of those efforts, for the legislature gave high priority to agricultural promotion throughout the nineteenth century.

Members of the agricultural community promoted "improvement" and "progress": "Onward and upward then must be our watchword. . . . God speed every hand and every mind to the bringing about of this great, this noble, this glorious result.''[16] The campaign was led by Winthrop's own Dr. Holmes, earning for him the title ''the Father of Maine agriculture.'' In local societies, state government, and the press he furthered innumerable innovations in farm practice. On his death an old resident noted, ''Winthrop knows not how to do without him. The whole town called on him for information and help. It was a common saying among us that Dr. Holmes knew everything, and was ever ready to impart his knowledge without money or price.''[17]

Even before 1820 (possibly in response to the ''cold season'') farmers organized their efforts. The Winthrop Agricultural Society was one of the first associations of its kind in the United States. Members considered organization itself a constructive step in stimulating pride and cooperation in a discouraging age.[18]

Throughout the period the society worked for the education of its members. They met regularly for discussions or lectures that extolled the yeoman's virtues and suggested ways he might handle his everyday challenges — how best to keep financial records, maximize farm yields, store produce, etc. Since the meetings were covered by local newspapers, information passed readily to the surrounding community. Reports of the society's activities, including committee and annual reports and lecture texts, appeared in full in the *Maine Farmer*. The society also published the first American manual on the diseases and management of sheep.[19] Its activities were highlighted by an annual cattle show and fair, where society committees awarded premiums for the best quantity and quality of produce, livestock, home manufactures, and farm implements. Competitors were generally required to submit detailed reports on how their entries were prepared. And after the fair the reports were published so that others might learn from the winners.[20]

But education was not the only cause for which farmers organized. Some called for more direct action against supposed economic predators — ''speculators,'' ''agents,'' and ''subagents'' — who pitted producers against each other and denied them a share of rising retail prices. In 1833, for example, a group simply called ''Wool Growers'' organized in Winthrop to boycott middlemen, establish base prices, and partially collectivize small flocks. Their policies, however, had little apparent effect.[21]

More significant to Winthrop was the increase in available agricultural information with the commencement of the *Maine Farmer* in 1833. Begun by Ezekiel Holmes with Agricultural Society encouragement, it was the first farm newspaper in Maine. Holmes edited the paper from its first issue in January of 1833 until his death in 1865.[22] Despite the weekly's title, it had a decidedly local focus, at least until 1844, when publication moved from Winthrop to Augusta. Until that time Winthrop, even in obituaries, was simply called "this town." Though the paper "borrowed" freely from other periodicals, most of its correspondents, advertisers, and, apparently, subscribers were Winthrop residents. Impassioned letters from readers provide ample evidence that residents were deeply interested in its contents.[23]

The *Maine Farmer* was singular in avoiding the religious and political discussions that filled the pages of its competitors. Like the Agricultural Society it featured pride, cooperation, "improvement," and above all, "practical" matters. The paper's apolitical and nonsectarian stance make it a unique testimony to nineteenth-century daily life. As the editor, Holmes was unswerving in his avoidance of the usual divisive issues. Of religion, he vowed: "It is enough for us to allow the farmers space in our columns to quarrel occasionally about the merits of their calves, or the best breed of pumpkins. It would be wholly irrelevant to the designs of our paper to make it an arena for religious strife." Of "moral reform," he declared: "A full discussion . . . [would violate] the legitimate objects of the paper." And of politics: "Don't start, gentle reader — we are not going to meddle with *Whigism, Jacksonism, Whiteism, Websterism, Van Burenism,* nor *Rheumatism,* or any other of the useless and aggravating squabbles which have agitated the country for a few years past."[24] Viewing politics ("that 'troubled sea casting up mire and dirt' ") as only slightly below phrenology in relevance to daily existence, Holmes even went so far as to censor political references out of letters to the editor:[25] "It is a journal devoted to the practical interests of the Farmer and Mechanic. A medium of communication with one another — a sort of savings bank of the 'odds and ends' of knowledge . . . 'the stuff that life is made of.' "[26]

Articles dealt in detail with everything from fence mending and recipes to the construction and use of hay rakes, in sum constituting a catalogue of ideals for daily life. Nearly a quarter of the copy was devoted to letters from residents documenting their experiences with the ideals. This information passed to an ever growing readership. The old hand-inked screw press, which printed two hundred copies of the first number, was replaced in 1846 by a power press that turned out more than a thousand papers per hour.[27]

The promoters of "agricultural improvement" claimed tangible results for their efforts. By 1850 they could refer to "the momentum . . . of the last fifty years": "The progress of improvement is slow but sure and though we may not realize at first the effect of the changes that are going on about us, yet as we pause and look back, we . . . feel ourselves cheered and encouraged. We see the footsteps of improvement."[28]

Among the "advantages afforded" they counted successful state lobbying campaigns (e.g., for laws promoting agricultural societies, wheat and corn bounties, and a tax on stud horses), better animal and plant varieties (e.g., Devonshire and Cotswold sheep, Jersey cattle, a host of apple varieties, and winning trotters descendant from "Winthrop Messenger"), advances in equipment technology (e.g., iron plows, pumps, horsepowers, and threshers), and refinements in everyday farm practices (e.g., fence maintenance, composting, and veterinary medicine).[29] Local "agriculturalists" did more than keep up with national developments. Samuel Cole's *American Fruit Book,* for instance, listed four apple varieties that were originated by Winthrop farmers. Three of the four, moreover — the "Fairbanks," "Moses Wood," and "Winthrop Pearman" — were among the seven varieties recommended by the Maine Pomological Society.[30]

There were thus significant agricultural changes during the period. On the one hand there was a decline in the number of farmers and in subsistence farming, in general, amidst economic and ecological hardship. On the other there was a corps of better-organized and better-informed agriculturalists operating more commercial and technologically sophisticated farms. The competing claims of "hard times" and "progress" provide the context for most farm writings in Winthrop from 1820 to 1850.

WINTHROP residents could recognize anyone who grew things as a "farmer," with few exceptions. The term was, for example, reserved for those who followed cultivation procedures all the way from preparation to harvest. ("Farmers" could thus be distinguished from "lumbermen," "fishermen," or "hunters" who merely harvested and from "hired hands" who were responsible for parts of the farm operation.) Yet the equation between agriculture and the label "farmer" was not a simple one. Many "mechanics" and "professional men" raised produce for their tables, while "farmers" took in piecework from the factories for extra cash. In some situations both the farming operative and the operative farmer might claim a common identity. (When talking about his potatoes, for instance, either might say, "As a practical farmer, I think deep planting is best.") In a wider set of circumstances, however, only the latter would properly be called a "farmer." Holmes appealed to such circumstances in contrasting those who "may do it [agriculture] as an occasional relaxation — as a change from the monotony of their trade or profession" and "farmers, whose trade, whose occupation, and whose duty it is to raise enough for supply."[31]

This problem of contextual variation is important in understanding nearly all the occupational terminology. When referring to a specific activity, speakers often invoke the label corresponding to its professional performance, even if the use of the occupational title might not otherwise be proper. (A modern analogue would be the aspirin-taking cold victim who declares, "I will be my own doctor.") In the general case, however, an occupational title signifies not so much what one does for a living as what one does *predominantly*. In an age of lesser specialization this was an important consideration. The bounds of nearly every occupational category hang on this notion of predominance. Obviously, it does not provide the kind of keen dividing line to which we are accustomed, but it apparently did not bother those who used the categories. Note, for example, a minister's easy remark: "You have frequently seen men leave my profession and go to the farm — and some indeed without leaving the profession."[32]

In agriculture, the notion of predominance is clearly manifest in the terminology itself, as shown in Figure 3. Categories in the "farmer" domain could be distinguished by the amount of time, and thus energy, a person spent physically working on the farm. The importance of those hours of toil for the "farmer" lexicon is mapped in Figure 4.

FIGURE 3

A Taxonomy of the "Farmer" Domain

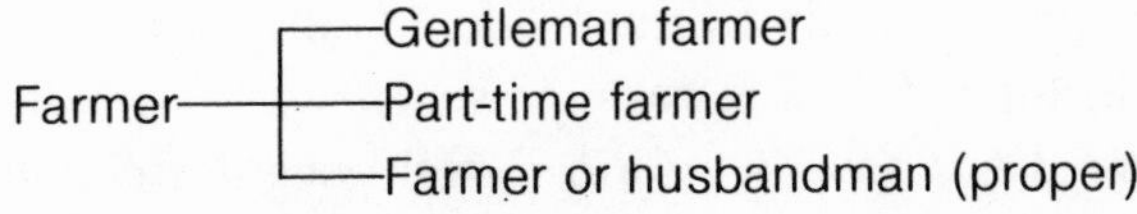

FIGURE 4

A Paradigm of the "Farmer" Domain: Time

Working Time in Manual Farm Labor

None ← → All

Gentleman farmer	Part-time farmer	Farmer (proper)

A "gentleman farmer" was, typically, a wealthy man, a "gentleman," who operated a large commercial farm but did little of the manual labor. Instead, he became an "employer"; he hired or leased his farm to an "overseer" or "farmer" (proper). Though the "gentleman farmer" might spend many hours in agricultural concerns, they were not hours of physical work, the relevant semantic variable: "The gentleman farmer, he who puts not his hand to labor but who overlooks and instructs others, is commendable as doing a duty sometimes sufficiently onerous, and frequently the extensive cares of a farm may require an oversight that will forbid the manual labor of its owner."[33]

"Part-time farmers" were generally of the type mentioned above — men who cultivated fields of their own but who devoted the bulk of their efforts to other pursuits. Generally they assumed other occupational identities.

"Farmers" (proper), on the other hand, were full-time tillers of the soil. In an 1833 address printed in the *Maine Farmer,* Henry Colman outlined the features of these three "classes" of "farmers" and concluded: "The third class comprehends those with whom agriculture is an exclusive profession. . . . It is . . . this latter class who alone, properly speaking, deserve the name farmers."[34]

The boundaries of the "part-time farmer" category are not very clear. Residents apparently tolerated quite a bit of variation in the use of the label. For example, Colman classed all those whom we would call "subsistence farmers" with "part-time farmers." In their case, he accused, idleness was their other pursuit: "The second class is composed of those who, occupying small farms, look for nothing from their farms beyond the bare support of their families. . . . They are content with the most scanty returns."[35]

Only "farmers" (proper) made full claim to the qualities socially attributed to agricultural pursuits. As evidenced in the terminology, and the Colman variation in particular, "industry" was one of the most important qualities. The husbandman benefited from the supposed "healthful influence" of hard outdoor work. Since his activities followed the seasons, he was also spared the "monotony" of other professions, his attention was spread over "a thousand little nameless things." Unlike the "part-time farmer," he boasted full self-sufficiency. He would "shun the doors of a bank as he would an approach of the plague or cholera." He was said to have a common-sense knack for handling almost any domestic problem. He made miraculous ad hoc repairs on farm equipment, concocted remedies for family ailments, and the like. Whatever his ambition, even faced with sinful temptation, he remained steadfastly conservative and "plain" in his affairs, "determined to proceed, *'just as father did.'* " In sum, the farmer had a unique reputation for industry, diversity, independence, ingenuity, and conservatism.[36] He represented all the qualities that the label "Yankee" implied.[37]

This is not, of course, to say that Winthrop farmers actually displayed these qualities. Even the strongest advocates of the "Yankee" image complained of rampant idleness and folly.[38] Nor is it to say that everyone considered these qualities desirable. The improvement campaign included a frontal assault on yeoman conservatism. In typical fashion, Dr. Holmes complained:

> We often see this among farmers — they become persuaded that a certain course of procedure is much better than the old one which they have heretofore followed, but it is *new* — or it is *odd* and somebody will laugh, or it may not be fashionable, or at first too laborious — or too expensive, though promising an equivalent return in time. Hence they vacillate — and hesitate and "talk of it" and talk *about it,* but never do it and plod in the old way.[39]

Moreover, work that was plain and industrious for some was just drudgery for others. On considering his imminent return to Winthrop to farm, for instance, a seaman confided: "The dreariness of my farming life need not be particularized, suffice it to say that nought but sense of duty to my aged parents could possibly induce me to renounce the seafaring life for that of the farm."[40] And however admirable the farmer's character, nearly all conceded that his occupation was less esteemed than others, especially in the beginning of the period.[41] Probably, in this sense, the farmer's life was more glorious as a symbol than as an experience.

Even the Yankee farmers, jacks-of-all-trades, had their specialists, those who identified with a particular "branch" of agriculture. (See Figure 5.) Yet this identification was generally temporary and only for purposes of discussion. It would be quite proper, therefore, for a man to be a "corn grower" at one moment and an "ox keeper" the next, so long as he raised corn and oxen. Reference to a "shepherd" might only indicate that the subject under discussion was the kinds of things a farmer does or thinks about in raising sheep. Thus, for example, a farmer would state: "Not being much acquainted with the diseases of sheep, I applied to a near neighbor who is considerable of a shepherd for advice."[42]

Such expertise was referenced to the various farm commodities. The most marked division, the one that determined the label root, was that between plant and animal husbandry. To distinguish his specialty a farmer could be (and with few exceptions was) denoted by simply combining the root "cultivator," "grower," or "planter" (for plants), or the root "keeper," "breeder" or "herdsman" (for animals) with the name of the commodity in question.[43] (See Figure 6.)

FIGURE 5

A Taxonomy of the "Farmer" Domain

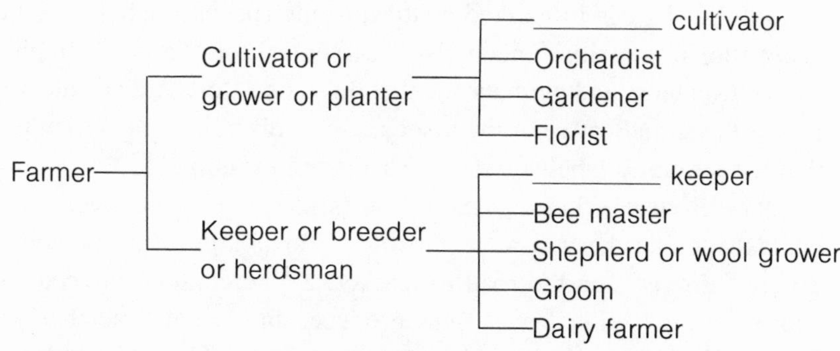

FIGURE 6

A Paradigm of the "Farmer" Domain: Branches of Agriculture

Branch of Agriculture				
Plant	Fruits			Orchardist
	Vegetables	______	cultivator	Gardener
	Flowers			Florist
Stock	Sheep			Shepherd or wool grower
	Bees	______	keeper	Bee master
	Horses			Groom
	Cows			Dairy farmer

Not surprisingly, then, the terminology reflects the farmer's relationship with his environment. His specialty depended on his experience with farm stock and the soil. Yet it is probably more significant that this specialized identity was so temporary and so contextually restrained. The general term "farmer," unlike "mechanic" or "professional man," remained dominant. A specialty label referred only to one item in a farmer's repertoire. Residents apparently assumed that he had others. This is in marked contrast to the specialty labels in other occupational domains. Labels like "carpenter" or "lawyer" implied an exclusiveness and permanence that those like "orchardist" did not. It is, I think, indicative of the association of diversity with agriculture that the specialty labels carried such limited meaning.

There were other names for a farmer that were even more context-specific: he was a "competitor" for premiums at the county fair, a "drover" on the road to market, a "purchaser" of seed and equipment, a "seller" of surplus produce, an elected "member" or "officer" of the Agricultural Society. In boasting of his independence, he was a "freeholder," "owner" of the land and stock that supported him. He was an "employer" to the "hired help."[44]

The use of these agricultural labels engendered little controversy. "Apple growers" and "competitors" were, first and foremost, "farmers." They had common values as well as a common public image.

Whatever their temporal commitment or specialty, farmers wanted "success." "Success," of course, could be variously defined, but there was wide consensus on its main components: property and reputation. Throughout the agricultural writings, innovative farm practices are recommended with the sanction of "prosperous" and "noted" farmers. Of the two, clearly property was the primary. Simply put: "The returns for labor and capital, the profit, is what we all seek." Hence, arguments over the value of a particular practice usually rested on a discussion of profitability; for instance: "merinoes [a breed of sheep] . . . are most profitable and therefore best for our farmers."[45] Honor was a kind of extra, the wealthy yeoman's just reward.[46]

Winthrop farmers aspired to varying amounts of wealth. Yet, whether the end was to become opulent or just debt-free, they tended to stress industry and efficiency, "the greatest product from the least expense," as the means. "Character," as one explained, was the key: "[For] a prudent economical farmer . . . everything bespeaks attention to business, and comfort, reputation and wealth follow."[47]

Hence, the farm was a showcase for its owner's "character." The successful farmer maintained his tools, fences, and buildings, while keeping his family well clothed and fed. A bad farmer, on the other hand, was a "slothful servant" whose yard was littered with wasted manure and stones, his fields poorly drained, and his fruit trees overgrown.[48]

Other values occasioned considerably more controversy. The improvement campaign, in particular, challenged basic concepts of "character" — concepts that defined what kind of "farmer" one was. (See Figure 7.)

FIGURE 7

A Taxonomy of the "Farmer" Domain

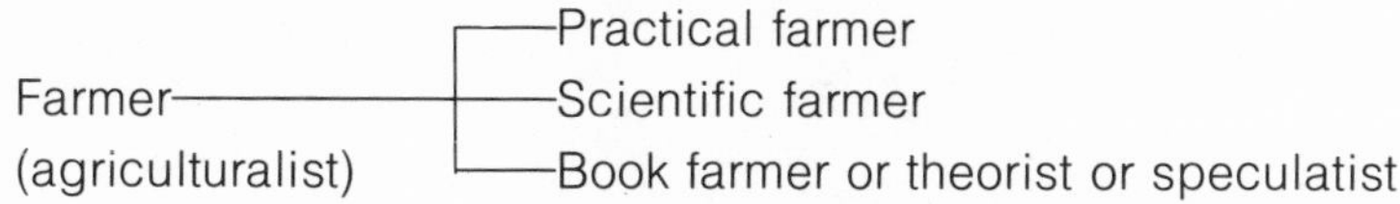

Traditionally, it was said, a "practical farmer" was good (i.e., he thought and acted in a way likely to yield "success"), while a "book farmer" was bad, or at least foolish. The first was a sensible man, a paragon of Yankee virtue, the latter his foil. In a typical exchange, one correspondent rejected another by charging: "The writer [is] a theorist. . . . His piddling mode . . . is deviating from known and well established practice. . . . [His advice] would be liable to lead many an innocent farmer astray from the true principles. . . . The author was not a practical farmer. . . . People should not be misguided."[49]

The two categories thus provided complementary ideals for daily life, one to be emulated and the other avoided. It should be no surprise that residents commonly introduced themselves and recommended their friends as "practical farmers" and accused only their adversaries of being "book farmers." These categories signified a configuration in values that was hardly convenient for the "progressive agriculturalist." (See Figure 8.)

FIGURE 8

A Paradigm of the "Farmer" Domain: Character

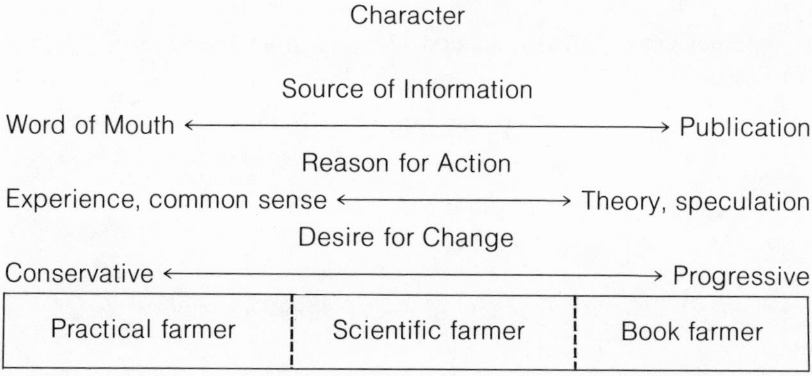

Character

Source of Information

Word of Mouth ←——→ Publication

Reason for Action

Experience, common sense ←——→ Theory, speculation

Desire for Change

Conservative ←——→ Progressive

Practical farmer	Scientific farmer	Book farmer

A "practical farmer" was one who mistrusted formal education. Sound agriculture, he would claim, is not to be found in the pages of a book: "A few cultivators of the earth agree to communicate to each other the results of their experience in farming. . . . These results are committed to writing, go through the press, and become a book. He who chooses to follow the results . . . as there detailed is guilty of book farming."[50]

"Practical farmers" knew "that you cannot *make* a farmer, he must be brought up to it, or he cannot succeed." His father and his neighbors were his only teachers: hence, he was often said to have been "bred a farmer."[51] A "book farmer," on the other hand, would make constant reference to "authorities," "philosophers," or other "men of science," precisely the people whom a "practical farmer" would dismiss out of hand.[52]

Residents explained that a practical farmer could trust informal education because its fruits were so readily apparent. In a father's or neighbor's fields were handy illustrations of the tried and true. As long as he kept within the limits of his own experience and "common sense," the "practical farmer" could be spared a lesson at harvest time. At a meeting to promote agricultural improvement, one cynic explained: "A common sense, practical man by his observations ascertains the best way to perform a certain agricultural operation. He tells it to his neighbors, to A, to B, and to C, and it is still all common sense, but if he record it on paper and that record be published it is no longer common sense, but book farming."[53]

The "book farmer" suffered under the illusion that agricultural practices could be deduced from scientific theory. (Thus, he was also called a "theorist" or "speculatist.") His recommendations were assumed to have less than a fair chance of yielding "success" in practice: "Theory of all kinds, and applied to all subjects is worthless without practice and . . . mere 'Book Farming,' as it is called, has justly the prejudice of all arrayed against it."[54]

Naturally, with action so tied to tradition, "practical farmers" were the ones most "determined to proceed *'just as father did.'* " They scoffed at the "book farmer" 's experimentalism as merely "aimed at creating an excitement."[55] Changes were thus greeted in conflicting terms. While, for instance, one group hailed "improvements in agricultural implements," the other derided attempts to "farm it by machinery."[56]

For those who adhered to the simple good-bad, "practical farmer"–"book farmer" dichotomy, evaluating relevant issues of "character" (one's own or others') was relatively simple. A substantial number of Winthrop residents, however, were at best uncomfortable with this conception. These were men like Ezekiel Holmes, Samuel Wood, the Snells, and the Metcalfs — names still familiar to Winthrop citizens — who championed the cause of agricultural improvement. They could be easily identified in discourse by their tendency to use the title "agriculturalist" in place of "farmer."[57]

The position they expounded placed them squarely with "book farmers" in the minds of their opponents. In regard to sources of information, these "agriculturalists" asked yeoman to be better read, and even called for the formation of a state agricultural school: "It is time, that the idea was banished that, because a man has spent four years at a College, he was fitted for some other employment, and therefore must not be a farmer."[58] They urged their "brothers" to turn to "men of science" instead of their neighbors in learning how to farm.[59] In regard to reasons for action, they heralded progress through "the application of the well settled principles of science."[60] And in regard to change, they stood forthrightly for "improvement" in every aspect of husbandry, particularly in the use of machines. In a kind of agriculturalist's prayer, for instance, editor Holmes pleaded: "Let us turn our eyes upon the field of the farmer, and we find instead of the clumsy wooden plough, a neat cast iron one, and that all his other implements met with an equal change; and in the performance of all the operations about his farm a corresponding improvement has been made."[61]

The epithet "book farmer" was one of the greatest obstacles men like Holmes had to face. It was more than a matter of name-calling, for the label invoked standards that were salient in almost every aspect of farm life. In refusing to be dismissed as "book farmers," "progressive agriculturalists" were promoting profound cultural change.

At times their defense constituted a blatant and direct challenge to traditional values and the two categories in which they were classed. This is not, of course, to say that these "agriculturalists" were battling terminology. What they wanted was "progress" — this necessitated the modification of some common ideas that (not surprisingly) had names. At the same time, however, they were aware of the purely linguistic problems in their campaign. In recommending "science" to farmers, for example, Dr. Holmes advised: "If you have a prejudice against the term science, and think it smells too much of 'Book Farming,' you may call it *Good Farming*."[62]

They denied the distinction between the "practical" and "book farmer" by arguing, for instance, that common sense and science or spoken and published advice were really the same. More often they simply rejected the dichotomy as "superstition": "The opposition against book farming rests on the shoulders of two monsters, ignorance and prejudice."[63] This campaign was apparently effective. As early as

1835, Ezekiel Holmes could gleefully report, "A book farmer is beginning to be looked upon with less horror than formerly."[64]

As a replacement for the old dichotomy, "agriculturalists" suggested a new ideal, the "scientific farmer." He was a man whose character represented the best of both worlds, a synthesis of "practical" and "book farmer" virtues. A "scientific farmer" improved on the advice of family and friends through serious study; he added theory to his common sense and speculation to his experience; he did not hesitate to experiment while preserving the tried and true.[65]

Acceptance of this category was, of course, less than universal. There were those who continued to charge that the title "scientific farmer" was simply an alias for "book farmer." Yet such charges were increasingly rare by 1850. As the "prejudice" against "book farmers" waned, "scientific farmers" received increasing and more flattering attention.

This trend paralleled agricultural "progress" in Winthrop from 1820 to 1850. The "scientific farmer" was better suited to developing commercial and technological farms than the "practical farmer." While residents continued to stress such fundamental farm values as industry and diversity, "improvement" made new demands on the yeoman's "character" — demands that he could meet by emulating a "scientific farmer."

The changes in the terminological system signal important cultural changes which did not escape the residents' attention. As Winthrop's B. F. Robbins observed: "The improvements have been many — not only as it regards the actual condition of farms, value and profits of animals, crops, &c., but what is no less important, a change in the views and feelings — in the minds of the Farmers themselves."[66] This change was, in large measure, a change of ideals, from the old "practical farmer" to the new "scientific farmer."

CHAPTER 5

Farm Help

THE LOWLY HAND

The yeoman's claims of self-sufficiency did not preclude his regular call for help in laboring on the farm. With such a short growing season planters wanted to get crops quickly in the ground and leave them there as long as possible. The spring thaw brought on a frenzy of sowing, and imminent autumn frosts a frenzy of reaping. With assistance Winthrop farmers could extend the productivity of their fields for vital days or weeks.

To meet these and other demands, they turned first to their families, and especially to their sons. Helping on the farm was considered an important part of growing up for any farmer's son. Even as an infant a boy played with little tools or wagons, while his sister played with dolls. Before the age of ten he could help feed the pigs, pick potatoes, or the like. As he grew older and stronger, he would share in more and more of the heavy labor at planting and harvest time. When the work was done at home, his father could "hire him out" to neighbors and thereby supplement the family income.[1]

This process was described as beneficial to both father and son. The older man received earnest labor and extra cash from the younger, who, in return, was "bred a farmer." As a result, William H. Parlin recalled, "the boys . . . worked with a will on the farm, assisting their father in his arduous labor. . . . They felt a personal and individual interest in the matter, and labored accordingly." A boy might also expect to be provided eventually with his own acreage. Fathers were urged: "If you are a farmer, make them farmers also: divide your land with them, hire land for them to cultivate, teach them to labor, economise, and grow rich; make them thus happy and independent."[2]

There was no such arrangement between the farmer and his daughter or wife. "Females," young or old, were described as "the feebler sex," even by those in the forefront of the supposedly progressive "female education" movement: "The whole physical structure of the female sex, as well as their obvious destination, clearly indicates that they are formed for employments which require less strength — less muscular exertion — than males."[3]

Residents concluded that outside farm work was, for the most part, too strenuous for women of any age. A farmer's daughter might drop seeds in the spring or help gather straw in the fall, but plowing, hoeing, or mowing were considered the realm of boys and men. She was not delegated even light chores unless "the work . . . pressed more without than within."[4]

As she grew older, her outdoor responsibilities remained meager. To recommend innovative farm practices, such as silk culture, for example, agriculturalists boasted that even women could do them: "The women and children, old people, and cripples could feed the worms and reel the silk. . . . A very pretty sum [is] to be raised up from the earth, and that too by women and children and invalids that could not wield a pitchfork or hoe."[5]

The wives of Winthrop husbandmen had many duties on the farm, but they were not described as "farming." The common label "dairy woman," for instance, was not included in the "farmer" domain. By milking cows or making butter and cheese, a "dairy woman" performed what was called a "domestic" as opposed to an "agricultural" service.[6]

Often, too, a farmer's wife had her own "garden" in which she raised vegetables, flowers, and herbs. But this was portrayed as recreation more than production. In an address to a female seminary, for example, a minister outlined the predetermined "spheres" of the sexes and explained: "He has a wide field upon which he labors and over which he vexes himself. She has a garden which is beautiful and in order without anxiety." Her efforts were apparently not recognized as a very serious aid to her husband.[7]

When necessary, Winthrop farmers added "hired help" to their family work force. They would employ "day-laborers," such as "ditchers," when clearing new fields, and "boys" or "hands" at planting and harvest time. These labels were rarely used as occupational titles, probably because it was too temporary and low-paying to be a man's predominant employment.[8]

Often a yeoman merely bartered with a neighbor for a few days of his son's services. Larger farms, of course, made more extensive use of outside "help," yet in both cases wages accounted for a significant part of the farm budget. Competition for unskilled labor in the growing industrial sector and general inflation thus had a direct impact on agricultural profits. The fluctuations were often tremendous. In 1835 and 1836, for example, salaries for farm "help" sky-rocketed, only to crash in the 1837 depression. Farmers, no less than the "hands" themselves, felt victimized by the unstable situation:

> Perhaps there is not one question of more importance or that has a greater influence upon the profits of agricultural operations than the wages paid to what are familiarly called "hired hands" or "help." . . . It often happens . . . that extraneous circumstances [i.e., other than the price of produce] influence the rate of wages. If, for instance, some mechanical or commercial pursuit should suddenly rise . . . and draw off large numbers from the farm . . .; and if there should be an abundant harvest, produce [prices] would fall on the market. . . . When the season comes he [the farmer] must go forward and continue without stop until the harvest or [if he waits for wages to decline] all is lost.[9]

Unfortunately little information of a direct and personal nature on Winthrop's "hired hands" has survived. It seems that they were usually engaged through a simple over-the-fence offer and a nod.[10] Nevertheless, general references point to common notions about their character.

Few denied that the low wages paid to the "hired hand" brought him little prestige. "Progressive agriculturalists" mourned his lowly status and accompanying shame. Yet their cause could hardly advance while "abolitionists" touted the good fortune of the "day-laborer" by comparing him with a Southern "slave" — hardly a flattering comparison from the "laborer" 's point of view.[11]

"Hands" were assumed to have moral as well as economic justifications for their shame. Farmers complained that many of the "hired help" were too lazy, calling them "idlers," "loiterers," and "hangers-on," as well as too prone to drink. During the 1820s and early 1830s, residents debated whether it was even possible for "boys" to get in the hay without "the stimulating influence of ardent spirits." Some yeomen apparently felt it necessary to stipulate sobriety as a job requirement:

> DITCHER WANTED, a good ditcher — one who understands the business, and will attend to his work and *keep sober,* will find good encouragement here, a part, or all of the season. . . . N.B. None need apply who can't walk straight.[12]

The worst of the lot were portrayed as chronic grumblers and trouble-makers: "They are almost certain to do something tending to induce you to dismiss your help, or them to leave you. They will represent to your men that their work is too hard, their wages too low, or their privileges and treatment not equal to those enjoyed by themselves and others."[13] Men apparently often broke work agreements to seek better pay, causing some farmers to reminisce about the supposed "moral rectitude," "that faithfulness, that quiet love of subordination to employers," in former days.[14] With meager wages and a reputation marred by indolence, intemperance, and rebelliousness, "hired hands" had a less than honorable vocation.

Estimates of their agricultural expertise varied widely. Some, particularly "men" rather than "boys," were thought to have extensive farm knowledge. Elijah Wood, for example, one of Winthrop's most noted "scientific agriculturalists," advertised:

> NOTICE TO LABORERS. The subscriber wishes to hire a good, steady industrious *man* to labor on an old Farm, and the more he can teach me about farming the better.[15]

Dr. Holmes charged that "hands" sometimes pestered their employers with advice, that they were "too knowy."[16] Most often, however, being "hired out" was considered a form of "apprenticeship." On the job a "boy" could learn many of the skills that he would use if he became a "farmer."[17]

The "help" ("hired hands," "boys," "men," "workmen," or

"laborers") were given various names depending upon the particular tasks they performed. (See Figure 9.) These labels were even more temporary and context-specific than the lexicon of "farmer" specialists. A "farmer" might employ a single "hand" who would assume all these identities through the year, or, as an extension of common usage, he might employ no one and refer to himself in these terms. Whatever their special skills, "help" were generally assumed to be masters of the full range of farm chores. "Mower" or "ploughman," a "boy" was expected to work with speed and ease.

FIGURE 9

A Taxonomy of the "Hand" Domain

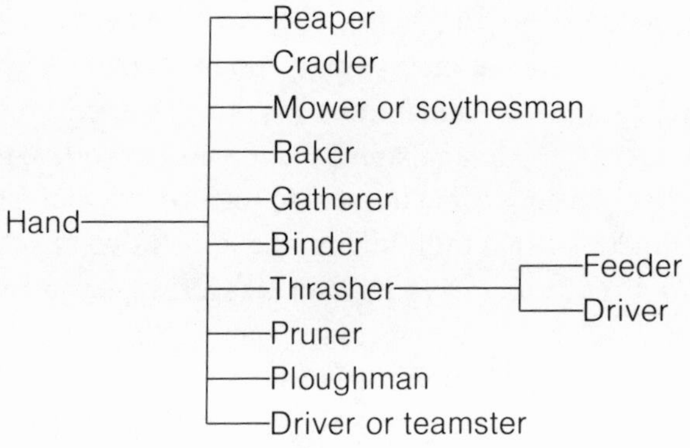

As shown in Figure 10, "hands" could be distinguished by the season in which they worked. The spring thaw brought a call for "pruners," who trimmed Winthrop orchards, and "ploughmen," who, with or without the assistance of a "driver," broke ground for planting.[18] The fall harvest required a fuller complement of "hands." (See Figure 11.) Step by step they brought in the crop: with a sweep of a blade the "reaper," "cradler," or "mower" cut his way from one side of the field to the other; the "raker" crossed his path combing piles of yield from the stubble; the "gatherer" bound the stalks of grain or hay in tidy sheaves; the "binder" arranged groups of sheaves in capped stands to air; finally, the "thrasher" beat the grain off the

FIGURE 10

A Paradigm of the "Hand" Domain: Work Seasons

Work Season		
Spring		Fall
Pruner Ploughman Driver or teamster	Reaper Cradler Mower or scythesman Raker Gatherer	Binder Thrasher Feeder Driver

FIGURE 11

A Paradigm of the "Hand" Domain: Harvest

Stage of the Harvest

Start ⟵⟶ Finish

Reaper Cradler Mower	Raker	Gatherer	Binder	Thrasher Feeder Driver

stalks. (With a horse-powered thresher, a "feeder" stuffed sheaves into the machine while a "driver" led the team that powered it.)[19]

There were, of course, many variations in the sequence, but the general pattern was common enough to structure the terminological system. Not only were the procedures represented — there were even the specific tools. Residents explained that a "reaper" used a sickle, a "cradler" a cradle, and a "mower" a scythe. (See Figure 12.) There were unique skills involved in wielding each implement, but all were applied toward the same end; thus, essentially, the tool defined the man.[20]

FIGURE 12

A Paradigm of the "Hand" Domain: Implements

Implement		
Sickle	Cradle	Scythe
Reaper	Cradler	Mower or scythesman

In sum, unlike "butchers" or "lawyers," "hands" did not sell particular skills or interests. They hired themselves to a "farmer" who, in delegating tasks and tools, assigned their identities.

It is consequently little surprise that "farmers" were more important than "hired help" in evaluating agricultural innovations. Although "hands" were probably more directly affected by the technology, they were not expected to play decision-making roles. In the mid-1830s, for instance, local cultivators largely abandoned their old preference for "reaping" and started "mowing." The procedures were vastly different from the "workman" 's point of view; the scythe demanded a strength and rhythm totally unlike those required by the sickle. Yet it was not appropriate for him to say, "I am a reaper; I don't do that kind of work.'' He was simply declared a ''mower,'' and his protestations dismissed as ungrateful ''sneering'' or ''croaking.''[21]

The ''hired hand'' 's labor, like that of his employer, was said to grant him the ''healthful influence'' of hard work out of doors. But that was about all that recommended it.

CHAPTER 6

Mechanics

THE HUMAN SIDE OF INDUSTRIALIZATION

Manufacturing was an important enterprise in Winthrop from its settlement. It was 1767 when John Chandler obtained a Plymouth Company land grant to build a sawmill and a gristmill, the town's first factories. Instead of locating at the old town hub, Winthrop Center, Chandler erected his mills on a stream farther west, in an area later to be dubbed "the Village." During the first half of the nineteenth century "manufacturing establishments" came to dominate the Village, and the Village to dominate the town.[1]

Winthrop offered obvious inducements to industrial development. There were excellent natural advantages: the swift waters of Snell Brook near Winthrop Center, the abundance of timber land to the north, and, above all, the falls in the Village. In but a half-mile the waters of Maranacook (or North or Chandler's Mill Pond) dropped nearly fifty feet to Lake Annabessacook (or South Pond). Even before 1790 at least four dams were erected to draw power off the water's southerly flow through the Village.[2] In addition, as agriculture declined and the population grew, there were plenty of strong hands to take over where gears, belts, and shafts left off.

Of course, power and personnel were not all that was required. Manufacturing, far more than agriculture, necessitated large amounts of capital, the kind of cash or easy credit that was seldom available between 1820 and 1850. In addition to national business slumps and the full depression of the late 1830s, Maine had its own special financial woes. Essentially a frontier, the state had little native capital, and what money it did attract tended to go for land speculation rather than

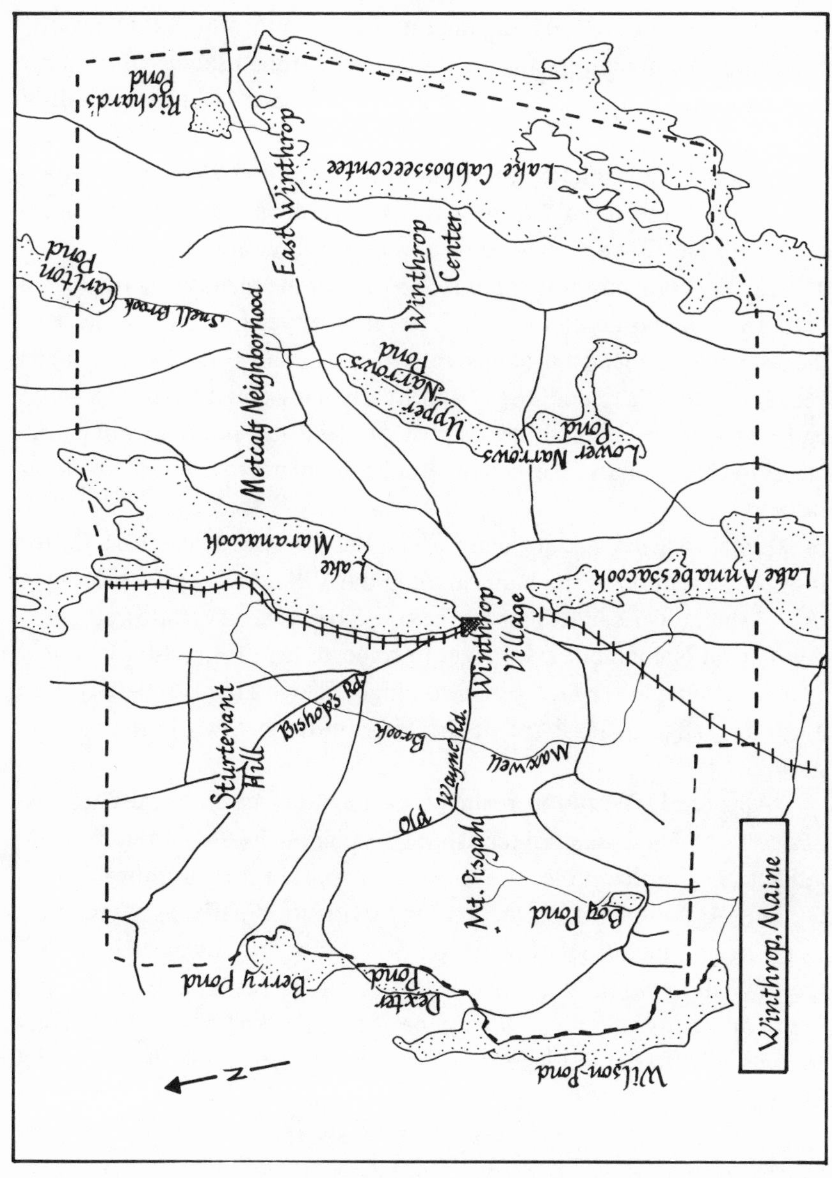
Richards Pond
East Winthrop
Lake Cobbosseecontee
Winthrop Center
Carlton Pond
Snell Brook
Metcalf Neighborhood
Upper Narrows Pond
Lower Narrows Pond
Lake Maranacook
Lake Annabessacook
Winthrop Village
Sturtevant Hill
Bishop's Rd.
Maxwell Brook
Old Wayne Rd.
Mt. Pisgah
Bog Pond
Berry Pond
Dexter Pond
Wilson Pond
N
Winthrop, Maine

industrial investment. By expanding slowly and reinvesting profits, Winthrop manufacturers were able to insulate themselves from many of the state's and the nation's business fluctuations — but hardly all of them.

Throughout its history the Winthrop Cotton and Woolen Manufactory, one of the town's largest mills, relied on "capitalists" from Hallowell and Boston, whose resources were, at best, unpredictable. Though the company was organized in 1809, the plant was not erected until 1813, and it failed to operate for another year. In its first decades the owners' financial problems caused it to change hands four times (1824, 1829, 1841, and 1850) and totally shut down twice (1837–42 and 1850–54).[3] Other mills did not rise and fall quite so often, but clearly "hard times" affected Winthrop manufacturers as well as farmers.

Local industry had its share of natural disasters, too. In 1832, for instance, a section of the main street in the Village collapsed, blocking one of the power canals that lay below. The owner, a Hallowell attorney named Nathaniel Perley, had to relocate his mill and build a new 150-foot flume to feed it.[4] Fire also plagued young industries. Between 1820 and 1850 at least six of the large mills in town burned to the ground.[5]

Apparently Winthrop residents were more ready to rally against agricultural than industrial hardship. Despite obvious community-wide advantages, for example, the town long resisted investing in fire protection. Agitation for protection was evident as early as 1826, but, aside from appointing "fire wards" to inspect stoves and chimneys, the town did not really act until 1832. After six years of fierce debate, the town finally purchased an engine, hose, ropes, hooks, and ladders to help guard the Village, the area most vulnerable to industrial blazes.[6]

Residents were somewhat more outspoken in promoting higher tariffs, which, they claimed, would benefit both manufacturer and farmer. In 1820 Sylvanus Thomas, then agent of the cotton mill, did not even let the census taker get away without registering the company's dissatisfaction with federal inaction. In 1842 the *Maine Farmer* made an exception to its normally apolitical stance to strongly endorse protectionism, and in the same year a supporting motion carried in town meeting. Though praising "free trade" as an ideal, residents voted to officially support a "judicious tariff" which, "unfortunately," the world situation and current depression required. Almost everyone greeted gleefully the high protective tariff that became law that year.[7]

One might at least expect the people engaged in craft or manufacture, "the mechanical arts," to organize for their common interests. But despite their growing number, these "mechanics" did not organize the kind of promotional campaign that agriculturalists did. Ezekiel Holmes repeatedly invited them to use the pages of his paper for "mutual improvement." In 1841 he announced that, "to render it more adapted to the interests of mechanics," he would devote a full page to manufacturing and would change the paper's title to the *Maine Farmer and Mechanic's Advocate*. Yet they remained for the most part silent and unorganized. There were scattered announcements about a Winthrop Mechanic Association in 1836, but it, too, was apparently a lame effort. A scant two years later residents were calling for the organization's "resuscitation."[8] Yet, with or without strong, organized support, Winthrop manufacturing continued to grow.

It should be emphasized, however, that industry was not just a matter of gigantic factories. As with agriculture, most of Winthrop's manufacturing operations were, and remained through the period, small and family owned. They supplied common household objects to the neighborhood and grew only with local demand. As late as 1836 a resident complained: "One who can make a common comb, a card, and umbrella, a scythe, a hoe, a rake, an ox-yoke; or a Morocco Shoe Maker, a Tinman, a Potter, a Cooper, and many other kinds of Mechanics are much needed. . . . Some of the above enumerated articles are sometimes manufactured in the village — but not followed as a steady employment."[9] At the turn of the century it was quite common in Winthrop for a farmer to begin a trade to profitably occupy his free time and a spare shed. As the population grew during the following years, his sons would turn it into a full-time business.[10] Though the number of such establishments increased in the period, the businesses remained small and had little division of labor.[11]

The manufacture of several other items, however, showed the kind of rapid growth that historians usually associate with the first half of the nineteenth century. The most marked expansion occurred in a network of related industries centering in the Village. Winthrop and neighboring sawmills produced lumber and valuable by-products for other operations. Waste slab, edging, and sawdust were burned and the ashes leached to make potash, which tanneries used to loosen the hair on skins before scraping. Ground hemlock bark was used to brew tannic acid and sprinkled between drying hides. The hides, in turn, went to boot and shoe factories, Winthrop's biggest growth industry. As a result, sawmills, potash plants, tanneries, and shoe factories lined the streets of the Village. The bigger shoe producers, such as Elias Clark and Horace Parlin, made leather as well as footwear. The success of each operation fed the others as well as associated trades. Artisans, for example, faced increased demands for shoe lasts and other instruments of production.[12]

Industries outside this network also arose during the period. Besides the cotton mill, there were large factories that printed oilcloth, for inexpensive table and floor covering, the precursor of linoleum. In typical fashion, production began in an outbuilding on Ezekiel Bailey's farm about 1830. One son, Daniel, taught his father the process as he learned it while working for Alton Pope in Vassalboro. Ezekiel's other sons, Charles and Moses, thereafter went extensively into the business, boarding dozens of workmen and producing hundreds of thousands of yards each year.[13]

John and Hiram Pitts and Luther Whitman (an associate until a bitter fight over patent rights) also introduced the large-scale manufacture of farm implements in the 1830s. It was probably this industry more than any other in Winthrop that profited from the increasing significance of machines in daily life. The Pitts brothers and Whitman patented improved endless chain pumps, horsepowers, grain separators, and corn grinders which found receptive local and, later, national markets with the new machine-buying public.[14]

The machine not only provided new demands; it helped the manufacturer meet them. Clearly, the growth of Winthrop's large-scale industry was accelerated through the efficient use of water power. This power, too, was used more efficiently as the period progressed. It is probably nowhere better exemplified than in the case of the Winthrop cotton factory. In 1841 Little, Wood, and Company of Boston purchased the cotton mill, which had been idle for four years, and retooled it from top to bottom. The resultant increase in productivity was indeed startling. The company wove about the same amount of cloth in 1850 as the previous owners did in 1832, but with fewer looms and spindles and about half as many employees. Even at the earlier date, Stephen Sewall, the mill agent, attributed rising profits to the "improvement in machinery."[15]

Yet the role of power in industrial development is, I think, too easily overemphasized. Most things were still made by hand in Winthrop even at the end of the period. This generalization holds for some of the large as well as small industries. Boot and shoe factories, for instance, increased annual production from twenty-five hundred to twenty-five thousand pairs from 1820 to 1850 without mechanizing their operations. By hiring more workers, arranging them more efficiently, and giving them better tools, the industry grew even faster than its water- or horse-powered contemporaries.[16]

In the most obvious sense, the development of Winthrop manufacturing was a change in things: water, timber, money, the landscape of the Village, products, and machinery. Winthrop just looked much more like a mill town at the end of the period than it did at the beginning.[17] But the human changes were no less significant. New skills and interests accompanied the changing material environment. The 1850 mechanic simply spent a very different working day than did his 1820 predecessor. Moreover, such changes affected an ever growing portion of the citizenry. By the end of the period the number of workers engaged in manufacturing or trades had grown more than sixfold. The kind of industrial change that could have affected the working lives of only one or two in ten affected the majority thirty years later.[18] Winthrop was becoming less the realm of the farmer and more the realm of the mechanic.

ANY MAN who made things could generally be labeled a "mechanic," but the qualifier *generally* is most important. The many variations in usage suggest how much more flexible the whole manufacturing lexicon was in early nineteenth-century Winthrop than it is commonly today.

Although, again generally, "mechanic" was a cover term for all those in manufacturing or trades, it was at times used in a much more limited sense.[19] Figure 13 shows a taxonomy of the "workingman" domain, which included "mechanic" in this narrow sense. Each label could signify a unique level of responsibility or authority in the manufacturing process. (See Figure 14.)

FIGURE 13

A Taxonomy of the "Workingman" Domain

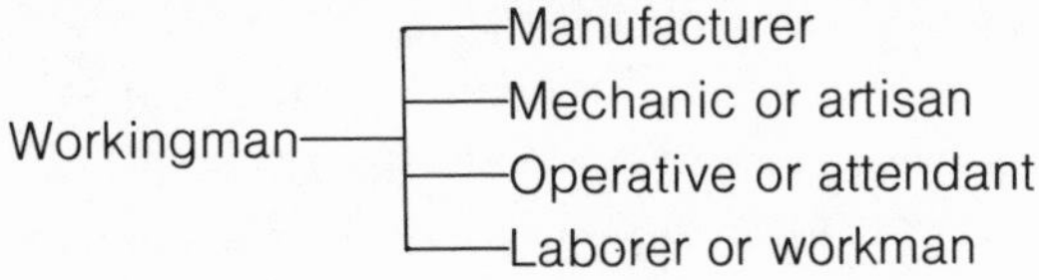

FIGURE 14

A Paradigm of the "Workingman" Domain: Responsibility

Responsibility

High ← → Low

Manufacturer	Mechanic or artisan	Operative or attendant	Laborer or workman

When drawing such status distinctions, residents would refer to the man who ran a mill or shop as a "manufacturer." He was the one who hired and fired, planned construction, directed production changes, or made similar important decisions. When, for example, the owners of the Winthrop Cotton and Woolen Manufactory, themselves "manufacturers," planned to retool the mill, they arranged to call in an "experienced Manufacturer" from Massachusetts for advice; in other words, his "experience" would qualify him to redirect an entire industrial operation.[20] Since "manufacturers" were assumed to have financial as well as mechanical responsibilities, they were often, too, considered "businessmen."[21]

"Mechanics" or "artisans," in the same reference context, were those who performed much of the production work but were not necessarily responsible for an entire establishment. Their authority was nonetheless extensive. A "mechanic" was highly trained, and residents viewed the quality of the finished product as a fairly direct indicator of the skill he had acquired. The difference between a "manufacturer" and a "mechanic" was, in this sense, more than a matter of wealth. Through both were numbered among the "producers," "mechanics" were the ones who more regularly soiled their hands in daily employment.[22] It is, I think, for this reason that references so often blur the ideal distinction between the two. "Manufacturers" could stress their membership in the "productive classes" and their "humble origins" by claiming to be "mechanics," while "mechanics" could emphasize the breadth of their responsibility by calling themselves "manufacturers." Both usage extensions suggest the value residents placed on manual labor and authority.[23]

"Operatives" or "attendants" were the prime victims or beneficiaries in the division of industrial labor. While an "artisan" was usually said to follow all the steps in production, an "operative" was responsible for but one or a few of those steps. He or she would do piecework or tend a machine as part of a larger operation. Though such tasks often required great skill, the "operative" 's responsibilities and training were limited.[24]

Nevertheless, "operatives," too, were frequently called "mechanics," both as a form of flattery and as a natural consequence of the fluid conditions at the time. Characterizations of the industrial revolution, I think, too often give the picture of the country cobbler awakening one day to find his quaint shop transformed into a massive factory. The developments in Winthrop, at least, were far less cataclysmic. The successful shoemaker might simply assemble a few of his less fortunate associates and expand his shop. He might or might not arrange them in assembly-line fashion. Thus, at any given time, each shop was in its own stage of implementing new technology. Just how much more mechanical or repetitive was a man's work, how much more limited his responsibilities, when he became more of an "operative" than a "mechanic"? The documents show little concern for an answer. Residents were apparently content to allow each person to set his own boundaries. This neglect could have contributed to Winthrop's rapid industrialization. Unlike the "practical farmer," the "mechanic" did not have to face a change in identity with the modernization of his duties. Though some people might begin to consider him an "operative," he could quite properly continue to think of himself as a "mechanic."[25]

"Laborers," or "common laborers" as they were so often described, seldom left their own mark on the historical record. Others characterized them in the same lowly terms as the farmer's "hired help." Residents tended to overlook the significance of the "laborers' " toil for Winthrop industry. Whatever their specific tasks, their responsibilities were supposed meager. For minimal pay they were usually expected to do a job that required little or no skill and then to be on their way. They were the one manufacturing group that could not properly lay claim to the "mechanic" 's virtues.[26]

Those who could claim to be "mechanics" associated themselves with the extensive training program that traditionally characterized the trades. Though the program was gradually falling out of practice, residents continued to speak of the orderly stages through which an "artisan" passed. (See Figure 15.) Each step marked the "me-

FIGURE 15

A Taxonomy of the "Mechanic" Domain

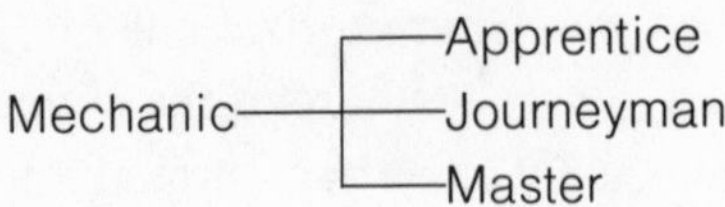

chanic'' 's increasing age, responsibility, skill, and, above all, independence; he was growing up. (See Figure 16.)

FIGURE 16

A Paradigm of the ''Mechanic'' Domain: Independence

Independence: Low ⟵⟶ High		
Apprentice	Journeyman	Master

Ideally, a boy took his first step toward occupational as well as social maturity when, in his early teens, he or his father arranged an apprenticeship. Over the next five to seven years an ''apprentice'' was, in a very real sense, prepared for adulthood.[27] Toward this end, his ''master'' exercised almost total control. An ''apprentice'' could not leave his service without the ''master'' 's consent, and such consent would generally be taken as a negative reflection on the ''apprentice,'' an indication that he was ''bungling'' and ''unfaithful.'' In 1836, for example, area printers found it difficult to agree that even criminal abuse was just cause for an ''apprentice'' to leave ''at his own caprice.'' *Maine Farmer* advertisements for the recovery of ''runaways,'' frequently offering as little as one-cent rewards, testify to the extent of the indenture as well as the community support for its preservation, at least in the advertisers' estimation.[28]

Residents were quite self-conscious in treating apprenticeship as a turning point in the maturing process. This is probably best exemplified in the letters that Winthrop's Congregational minister, David Thurston, sent to his son, an ''apprentice'' to a Portland printer in the 1830s. Thurston observed: ''Your departure from home to learn a trade is an important era in your life. Separated from the watchful, fostering care of the domestic circle, you are to form new acquaintances, new associations, and be brought under new influences. . . . Disappoint not the fond hopes of your fond father.'' He explained how a boy's relations with his God, parents, employers, and fellow apprentices in these crucial years would probably shape his character for the rest of his life. He warned against "youthful lusts" and the threat of any "impure, dishonest or untrue thought," emphasizing that even choices of diet or residence could be perilous.[29]

Only after successfully completing his service would an "apprentice" be ready for the most basic adult responsibilities: "*Apprentices . . . are not to marry. . . .* [You may wed only] when you have finished your apprenticeship, established yourself in business, and have a prospect of furnishing a comfortable support to a family." That liberty was the "apprentice" 's ultimate reward suggests the importance given independence. Residents regularly spoke of the "mechanic" 's life after apprenticeship as "the time you are free."[30]

If he continued his trade, the young "mechanic" could next contract to work as a "journeyman." Winthrop's large boot and shoe factories, for instance, hired dozens of "journeymen shoemakers." His training brought him more pay and independence than the "apprentice," but he was still obligated to an employer. Though less frequent and vehement, there were complaints about runaway "journeymen" as well as "apprentices."[31]

Having amassed sufficient skill and capital, a man might then become a "master mechanic." He would achieve the ultimate in independence by going to "work on his own account." He might work alone in a shop or employ his own "apprentices" and "journeymen." As Winthrop factories increased in number and size, the latter prospect became more likely, but this development meant fewer opportunities for "journeymen" to become "masters." Nevertheless, residents continued to stress the "mechanic" 's ability to attain skill and independence in his occupation.[32]

Like agriculture the "mechanical arts" implied a good measure of manual labor. Winthrop residents commonly expected an "artisan" to "be found during the day with leather apron on–coat off–shirt sleeves rolled up, toiling at the work bench." His was the "practical" world of tools, machines, and sweat.[33] To some extent this image was complimentary. Manual labor, aside from its special romantic appeal, was considered a good road to self-sufficiency. Unlike "businessmen" or "professional men," the "mechanic" was pictured "earning with his own hands, the means by which he supports himself"; the instruments of his independence were made rather than winnowed from fluctuating finance or service markets. Only a reliance on "customers" made his fortunes more tenuous than the "farmer" 's.[34]

Yet, many observed, it was also manual labor that accounted for the "mechanic" 's low position in the "social or political scale." A resident complained: "There is a strange dislike to the name of mechanic in this country . . . ; it would almost seem a disgrace to be an industrious and useful man. . . . Because he get 'his bread by the sweat of his brow,' [he] is not considered so good as a man who is too proud to labor."[35]

In promoting the honor of the "workingman," contributors to the *Maine Farmer* repeatedly blamed the folly of those blinded by "finery and show" for this opinion. One W. H. L., for instance, dedicated an article, appropriately entitled "Respect Thyself," to his fellow Winthrop "artisans." He declared: "There are those now who look upon the mechanic as one degree below those who have a living afforded them without manual labor; but that portion is small and weak. . . . The individual . . . who judges his fellow citizens by their ability to subsist without labor must be destitute of two important qualifications, *experience* and *common sense*." Yet, despite decades of such protest, estimates of the "mechanic" 's prestige were low in 1850 as well as 1820. The sweat that was an object of pride in the promoter's argument was often a disgrace in the parlor, where a "mechanic" could anticipate the muttered boast: "I can always smell a shoemaker, if there is one in the room."[36]

There were, too, additional negative aspects to the public image of the "mechanic." He was reputedly without the intellect or education that marked more prestigious vocations. The "practical artisan," like his agricultural counterpart, apparently viewed higher learning as at best irrelevant or at worst destructive in his trade: "The deeper branches of mathematics, the art of composition, eloquence, philosophy &c.? They have nothing to do with our profession. . . . We leave these branches of education to the Ministers, the Doctors and Lawyers of the land." In a folk biography of Eli Whitney, for example, a carpenter shows his surprise at Whitney's manual dexterity by exclaiming: "There was one good mechanic spoiled when you went to college.'' Even with seven years of intense training, the ''mechanic'' was still not, in the popular sense, ''learned.'' Some residents attacked this position by claiming, on the one hand, that the definition of ''learned'' was absurdly arbitrary and, on the other, that ''mechanics'' should seek the knowledge that would make them ''learned'' in the public eye. But parents who held high estimates of their sons' intellectual capacities could be expected to steer them away from the trades.[37]

Additional reasons for avoiding the ''mechanical arts'' were the well-known hazards involved:

> The mechanic is . . . — from the nature of his occupation — often placed in situations where a greater degree of care is required to preserve the health than is necessary for other classes. A portion labor in damp, unhealthy mines, in wells and cellars; some are perpetually exposed to the fumes of melted metals, which are well known to be poisonous; others again are liable to injury from the postures in which they are obliged to work, or even from the use of certain tools and instruments.

A local doctor reported a host of threats to health and longevity in each of the trades. Although some ''artisans'' hoped that mechanization would decrease the hazards, on-the-job safety was a continuing problem.[38]

If a man was fortunate enough to become a ''master mechanic,'' furthermore, he could face troublesome relations with his employees as well as customers. In ''hard times'' or with increasing competition he might even be unable to support himself: ''The mechanics . . . are continually plagued with captious and mean customers, untoward and lazy apprentices, or perhaps want of employment.''[39] Nevertheless, despite its relatively low and hazardous image, the ''mechanical arts'' attracted an increasing number of Winthrop men.

Those who did choose this path, regardless of the particular branch, had a very explicit set of values to guide them. For the most part, the finished product was the key evidence in distinguishing a ''good mechanic''; the product was a measure of the man. As in agriculture, there was an accent on both quantity and quality. In advertisements, for example, Winthrop ''mechanics'' used production figures and claims of ''fine'' or ''neat'' work to solicit business.[40]

Yet there was also a uniquely heavy accent on speed. The usual boast was not just that one made many good things, but that one made them in a very short time. Winthrop's shoe industry, for instance, even sported contests to distinguish the best ''cordwainers.'' In 1847 Mr. Fasset, a young Winthrop ''mechanic,'' was widely touted for fitting and putting the bottoms to twenty-four heavy, double-soled boots in a twenty-one hour marathon — an achievement that required setting no less than ninety-six hundred pegs. Time trials constituted a major justification for adopting new technology. It was thus the union of three features — quantity, quality, and speed — that marked the ''workmanlike manner'' of a good ''mechanic.''[41]

''Artisans'' were also to manifest a special sort of shop presence. Thurston, for example, advised his apprentice son: ''What then is the real excellence in one placed in your condition? It is not merely the greatest aptness in acquiring a knowledge of the trade; nor the most untiring application to business; nor the utmost punctuality; nor the highest trustworthiness. It is the union of all these.'' Prompt and courteous attention to customers would show that a ''mechanic'' was both industrious and trustworthy. His strict supervision of employees would show his uncompromising standards: ''He had his journeyman and his apprentices and was always present to oversee them and to be seen by his customers, as all master mechanics ought to be.''[42]

Proper craft skill and human relations together were said to yield the typical occupational rewards, wealth and fame. Thus, Winthrop success stories commonly outlined the ''workmanlike manner'' of a ''mechanic'' hero and his ensuing good fortune; for example: ''Charles Clemens never neglected his shop; never broke his promise; never slighted his work; never cheated a customer; and Charles Clemens soon had a purse full of dollars and cellar full of beef and cider; a house of his own and two or three handsome lots around it.'' Word of his success would soon spread to bring him an ever wider circle of customers.[43]

Although residents could identify a reputation and values characteristic of ''mechanics'' in general, individuals were usually identified with a particular specialty, as shown in Figure 17.

Clearly ''mechanic'' was a very general term.[44] It covered not

FIGURE 17

A Taxonomy of the "Mechanic" Domain

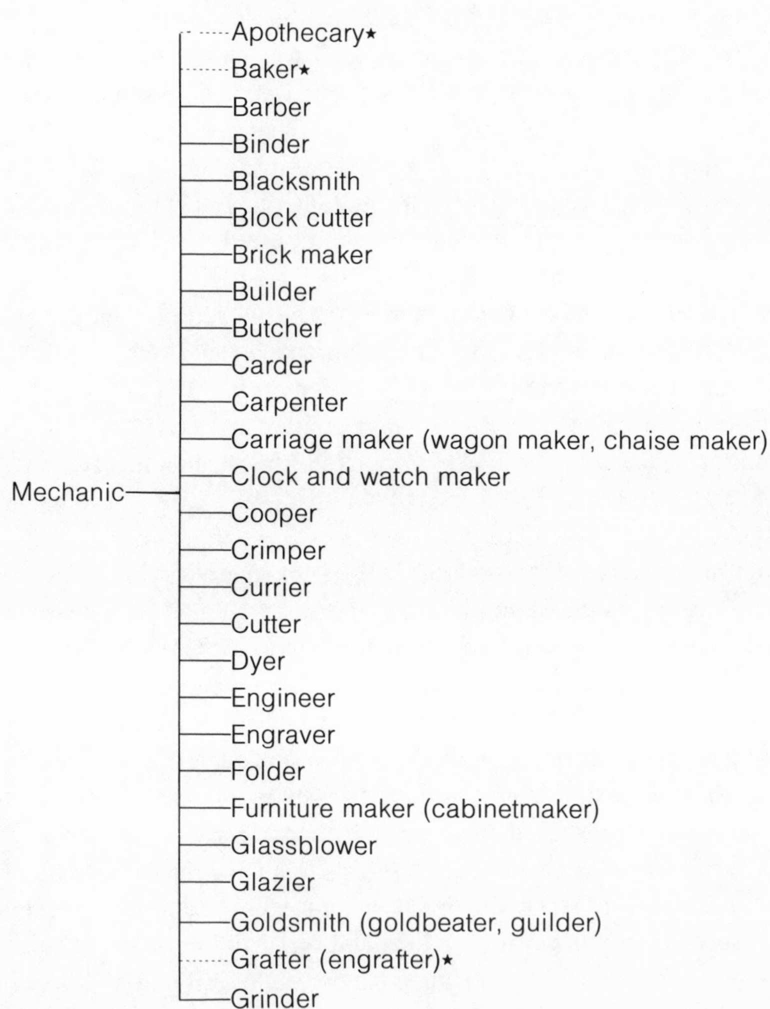

A Taxonomy of the "Mechanic" Domain (Cont.)

Mechanic
- Hatter
- Housewright
- Jeweler
- Joiner (wood workman, wright)
- Lapidary
- Machinist (mechanician)
- Miller
- Milliner
- Millwright
- Painter
- Polisher
- Printer
- Saddle and harness maker (saddler)
- Sawyer
- Shingle weaver
- Shoemaker (bootmaker, cordwainer, catwhipper, tapster)
- Silversmith
- Slater
- Spinner
- Stonecutter
- Surveyor
- Tailor (clothier)
- Tanner
- Tinman
- Weaver
- Wheelwright
- Whitesmith
- Woodturner

*The dotted line indicates the absence of clear documentation for inclusion in this domain.

only those who made a large variety of articles, but also those who may not have made anything at all. Despite the ideal "maker" definition, for example, the term was even used to designate "barbers."[45] In structural terms, then, "mechanic" served as a kind of holding category for skilled manual workers who were not "farmers." Yet residents repeatedly expounded the ideal definition, often using "maker" or "manufacturer" as a synonym for "mechanic." Neither did they make the now popular distinction between craft and industry. The labels "mechanic," "artisan," "tradesman," and "craftsman" were interchangeable; indeed, even "operatives" were at times called "artisans." This is but a further indication of the flexibility that characterized the entire domain.[46]

The greatest flexibility, however, is evident in the way the various specialties were constituted. Individual "mechanics" were simply identified by the type of materials they handled, as illustrated in Figure 18. Often the name of the finished product was just combined with the term "maker" or the like to yield such labels as "edge tool manufacturer."[47]

Technological considerations were thus largely irrelevant. As, for example, Winthrop "blacksmiths" gave up the sledge and anvil for the water-powered trip hammer, they remained "blacksmiths."[48] In this sense the terminology was inadequate. It failed to reflect the changes in day-to-day activity that industrialization required. A *Maine Farmer* correspondent probably put this most clearly when he observed:

> The carpet loom is a very complicated machine, requiring the closest attention on the part of the operatives, which would seem to be no easy task amid the clang of a hundred shuttles — each loom having a dozen or so . . . — and the jingling of as many little bells that ring at every change of color required. . . . The workmen look care-worn — and you have none of the songs of the "jolley weaver," to which the brisk shuttle used to beat time . . . ; the tread mill turneth out no music now-a-days, and "things isn't as they used to was!" However the *carpets* are beautiful — pattern colors and all — and if the *end* is but gained, what matters the *means?*[49]

So long as the identity of a "mechanic" was tied to the product and his success a matter of quantity, quality, and speed, the question is rhetorical; the means do not matter. The "mechanic" who tended a power loom was just a more productive "weaver" than his "jolley" predecessors.

Probably, then, the most significant thing about the lexicon is how little it changed. The apparent stability of the terminology masks the shifting occupational life of the community. Despite rapid industrial development, Winthrop remained a town of "blacksmiths" and "cordwainers."

The impact of industrialization on another group was far more turbulent. Traditional social ideals did not adequately allow for the increasing number of women engaged in manufacturing. Since the census, with few exceptions, failed to report the occupations of women, summary employment figures are hard to find, but the number of women in the mechanical arts was assuredly significant and growing. The Winthrop cotton factory alone in 1832 had ninety-five employees, and eighty-three of them were women.[50]

In the absence of clear community standards, residents were often at odds in their understanding of this development. On the one hand, "mechanics," those who made things, were male by definition. Note, for instance, the contrast implied in a statement about the Show of Manufactured Articles at the 1833 Cattle Show and Fair: "What articles were exhibited were good, but we really hope that the ladies, as well as our mechanics, will give us a better treat next year." In other words, both men and women could make things, but only men were considered "mechanics."[51]

On the other hand, residents recognized that women were taking their place in a number of specialties commonly included in the "mechanic" domain, such as: "binder," "bottomer," "folder," "milliner," "operative," "tailor," and "weaver." Women, too, were counted among Winthrop "apprentices," most often serving "tailors" or "milliners."[52]

Yet, such women could still not properly be referred to as "mechanics," or, for that matter, assigned any other general occupational identity. They were usually just called "girls," with some lengthy or relatively awkward qualifier, such as "warper girl."[53]

FIGURE 18

A Paradigm of the "Mechanic" Domain: Materials

Materials	
Barrels	Cooper
Books/papers	Printer, folder, cutter
Bread/cakes	Baker
Brick	Brick maker
Buildings	Builder, carpenter, housewright
Carriages	Carriage maker, wagon maker, chaise maker, wheelwright, painter, glazier
Cloth	Carder, spinner, weaver, dyer
Clothing	Tailor, clothier
Fine metals	Silversmith, goldsmith, goldbeater, whitesmith, guilder, engraver, tinman
Gems	Jeweler, lapidary
Glass	Glassblower, glazier
Grain	Miller
Hair	Barber
Hats	Hatter, milliner, binder
Iron	Blacksmith, grinder, polisher
Leather	Tanner, currier
Lumber	Sawyer, shingle weaver

A Paradigm of the "Mechanic" Domain: Materials (Cont.)

Materials	Machinery	Machinist, mechanician, millwright
	Meat	Butcher
	Oilcloth	Block cutter, painter, printer
	Remedies	Apothecary
	Roads	Engineer, surveyor
	Saddles	Saddle and harness maker, saddler
	Scions	Grafter, engrafter
	Shoes/boots	Shoemaker, bootmaker, cordwainer, tapster, catwhipper, crimper
	Stone	Stonecutter, slater
	Timepieces	Clock and watch maker
	Woodwork	Wood workman, cabinetmaker, furniture maker, joiner, wright, woodturner

Quite literally, then, Winthrop citizens did not know how, in what terms, to address a significant social change. Between 1820 and 1850, in a fairly self-conscious manner, they sought to fill the cultural gap. In 1833, for example, residents met to formally debate the question: "Is the Employment given to Females, in Manufactories, calculated to result in the benefit or injury of themselves and the Public?" They tried to develop a more complete set of standards to apply to the new group.[54]

A major resource in this effort was the limited but long-standing image of "female" as home "manufacturer." Furnishing family clothing traditionally constituted a wife's "domestic duty" and a daughter's "household education." Thus, carding, spinning, weaving, sewing, and knitting were quite proper activities for a woman in her family role: "The fingers of our industrious help-meets, and daughters, and sisters seldom tire." But this propriety was explicitly limited to what was called "domestic manufacture," that is, making things in the home for family use.[55]

The notion of women leaving the home for pay was a totally different matter. There were, of course, ample nonindustrial precedents for such action, but, both men and women agreed, these were hardly honorable. Even before factory work became available, many women worked as "seamstresses" or "domestics."[56] Yet it was assumed that these occupations were reserved for those threatened by poverty; only a desperate home economy could cause a woman to abandon her full-time "household duties." The desperation that was implied served as both an embarrassment to working women and a major obstacle to those who promoted new employment opportunities. The *Maine Farmer*, for example, which generally opposed the extension of "female labor," printed a reader's complaint:

> There are females, who have been so educated by their parents, that they look upon labor as something derogatory to their sex. . . . They do not care to associate with those of their own sex whom misfortune or poverty compel to take in work, or who labor in shops or factories. . . . Girls, if you know what belongs to your interest and your happiness, you will never be ashamed to work —

> you will never let the crimson mantle your cheeks when it is said, "She takes in work," or "She has entered a shop or factory."[57]

The work of "seamstress" or "domestic" yielded outrageously meager returns. The typical employer was pictured too often: "Obtaining services for the least compensation, many times giving scarcely sufficient to sustain life. . . . What do many day-laborers and seamstresses receive?"[58] Like the "day-laborer," too, women in traditional employments were said to be fearfully subject to "immoral temptations." Residents flaunted reports of urban scandals to buttress this image: "In our cities, heretofore, women employed as seamstresses have been poorly paid and have many times been so severely oppressed and abused by their extortionate employers, that they have been driven to desperation, and yielded to temptations which have ended in infamy and ruin."[59]

Thus, as residents evaluated the changing character of "female labor," its traditional associations with vice, poverty, desperation, and the dereliction of household duties became key issues. The addition of "factory girl" to the list of common occupations meant, to some, only the multiplication of threats to women and the community as a whole. Factory work, it was claimed, would compromise a girl's "domestic education," making her an inferior "wife" and "mother"; its health hazards were too severe for her "delicate constitution"; and there was the "vicious influence" of males and females congregated without parental supervision. Often the whole argument was hyphenated by the simple assertion that women, by divine design as well as tradition, are excluded from the occupational world.[60]

The reason someone would choose to become a "factory girl" was, from this standpoint, a mystery. Often such a choice was attributed to some "character" defect, a misdirected ambition or just a lack of intelligence. Samuel and Susanna Clark, for instance, reported to their son: "Martha is going to work in the factory tomorrow is tired of doing housework no other excuse that I know of." That such "excuse"-hunting should occur suggests again the troublesome absence of community standards for the "factory girl."[61]

A number of citizens, however, particularly the "factory girls" themselves, disputed this picture. Naturally they placed a heavy emphasis on the superiority of their position when compared to that of a "seamstress" or "domestic." One woman, for example, took issue with an editorial that contrasted the "virtue" of housekeeping with the "slavery" of mill work by declaring:

> Were I in search of employment I do not hesitate to aver that I should much prefer the *slavery* of a cotton factory to that of any domestic. . . . Girls that go out to do house work are not paid for their labor. Not one girl in ten can clothe herself decently with the wages allowed in this place. Then let no one say that poor girls are above doing house work till they receive suitable renumeration [*sic*] for their services.

From this standpoint, it was not misdirected but well-directed ambition that brought Winthrop women to the factory. Higher wages were repeatedly touted in disassociating "factory girls" from traditional female employments.[62]

Higher wages, in turn, would supposedly deter "immoral temptations." Less desperate in her dependence on her employer, the "factory girl" would also be less vulnerable to an "extortionate" one. Besides, many argued, her moral supervision was in the dedicated care of the "intelligent and high-minded men" who usually ran the mills.[63]

While admitting that the extension of "female labor" meant decreased devotion to the household, some residents preferred to view it as a gain for woman's freedom and self-respect. Those who associated with the "female education movement," in particular, pictured factory work as a rare opportunity for their advancement. In estimating the "value of female labor" in the future, for instance, one advocate predicted: "They will cease to be regarded merely as the creatures of man's pleasures and the slaves of his caprice . . . and they will rise to the condition in which God designed and Christianity tends to place them, not at the feet, but at the side of man." From this perspective, the "factory girl" constituted a fairly radical departure from the traditional conception of "God's design."[64] But hopes for new freedom were not limited to the pages of reformers' tracts. Note, for example, the composition "Song of the Factory Girl," by one of Winthrop's own representatives of "female labor":

Though to this noisy, tiresome room,
At early dawn, I take my way,
Where sterner fate has fixed my doom
To labor the live-long day —
Ye proudly great, sigh not for me,
For still my thoughts and will are free. . . .

I am not rich nor wish to be
For now my love, my acts, are free.[65]

The advocates and opponents of "female labor" continued their debate long after 1850. If Winthrop citizens reached any new consensus on their expectations of these women, it is not apparent. What is apparent, for men as well as women, is how little the terminology had adapted to industrial changes. Thus, one might well expect some future adaptation, some cultural change that would make these categories correspond more precisely to new manufacturing roles.

CHAPTER 7

Workingmen and Gentlemen

THE DYNAMICS OF STANDING

As indicated in the agricultural and manufacturing terminology, a man's occupational identity was largely determined by the particular materials, responsibilities, and "character" he displayed in his work. By considering these types of factors, residents could know generally what to expect of their "farmers" and "mechanics." Many expectations were also formed on the basis of such traditional sociological variables as wealth, prestige (or "honor"), and sex. It was these factors, for instance, that were often invoked in discriminating "females," "hired hands," and "laborers" from others who toiled in similar settings.

I hesitate to refer to these as status distinctions, since "status" was hardly a common term in Winthrop, but the word does correctly suggest how important "wealth" and "honor" were in the occupational structure. Residents regularly spoke of the "standing" of an occupation, its place "above" or "below" another. The evaluation was usually based on the expected amount of returns in riches and reputation which, it was assumed, went together: "We Yankees especially, and men generally, look very much at the profits derived from an employment, and consider it honorable in proportion to the dollars and cents derived from it." Thus a marked difference in "standing" separated "agriculturalists" and "mechanics" from their "hands" and "laborers."[1]

A similar distinction was drawn between what were sometimes called "producers" and "nonproducers."[2] (See Figure 19.) The mark of a "producer" (or "workingman") was the physical rather than mental nature of his work; his was a direct contribution to the material world. Residents commonly contrasted "the mechanic [or farmer] who depends upon the labor of his hands for a living; or the merchant who looks to his gains for a livelihood; or the professional man who depends upon HEADWORK for the supplies to his family."[3]

FIGURE 19

A Taxonomy of the "Man" Domain

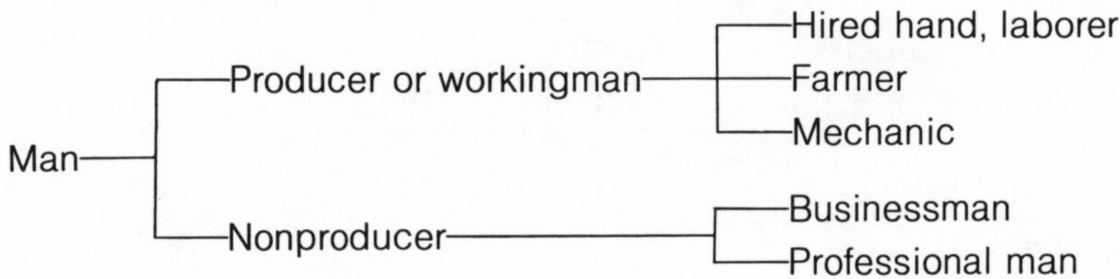

Yet, despite the general appeal of "practical" or "manual labor," the "standing" of the "workingman" was decidedly lower than that of the "businessman" or "professional man." Those who pleaded the cause of the "workingman" protested: "It seems to us wrong, that in this country of at least theoretical equality, the ingenious fabricator of an article or mechanism should be placed in the social or political scale below the merchant. . . . Yet so it is: the mere trafficker . . . generally stands a little ahead of the ingenious, talented, thinking, hard-working mechanic."[4] (See Figure 20.)

Naturally, then, those who opposed this conception attacked it on two fronts — the overemphasis of wealth and the underemphasis of manual labor. Rich "gentlemen," they claimed, too often displayed a passion for "fashion," "gaming," and other "folly" that should disqualify them from "high standing." Such an emulated position should be reserved for those who, by definition, "rise" only by displaying the highest virtues — "skill" and "industry." It was thus with considerable moral outrage that Holmes asked, "Is it a fact that the productive classes, which are the most numerous, are ruled by the non-producers?" and unequivocably answered, yes.[5]

FIGURE 20

A Paradigm of the "Man" Domain: Standing

Standing (Honor and Wealth)

Low ⟵⟶ High

Labor: Manual		Labor: Not Manual
Workingman		Nonproducer
Laborer	Farmer	Businessman
Hired hand	Mechanic	Professional man

Advocates of change begged "workingmen" to become more industrious and skillful, and thereby, it was assumed, to get rich, in order to break the exclusive hold of the "nonproducers" on "high" position. If successful, they would be worthy of even greater esteem, since they would have used more virtuous means to achieve the same end. Thus, typical references to "self-made men" were applied not to successful "merchants" or "lawyers" but to successful "workingmen," usually "farmers" or "mechanics." A "self-made man" might end up in a business or profession, but, significantly, he began as an industrious member of the "productive classes." Tales like those that appeared in the *Maine Farmer* or the *Lives of Distinguished Shoemakers,* a work assembled by a Winthrop cordwainer and a machinist, stress "character" rather than occupation as the model determinant of "standing."[6]

The debate in Winthrop provides some clarification of the role of the "common man" in what has been so often declared his age. First of all, it should be emphasized that the label was exceedingly rare. Any reference to Winthrop's early nineteenth century as "the age of the common man'' might be of heuristic value but is hardly of great cultural relevance.

Second, on those few occasions when it was used, the label had neither a special significance nor a clear referent. ''Common man'' did, of course, imply, in some sense, a ''lower standing,'' but serious semantic questions remain. Did the speaker or an unjust ''society'' deem the ''common man'' ''lower''? What features of the individual made him ''lower''? And relative to whom? ''Common man'' was at times even used in a simple mathematical sense to denote ''workingman''; constituting at least 90 percent of the adult male population, ''workingmen'' were, after all, quite common. For those (apparently most) who assumed that ''standing'' had occupational correlates, ''common men'' were also ''producers,'' but, from this standpoint, ''common'' did not necessarily imply relative poverty. Since some ''farmers'' and ''mechanics'' amassed great fortunes, there were wealthy ''common men,'' even if they would be considered highly uncommon by modern standards. Those who rejected the occupational barriers to honor could call ''workingmen'' ''common men'' to parody community standards or use it more generally to refer to less ''successful'' members of any occupation. Whatever the most proper definition and role of the ''common man,'' he apparently did not occupy much attention in Winthrop from 1820 to 1850.[7]

A figure who loomed more prominently in the discussions of occupation and ''standing'' was the ''gentleman.'' Since he was by definition a man of ''high position,'' evaluations of his ideal or expected ''character'' were, as well, evaluations of the basic nature of ''standing'' in the community.

In its most general usage, ''gentleman'' was a title of respect. In honoring their audience, for example, orators commonly addressed their remarks to ''ladies and gentlemen.'' Those who anticipated the ''elevation'' of the ''workingman'' promised, ''The time is not far distant when *our mechanics* will be entitled, *in the very best sense of the word* to the name of *gentleman*.'' Note, however, that this remark admits both multiple ''senses'' of the word and occupational bounds to its application.[8]

''Gentleman,'' as an occupational term, was usually reserved for ''businessmen'' and ''professional men'' or, more specifically, for men free of regular employment responsibilities. They were "capitalists," "speculators," or "heirs" to great estates who were so wealthy that they did not have to "go to work." Thus, for example, a Winthrop census taker could report that by profession Stephen Sewall was simply a "gentleman."[9] That "gentleman" could be a general term of respect, yet be limited in application to rich men in certain vocations, was a source of considerable conflict.

Significantly, though, the importance of wealth was not seriously questioned. Residents could agree that men of "high standing" should be "successful" by the same economic standard that distinguished men of any vocation. Thus, "gentlemen" were pictured commonly and quite properly midst an array of fine possessions and attending "servants."[10] What was more open to question was the importance of "character" in defining a "gentleman," the way he acquired and lived with his wealth. (See Figure 21.)

FIGURE 21

A Taxonomy of the "Gentleman" Domain

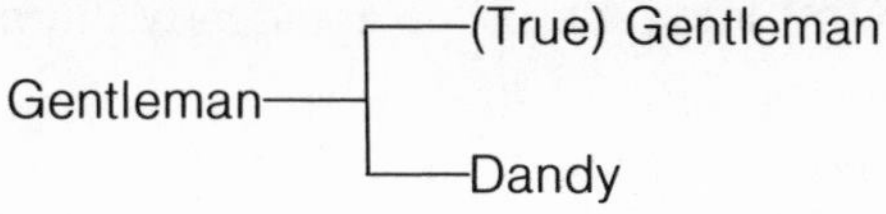

Ideally, a "true gentleman" would adhere strictly to community standards in all his affairs: "He who is a gentleman, whatever he may think of himself, will conform to the customs of the society he associates with as far as he can conscientiously, and the more of a gentleman a man is, the more easy, modest, and unassuming, and the more strict in the observance of order." He was thoroughly "respectable."[11] (See Figure 22.)

He could be expected to display his model "character" in a number of ways, not the least of which was generosity. The common identity of "gentleman" as "philanthropist," for instance, is evidenced in a "practical exercise" in arithmetic assigned to students in

FIGURE 22

A Paradigm of the "Gentleman" Domain: Character

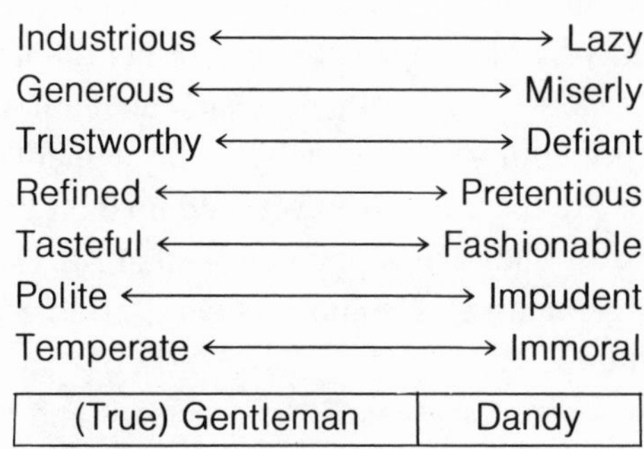

Winthrop schools: "A gentleman has an annuity of $2,000 per annum; I wish to know how much he may spend daily, that, at the years end, he may lay up 90 guineas, and give 20 cents per day to the poor of his own neighborhood." He was to be trustworthy in all his financial affairs, faithful to "creditors" and "debtors" as well as employees. He was to show moderate, "cultivated" taste in dress and diet, a temperate regard for "fashion," and continuing "industry" or vigor in life. His entire social presence would bespeak propriety and European grace. A correspondent to the *Maine Farmer* explained:

> True gentility or high breeding is unmistakable. . . . Refined and condescending deportment, a kind bearing to every one, absence of all stiff and unbending reserve . . . together with a uniform regard for superior intelligence and moral worth in *whomsoever found* — these characteristics, in our esteem, constitute the true lady or gentleman. . . . The finest models of this sort of people that the world can show come from *France*.

Despite the egalitarianism suggested here, the ultimate mark of a "gentleman" was the special treatment he gave to "ladies." There was a large stock of "feelings and proceedings" that "no true gentleman" would direct "towards the weaker sex."[12]

He was, in short, the ideal representative of "success" and "virtue" in his community, and, as an ideal, a proper subject of wide emulation. "Fashion" in Winthrop was explicitly tied to the supposed style and appearance of "gentlemen." Yet it was a common complaint, particularly by older against younger men, that the emphasis on "fashion" or "exterior" rather than "character" amounted to "a false standard of respectability." Holmes typically lamented: "How many heartless villains are there . . . who yet hold up their heads for no other reason than because they are gentlemen — that is to say, they possess the exterior of gentlemen, a comely person, affable manners, and a good suit of clothes."[13]

In a society where "success," "character," and "high standing" were assumed to be indivisible traits, the admission of "gentlemen" with less than ideal "character" bordered on blasphemy. Such complaints, which accelerated in the late 1830s and 1840s, foreshadow the rise, not of a European gentility, but of a Victorian bourgeoisie. In 1844, for example, the *Maine Farmer* offered the following definition "not to be found in Webster's last edition" but nonetheless applicable "to the present day and generation":

> Gentleman — a male person who has got above labor; who dresses in the top of fashion; who has learnt to suck the smoke through a lighted piece of tobacco with much ease and grace; who devotes the greater part of his time and a good share of his money to the ladies, in riding, &c. — to the neglect of his own business; who talks loud in company, uttering witty things; who has been to Niagara Falls and Saratoga Springs; who attends the popular church on Sabbath, and who generally leaves town without paying his bills.

Absent is the "character" that would distinguish a "true gentleman." Residents could assert: "Is there not a false standard of respectability . . . ? This standard appears to be idleness and a fine coat; and consequently, the more idle a man can be, and the finer the dress, the more of a gentleman. Not so. Respectability should consist in an improved mind, and skillful and industrious hands."[14]

In decrying undue attention to a man's "exterior," residents often contrasted the "opposite character of the 'true gentleman of worth' and the 'dandy.' " Unlike his ideal counterpart, the "dandy" or "fop" betrayed his responsibility for moral leadership as a man of "success."[15]

His boasted freedom from "useful labor," for instance, made him liable to the charge of "loafer" or "idler." Some residents pleaded "to induce some of the *gentleman loafers* who are trying to gull the world out of a living — without labor, to listen to common sense and go to work. Idleness seems to be the besetting sin of our natures, if it be not the principal ingredient of Original sin itself, and it has now become so leagued in with fashion that it is hard to persuade one that it is not the very pink and essence of gentility itself, especially if it be covered with a decent coat." In a society that paid such frequent homage to "industry" and "labor," it is little surprise that the "dandy" 's conspicuous leisure could be considered a sin.[16]

It seemed dangerous both as a social precedent and as a threat to the "dandy" himself. Without the healthful influence of "labor" or vigorous attention to business, "hearty gentlemen" degenerated into "the pale dyspeptics and chicken fisted dandies of the present day."[17] Also, by the traditional logic of "success," their idleness as well as general financial irresponsibility would result in their eventual economic demise. A Winthrop correspondent, for example, gave the following ideal life history of a "dandy," the lowest "grade of idler":

> [He is] a young man who has been brought up in affluent circumstances, over whom the reins of government have been kept rather loose, not having been kept to labor for a living, consequently not realizing from whence cometh his support. . . . His father dies, perhaps leaves him a dowry of some thousands of dollars, he is thrown upon the world without a parent's guardian care, to pursue his own wayward course. He riots in luxury a few years, becomes a degraded and reckless man; his funds become exhausted.

Note that here, as in similar references, the "dandy" 's original "success" is attained not through his own "labor" but through inheritance (or speculation). Without the requisite "character" his fortunes are naturally attributed to exceptional circumstances and their demise is totally predictable. They are maintained for a short while only by gouging the public and "setting his creditors at defiance." Unlike a "true gentleman," "he is idle in the performance of all deeds of a philanthropic or patriotic nature, except where his own personal agrandizement is interested." Residents lamented that the "dandy," rather than representing proper ideals, undermined them: "He is idle in the strongest acceptation of the term as rural or useful pursuits, he is idle in the education of his children . . . his family is brought up in idleness like himself . . . and become a pest and nuisance to the community."[18]

Conspicuous consumption also figured in the "dandy" 's predicted downfall. Winthrop's young men were apparently acquiring an appetite for costly possessions, flaunted as the mark of a "gentleman." A resident charged: "There is quite a large class of odd chaps who on making their appearance in the streets, would almost claim the title of dandies, who make dress their first consideration or perhaps even the tie of the neck handkerchief." Rather than displaying the moderate, fine taste of a "true gentleman," they wore "gaudy" clothes, drove "pretentious" carriages, and "washed in cologne." "Fashion," to those who protested, meant a foolish obsession with the "exterior" and "what is new."[19]

Naturally, the neglect of "character" was assumed to have moral consequences:

> . . . being Gentlemen by Trade
> They will not touch an ax or spade,
> But useful labor shunning,
> They lounge about in lazy bands,
> Throng tipplers' shops and tavern stands,
> Like rattle-snakes a sunning.

Many Winthrop men who claimed to be "gentlemen" were reputedly intemperate and ill-mannered. They were "odd professional fellows who congregate in a bar room and small clubs to relate stale jests and pass off low tricks upon one another. One slyly fastens some paper or a string to the coat of another, or substitutes salt for sugar in his friend's dram, or tries to be witty at the expense of some of his companions, and the like, &c."[20]

Absent, as well, was true gentility toward the "ladies." A facetious advertisement in the *Maine Farmer* reflects growing disagreement over standards of "respectability" in the community:

> Wanted — A few spruce young Dandies to stand at the Meeting-house doors, at the assembly of the congregation, for the devout purpose of staring the ladies out of countenance. No other qualification than a share of impudence is requisite for his employment — If, however, to this should be added a complete destitution of propriety, or a talent for making polite remarks upon each lady as she passes — or even a capability of exciting a laugh among his comrades at her expense — the applicant will be considered as most eminently qualified for his station.

Note here not only the use of such categories as "dandy" and "lady" but also the role of what is devout, impudent, polite, or humorous (i.e., "character" considerations) in determining their proper use.[21]

Such behavior, whether in taverns, at the meetinghouse, or in the street, presented a clear contradiction to those who sought to preserve traditional ideals, particularly the unity of "success," "character," and "standing" that the "gentleman" represented. The prospect of "dandies" appointing themselves "gentlemen" led many residents to loudly protest the blurring of an important distinction. One argued: "There is a false standard of gentility set up in society. . . . Thus it is no uncommon thing to see a man who can drink, gamble, swear, and commit any other species of vice and still be a 'gentleman.' "[22]

Of course, the debates over the proper identity of a "gentleman," like most other cultural conflicts, did not end with some definitive public pronouncement. Charges that "the rising generation" confused "dandies" with "gentlemen" continued to appear in Winthrop at least until 1850.

If my interpretation is correct (i.e., psychologically valid), the argument was long and vehement because there was more than a simple semantic point to be made. At stake were basic social values. Some, particularly older residents, described an increasing disparity between what they saw and what they hoped to see in Winthrop's young men of "high standing." Since the disparity was largely attributed to an increasing emphasis on the "exterior" to the neglect of "character," it amounted to no less than a corruption of the whole structure of "honor" in the society. The central promise of the campaign for occupational "improvement," that "successful workingmen" were both richer and better men, would erode if "character" was divorced from "respectability." If the observations of so many residents were accurate, this is precisely what was happening. Only the naive would trust "virtue" as a route to "success," and wealth or occupation would loom as barriers to their rise in "standing." The torch of moral leadership would be passed to "dandies" obsessed with the human "exterior" or left to "moralists" scrambling for their own special recognition.

CHAPTER 8

Businessmen

CAPITALISM'S MIXED BLESSING

The proximity of Hallowell, central Maine's most active trade center, was a distinct merchantile advantage to early Winthrop. The Kennebec River port provided ready access to markets and suppliers on the Atlantic seaboard. Moreover, since the only major road north or west of Hallowell passed through Winthrop, residents could capitalize on the flow of traffic to and from Maine's interior. It was largely for this purpose that inns and merchants clustered in Winthrop Center in the eighteenth century. The growth of that "neighborhood" signals the historic significance of commerce in the community. Though never accounting for more than 1 or 2 percent of the town's labor force, the business sector continued to figure prominently in the nineteenth century.[1]

Of course, "hard times" affected commerce as well as agriculture and manufacturing, but in many ways business opportunities were increasing. On the one hand, the Hallowell traffic was growing with the further settlement of the interior and exploitation of its woodland. On the other hand, Winthrop's own trade was becoming more valuable. As farmers turned to cash crops and manufacturers to large-scale production, the call for merchants increased. Nineteenth-century tanners, for instance, could no longer simply barter with local butchers for steer hides. To meet the volume demands of new industry, men like Samuel Clark turned to "dealers" who would fill New Orleans bound ships with shoes and have them return with tons of southern hides. Similarly, as family resources proved less adequate in financing further development, Winthrop manufacturers intensified their dealings with capital markets and "the New York store."[2]

Winthrop businessmen benefited from improved communication networks. Mail and stage coach services were becoming more rapid and reliable during the first half of the nineteenth century, creating more ready access to sound business information. At a time when the town's fortunes were increasingly tied to distant financial conditions, this was an important development.[3]

At the same time transportation routes were the subject of concerted improvement campaigns. In 1821, for example, when the Hallowell traffic began to show a preference for a more direct route (through the Forks, the road junction in Manchester, rather than the Village), a storekeeper named Nathaniel Bishop lead a long, successful fight to upgrade the heart of the old route, the road from Wayne to the Village. The improvement of Bishop's Road guaranteed continuing trade with northern sections of the Androscoggin River valley and Oxford County. Throughout the period the town budget gave highway maintenance top priority.[4]

Many residents also showed a passion for the grander sort of "internal improvements" that were receiving state and national political attention. As early as 1807 some residents joined a regional group lobbying for canals to link the lakes and rivers stretching from Wayne through Winthrop to Gardiner. By an 1826 proposal the waterway would extend all the way from Farmington to the sea: from the Sandy River to Androscoggin River and thence to Dead River, Androscoggin Lake, Wilson Pond, Wilson Stream, Lake Annabessacook, Cobbosseecontee Lake, Cobbosseecontee Stream, Kennebec River, and finally Casco Bay on the Atlantic. This incredibly ambitious plan was never realized, nor were even more modest proposals, such as one in 1836 for a canal with locks between Maranacook and Cobbosseecontee. Nevertheless, residents continued to agitate for a navigable waterway to link Winthrop with the sea.[5]

In the 1840s their attention shifted from canals to the railway. Of course, the development of Maine rail service was a broad, complex affair commencing much earlier in the century. It involved intricate dealings in finance and government policy, competition between the Kennebec and Portland Railroad Company and the Androscoggin and

Kennebec Railroad Company, debates over narrow- versus broad-gauge track, and the future of regional commercial relations with Canada versus Portland, Boston, or New York.[6]

Though clearly these were much more than local developments, townspeople in general and businessmen in particular demonstrated a deep interest in bringing rail service to Winthrop. From 1846 on, Holmes described widespread "excitement about the railroad." The *Maine Farmer* gave extensive coverage to each rail development, and Winthrop delegates apparently attended every Androscoggin and Kennebec corporate meeting. In 1847, when the Androscoggin and Kennebec incorporated, a recent emigrant, Josiah Little, Jr., and a current citizen, Samuel P. Benson (six years later president of the corporation), served on the first board of directors. Residents contributed some thirty thousand dollars to the company's stock, and when the shareholders assembled in Winthrop, they more than filled the Congregational meetinghouse.[7]

The rationale for their excitement was explicitly commercial. One villager, for instance, reported to a Boston paper: "The worthy people here are promising themselves much from the railroad, and apparently with good reason. Besides bettering their manufactures it will furnish a ready market for the produce of their farms." The railway was assumed to mean more active trade, which in turn would benefit every sector of the town's increasingly trade-dependent economy.[8]

Thus, residents welcomed the 1849 completion of the Androscoggin and Kennebec's broad-gauge line to Winthrop. The formal opening on July fourth was a wild celebration.[9]

Residents immediately noted profound effects of the railroad's arrival. Most obvious was the expansion of Winthrop's social horizons. Such industrial centers as Lewiston and Waterville, once accessible only by long stagecoach or horseback passage, were now within an hour's ride. Six days a week citizens could ride to Boston for a mere $2.25. Unexpectedly, travel in the opposite direction was to prove even more significant. In the late nineteenth century passengers from southern New England and New York found Winthrop an attractive vacation spot, heralding the town's future as a resort center.[10]

The railroad even served as a rallying point for area feminists. When local women, many of them stockholders, discovered that they were denied passage, they took immediate action. In December 1849, "they put themselves 'on women's rights' " and boarded the train en masse. The brief freedom ride from Waterville to Winthrop broke once and for all sex barriers to travel on the Androscoggin and Kennebec.[11]

There were also new employment opportunities. In the ensuing decades young men in Winthrop could join the railroad's payroll or find related contract work.[12]

Yet in retrospect, as in anticipation, residents mainly touted the railway's commercial value. As one explained:

> Both of these roads thus far opened [the rail lines from North Yarmouth to Bath and from Lewiston to Winthrop] will have an immense influence upon the future interests and prosperity of Kennebec. They both open new awareness of travel and transportation from her to the great centers of business in different parts of the Union, and connect her with iron bands to the remotest verge of railroad extent on our Continent. From this time she can equal any other section of the nation in the facilities of intercommunication and travel to and from the several markets as cheap and as quick as any other community.

Where, then, were the trains going? — To "centers of business" and "markets."[13]

Residents could easily see the railway's commercial advantages. Whitman's horsepowers and threshers, for example, which had been bound to local markets withering with the onslaught of the midge, were now loaded on freight cars destined for New York. Improving business prospects were probably best symbolized by the formation of the successful Bank of Winthrop in 1853. The only previous banking experiment was the Winthrop Bank, which incorporated in 1824 and collapsed the same year.[14]

In sum, cash cropping, industrialization, and improved communication and transportation as well as a modest growth in population facilitated the extension of Winthrop's commercial activities. The people for whom these activities were a vocation were guaranteed a prominent place in the community.

A PROFESSIONAL career in capital speculation or trade was the defining attribute of a "businessman." (Figure 23 shows a taxonomy of this domain.) It should be emphasized again, however, that to some extent most men fit this definition. Trade was common in all vocations, but the label "businessman" was reserved for those whose time and energy was *predominantly* dedicated to commerce. Despite a variety of special interests, these "men of business" were assumed to share a unique regard for money matters and pursuant gains.[15]

FIGURE 23

A Taxonomy of the "Businessman" Domain

They were resolved into various types by the "branch of business" in which those "gains" were to be made, as shown in Figure 24. Thus, "capitalists" engaged in "speculation" and "merchants" in "trade." "Merchants" (or "dealers") could be more specifically

FIGURE 24

A Paradigm of the "Businessman" Domain: Branches of Business

Branch of Business		
Speculation	Trade	
	Wholesale	Retail
Capitalist	Merchant	
	Agent	Shopkeeper

identified with the particular commodities they handled. This was, for example, the function of such labels as "grocer" or any of a number of combination forms like "leather dealer." More generally, "merchants" were resolved into those whose trade was wholesale ("agents") versus retail ("shopkeepers"). The difference was more than one of economic function, for the "retailer" 's shop was a town fixture, while "agents" could be expected to roam the countryside in search of trade.[16]

Residents recognized some features common to all "businessmen," whether "merchants" or "speculators." First, as "nonproducers" they were subject to the predictable comparisons with "workingmen." Second, as the phrase suggests, "men of business" were expected to be just that, men. Women were excluded from commercial life in principle, if not in fact, by community sanction as well as the supposed divine order. One minister declared:

> The question as to the equality of the sexes . . . is clearly settled . . . by a higher arbiter than man. . . . By his firmer texture, by his more comprehensive plans, by his more energetic powers, man will ever sway the destiny of the nation, grasp the helm of the ship in the storm, draw out the army in battle array, and control the commerce, the national intercourse, and the finances of the world: while woman will move in her own sphere.[17]

If "businessmen" were the troops of world finance, "capitalists" were the commanders. "Speculators" were assumed to wield tremendous power, stimulating economic growth where they chose to invest. The settlement of new territory, industrialization, or the like was attributed to their "enlightened interest": "The capitalist . . . calls forth the dormant energies of iron mines and gives profitable employment to the strength of streams that have for ages been running to waste." At a time when so many residents identified "progress" with economic growth, the "capitalist" had a unique responsibility and value.[18]

Indeed, "capitalists" were treated in quasi-supernatural terms. They were said, quite literally, to move mountains and shape the destiny of cities, yet there was a remarkable lack of specificity as to who they were. Citizens of Winthrop attributed great developments simply to "Boston and Hallowell capitalists." In prayerlike pleas, contributors to the *Maine Farmer* begged them to stimulate Winthrop's growth as they were assumed to have done elsewhere.[19]

Yet, despite lordly powers and the reverence they engendered, "capitalists" were not immune from human frailties. Too often, residents charged, they neglected their responsibilities to society by engaging in petty profiteering. Residents asked: "Will not every man of capital turn his funds to this end [Maine industry] instead of shaving notes and inundating the state with stores . . . bringing those very articles here, to excite us to buy, instead of doing what we can to cause them to be manufactured among us?" The self-serving so-called "fortune hunter" betrayed the doctrine of the "capitalist" 's social commitment. He would "shave notes" or spread misleading information in search of quick profits rather than contributing to community growth. This was, for example, a major complaint against "monopolists" who speculated in western lands. There were likewise charges that "speculators" were too conservative, unwilling to make the type of moderate-gain, long-term investment that local development required.[20]

Whatever the net attractiveness of their position, "capitalists" continued to be touted as the catalysts of "progress." Apparently, however, Winthrop residents did not (and probably could not realistically) hope to become "capitalists." Members of this class were assumed to be "gentlemen" of truly extraordinary wealth, the kind only to be found in Hallowell, Boston, or New York. Aspiring local young "men of business" looked to trade rather than speculation for their fortunes. In local experience "merchants" were the representatives of "businessmen."

The "merchant" 's life, like that of other "nonproducers," had distinctively desirable features. In contrast with the "productive classes," the merchant had a more "tidy," "respectable," and in some ways "easier" employment. He was spared the leather apron and sweat that symbolized the "workingman." Probably more significantly, he had a chance to get rich quick or at least shorten the road to "success." These were, for example, the types of considerations normally attributed to "workingmen" turned "dealers."[21]

On the other hand, there were those who felt that "merchants," like "gentlemen," suffered from comparison with "producers."

Theirs was the life not of ease but of laziness. Frequent entries in the *Maine Farmer,* like the following riddle, raise again and again the charge of "idler" against the "merchant":

Q: Who is the man of business?
A: He that makes the most bustle and does nothing.

Residents could conclude that the "dealer" "creates nothing. . . . He merely causes property to shift hands." They could lament, "Many of our young men, and of our old men too, are exceedingly anxious to make a fortune by their wits, rather than their industry." "Merchants" were thus thought prone to the "dandy" 's folly.[22]

Moral objections were also raised against the "dealer" 's involvement in the liquor traffic. The seriousness of such an objection can hardly be overemphasized in view of the strong temperance sentiment in town. Beginning as early as 1815, various local reform groups promoted "total abstinence." Throughout the period their memberships and number rapidly increased: the Winthrop Society for the Promotion of Good Morals (1815), the Winthrop Temperance Union Society (1834), the Winthrop Washingtonian and Martha Washington Societies (1841), the Sons of Temperance (1846), the Watchman's Club (1850), plus various unchartered "juvenile" and "daughters of temperance" groups. Deacon Daniel Carr's hotel in Winthrop, founded in 1820, was the first "temperance tavern" in Maine. But the movement was also reflected in more inclusive community institutions. In 1835 Congregationalists, under the leadership of the Reverend David Thurston, one of the town's most rabid reformers, stipulated total abstinence, even from wine or beer, as a prerequisite for church membership. The Reverend Mr. Thurston went so far as to abolish the use of wine in the Sacraments. A year earlier the Winthrop Agricultural Society had barred distilled liquor sales from cattle shows and fairs. Local sentiment was clearly reflected in a series of increasingly stringent resolutions passed at town meeting: prohibition of liquor sales to "known drunks," their names posted about town, in 1819; prohibition of "dram drinking," i.e., in stores or shops, in 1830; stronger enforcement measures in 1832; prohibition of liquor sales in less than twenty-eight-gallon lots in 1836; and finally the ban on all liquor sales (except by one "medicinal license") in 1840.

Hence, though the 1850 "Maine Law" is a noted early precedent for prohibition, Winthrop went "dry" some ten years earlier.[23]

A resident could reasonably charge that liquor traffic was "the cause of half the Insanity, a very large proportion of the Pauperism, and almost all the Crime in this county." It is no wonder, then, that those who promoted the traffic were subject to wide disdain. The disparaging title of "trafficker" or "vender" signified "merchants" who brought spirit-filled casks into town or parceled out drams in their shops. They were accused of "making drunkards"; they profited by preying on the virtue of their neighbors.[24]

Some residents claimed that they were victims of "merchants" in an economic as well as moral sense. To some extent these complaints were part of the traditional Western concern for the underdog. A minister could observe that the nameless "rich oppress the poor, the strong the weak, the creditor the debtor."[25] But residents had more specific complaints, which they aimed particularly at the growing number of middlemen or "agents" operating between the "farmer" and the "manufacturer." A group of Winthrop shepherds resolved: "The wool grower . . . has been passive prey to the cupidity and extortion of Itinerant agents which annually throng the county."[26]

It was not that "traders" were necessarily bad. Residents readily admitted that they served some purpose: "The merchant . . . advances the comfort and welfare of his neighbors by bringing useful commodities to their accommodation." Nor would anyone have seriously challenged the profit motive. Residents even acknowledged the necessity of an "agent" between the "producer" and distant "buyer" as well as "subagents" where large territories were involved. A dissident, for example, described the "system" as a simple adaptation to the Maine environment: "A manufacturer sends to an Agent in a distant town to procure a certain amount of wool. He (the Agent) starts off his deputy agents throughout the country, and these buy up whatever they can find."[27]

What they did object to was the "unnecessary" multiplication of "minor speculators": "We readily acknowledge the propriety and necessity of a capitalist or agent between the wool grower and the manufacturer, but . . . one is enough." It was apparently considered acceptable for a "dealer" to profit if he facilitated trade, but mere "speculative intrigue" would be subject to protest. "Agents" who traded among themselves, each time extracting a "fee," were accused of being "sharpers," of simultaneously depressing farm prices and inflating prices paid at the mill: "It is not so much the manufacturer who causes this fluctuation [in prices] as it is his agents and sub-agents and deputy deputy agents. These go about the country telling woeful stories and offering small prices and deceiving the community."[28]

Such objections constituted far more than the grumbling of a few "wool growers." Some residents felt that the "hard times" which affected the whole community were directly attributable to *"the increase of Speculators and decrease of Producers."* This was, for example, the argument Holmes used to explain the depression in 1837: "When in 1835 so many splendid fortunes were floating about . . . hundreds and hundreds left the farm and the workshop — and launched into the abyss of speculation. . . . Incidental causes may have concurred to hasten the result, but it would nevertheless have come."[29] To a limited extent, then, "merchants" were considered morally and economically detrimental to the community.

But there were more selfish reasons to avoid the career of a "merchant." Although one might soon attain wealth, ease, and respectability, there was assumed to be an equal chance of disaster: "He may, by a single speculation, gain his thousands, and by another lose the whole. His mind is ever agitated with the fluctuation of prices — the fear of losses at sea and failures on the land." Residents frequently cautioned their young to beware of the risks and anxieties that plagued the "man of business."[30]

To succeed business aspirants would ideally have to acquire great skill. Toward this end parents could set about grooming their sons at an early age, a process revealed in some of the highly personal papers of a Winthrop "businessman" and "manufacturer," Samuel L. Clark. Clark hoped that his sons, Harrison, Miller, and Lewis, would follow business careers. When they resisted his efforts, Samuel appealed to friends to help properly prepare the boys for business, despite their own desires. The "character" training that Samuel directed was intense. He went so far as to send his teenage son, Lewis, to Virginia for several years, paying a Dr. Bezer Snell to see that Lewis became "acquainted with the general concern of doing business": "Sir, I send him to you that you will take him under your care, advise, direct and admonish him as a faithful father would his son and may God direct you." Clark's instructions to Dr. Snell and other influential parties indicate a set of ideal features for a "man of business." Through his agents Clark pressured his sons to "love College," associate with "the business class," avoid "lowly" male and female company, and resign all "passion for novelty." Ideally each son would develop a "character" of "consistency" and respectability. Clark declared, "We will prepare him for business."[31]

Examples like that set by the Clark family supported the common notion that wealthy, business-oriented parents could engage the right teachers and friends to give their sons an advantage. A resident's story, for instance, carried the moral: "Those who had been bred to business proved more successful rivals."[32]

Regardless of a boy's prior training, he could be expected to gain his first real commercial experience as a "clerk" for a nearby "merchant." As he arranged stock, balanced the books, or waited on "customers," he served a kind of apprenticeship; he would learn the rudiments of business. Failure to strictly "supervise" his employees made the "merchant," like the "master mechanic," liable to the charge of "idler." Young "scholars" in Winthrop schools worked out sample financial dealings that would allow a "clerk" to "set himself up as a merchant."[33]

The key to these dealings was acquiring credit and, thus, the "merchant" 's identity as "debtor" to his "creditors." When the young "man of business" signed his first "notes," he began a long, anxious relationship with his "creditors." This anxiety was an important aspect of the "businessman" 's public image: "Look with scrutinizing gaze upon the man of business with furrowed brow and swollen eye. Swollen by restlessness and want of sleep. Perhaps he may have slept a few hours, dreaming as he slept of some competitor getting the advantage over him, or of a note becoming due at the bank, without prospect of meeting it . . . the haunts of ambitious men."[34]

If his business began to "fail," he would be late in paying his debts; he would become a "delinquent." If he were to suffer further "embarrassment," his "creditors" could "sue" and take all his property; he would become a "bankrupt": "His creditor *calls* for pay

— the trader fails . . . and his store is broken up — he is no longer a merchant.'' There were, of course, many complex strategies for ''putting off'' one's ''creditors,'' but ''failure'' and ''embarrassment'' remained common concerns. Bankruptcy suits were noted regularly in the newspaper, and Winthrop schools gave lessons on how to handle them.[35]

''Creditors'' were at times the subject not only of anxiety but of outright hatred. Those who were ''merciless,'' who ''pressed'' too hard for payment, were given insulting names, such as ''Jew'' or ''harpy.''[36]

Nevertheless residents greatly emphasized the virtue of paying one's debts, not only as a way to achieve ''independence,'' but also as a ''sacred duty'' in itself: ''When we see a man counselling with his lawyer and contriving how he may cheat his creditors, we remember the saying [''owe no man'']. . . . You had better pay your debts honestly.'' Moreover, in arbitrating ''debtor''-''creditor'' controversies among its members, local churches sought to give equal consideration to both parties. It was an alternative to the courts, but the result would probably be the same. The ''debtor'' was only to be spared legal fees.[37]

In sum, from the outset aspiring ''men of business'' were in the risky role of ''debtors.'' A worrisome relationship with ''creditors'' served as a mark of their profession and a warning to the ambitious. A typical Winthrop story, for instance, documents the ''merchant'' 's potential course:

> Tom had rather high notions from his boyhood; and persuaded his father to put him to a *merchant* [i.e., as a ''clerk''] — In due time Tom became the master of a shop of goods, was attentive and fortunate, and acquired a snug estate. . . . But pride got the better of prudence, and persuaded him that he might DO BETTER at New York. He went there, figured as a *wholesale* merchant, for which neither capital nor his experience were adequate, for three years, and then came the notice in the state paper for his creditors to show cause, &c.

The author apparently felt that the tale of doom was so familiar that an

"&c." would carry the message. Predictably, it is Tom's "creditors" who punish him for his mistakes.[38]

Yet the "merchant" 's supposed difficulties were not limited to his identity as "debtor." To be successful he would have to become skillful in a variety of human relations. He would learn how to deal with "auctioneers" as a "bidder," judge "sellers" as a "buyer," watch for "shoplifters" as a "vender," manage "clerks" as an "employer" (or "master"), contract with "customers" as a "creditor," and generally match his "rivals" (or "competitors") in all affairs.[39] In these relations his fortunes might depend on his strict attention to the subtlest nuances. He would learn, for instance, to "beware . . . the seller [who] declines to name the price . . . and says, 'there will be no difficulty about it,' " or to see that a "customer" drives a "good fat horse" before letting him buy on credit.[40]

Clearly by requirement as well as reputation successful "businessmen" were a shrewd lot. Apparently their skill was not necessarily matched by honesty. Residents charged that "men of business" too often raised "an ideal value upon things which are destitute of intrinsic worth," slandered their "competitors," lied to "creditors," and even occasionally put a thumb on the scale. In a thinly disguised attack, one resident declared: "If I was a merchant, I would have an established price for my goods, and not undersell or injure my neighbors; I would sell at a moderate profit, giving good weight and measure, and deal as honestly as possible." Apparently those who truly were "merchants" were less than faithful to these ideals.[41]

Overall, then, Winthrop residents tended to view the "businessman" as a mixed blessing. He could be at once a moral and economic parasite to the community and a vital catalyst to its growth. His career could offer a ready route to wealth, ease, and respectability or an anxiety-ridden road to disaster, to "failure" and "embarrassment." Nonetheless, a man who was "successful" in his business could expect to be honored as "ingenious," well-informed, and above all "skillful" in human relations.[42] Along with wealth, he might well enjoy the "high standing" due a "gentleman."

CHAPTER 9

Professional Men

WINTHROP'S BEST

When the census taker reported Winthrop occupations in 1840 and 1850, he found only about fifteen people who could claim to be "professional men."[1] Yet this small group attracted a good deal of attention. It included some of the town's most prominent citizens, its "doctors," "lawyers," and "ministers." (See Figure 25.) In 1854, for example, when the town called on David Thurston to compile a community history, he chose to elaborate, not only every "professional man" who ever practiced in Winthrop, but also every one "born or brought up" there, even if he practiced elsewhere. This was the only occupational group that received such biographical recognition. Thurston boasted of the number of people that "Winthrop raised" into the professions.[2]

FIGURE 25

A Taxonomy of the "Professional Man" Domain

Professional man (professional gentleman or practitioner)
- Doctor
- Lawyer
- Minister

Many other residents apparently also felt that the number was a community distinction. Though the absolute number seems small, it was considered large for a town of Winthrop's size. Note, for instance, a joke appearing in the local newspaper:

> The following superscription of a letter came
> to the post office in this town the other day:
>
> 'Please Mr. Postmaster, pass this along
> To the land of Jack Downing. It can't go wrong.
> To the Village of Winthrop, the fairest in Maine.
> Where Lawyers and Doctors are plenty as rain.'

Evidently the presence of a mere handful of "professional men" was sufficient to distinguish an entire town. Similarly, "reformers" could seek to distinguish their cause by marshaling such men into their ranks.[3]

Possibly even more than the "businessman," the "professional man" was explicitly associated with "wealth" and "honor." Some claimed that, since he moved "in a more public sphere" than "workingmen" and had "more numerous acquaintances among the fashionable and opulent," his job required rich possessions and a measure of "impudence": "His family must dress in the highest style of fashion; his furniture must be more elegant, and his table spread with dainties to please the taste." One resident observed: "In the path of notoriety and eminence . . . those who have neither great impudence nor superior talents are in a hopeless condition." In this sense, becoming a "professional man" was a "success" in itself.[4] It is thus little surprise that those with "high ambition" and sufficient means could be expected to prepare themselves or their children for the "professions."[5]

Yet the difference between the "professional" and the "businessman" was less a matter of "standing" than of the kind of work each regularly performed. Both, of course, were considered "nonproducers," but to some extent the "professional man" was even less productive than his business counterpart. Though "merchants" did not really make anything, they at least helped others to do so by moving the necessary capital and materials. "Professional men," on the other hand, reputedly failed to make even such an indirect contribution to production. This was the distinction defined when a resident explained, "The professional man . . . depends upon HEADWORK for the supplies to his family."[6]

"Professional men," supposedly more than any other occupational group, were ignorant of the "agricultural" and "mechanical arts." As one farmer quipped: "I was much pleased to see last year, some experiments published by S. F. B., who, if I 'guess right,' is a Lawyer, on the subject of raising potatoes. Such experiments are worth whole columns of trash."[7] This ignorance meant that they did not have "a trade or an art, upon which they can always depend for a respectable living."[8] But since the professions were usually assumed to provide a "respectable living," the belief that "professional men" had "interesting," that is, mentally engaging, work probably had a greater influence than did financial concerns on those able to choose a career. The economic risks were small while the intellectual challenge was great: "Professional gentlemen are operated upon by the double motive of interest and honorable distinction."[9]

Much of the exclusiveness of professional life was a result of its educational prerequisites; "professional men" were by definition "learned." This characteristic distinguished them from men in any other occupation; they belonged, as it was so often put, to the "learned professions." The difference between "professional" and other men was formalized in a full set of separate educational institutions.

Generally, formal education in Winthrop consisted of neighborhood "common schools" which boys and girls attended voluntarily. The schools operated with minimal town control or support. The quality of instruction, the choice of textbooks, and even the length of the school term varied widely from year to year and from district to district. It was education on the familiar little-red-schoolhouse model, accenting the three Rs and discipline. Occupational training was left to a child's parents or employers.[10]

"Professional men," however, received or, more accurately, bought private instruction. Parents engaged "tutors" for their sons or sent them to an "academy" where they were explicitly "fit for the professions." They were taught the standard "common school" fare as well as the "higher arts" such as oratory, the ancient languages, philosophy, or political economy. Unlike other Winthrop residents, these "scholars" would continue instruction into their late teens and then go to "college." Indeed, "college" was considered *their* institution, "granting benefits to a few only who intend to become professional men.'' Though some ''clergymen'' attended ''seminaries'' rather than ''colleges,'' and a few had no ''higher'' education at all, ''college'' training was assumed a distinctive achievement of all ''professional men.'' They were ''learned'' because they were ''graduates.''[11]

''Professional men'' thus had a firm hold both on the quality of being ''learned'' and on the institutions that could award it. Those without the resources necessary for extensive schooling were excluded: ''Students in . . . these professions have to expend much time and money to qualify them to perform such services.''[12]

As one might expect, women were particularly excluded from the ''learned professions.'' As with other occupations, the exclusion was manifest in informal community sanctions (i.e., the professions were not in their ''sphere''), but in this case there were formidable economic and institutional barriers as well. Women were rarely allowed to control family finances and, even if they could, they were not admitted to the ''colleges'' and ''seminaries'' where Winthrop's young men became ''learned.''[13]

Even the movement for ''female education'' was little help. ''Female seminaries,'' like the one operated by the Reverend John Butler in East Winthrop, 1825–1832, offered women a new opportunity for private schooling similar to male ''academies'' in organization. But the similarity did not extend to the quality of instruction. Their differing purposes are well illustrated in an 1835 advertisement in the *Maine Farmer* for Augusta High School:

> In the MALE DEPT. will be taught all the branches of learning necessary to fit young men for College, or qualify them for the business of life, including instruction not only in the ancient languages but also in French, Spanish, Italian, and German. In the FEMALE DEPT. instruction will be given in all the branches usually taught in the highest Female Seminaries in the Country, including the modern languages–painting–drawing and the ornamental branches of education.

In short, while men were becoming occupationally ''fit,'' women were learning the ''ornamental'' arts. A farmer could charge that women learned ''the debilitating discipline of the yellow bird and canary bird''; women learned, not to join the professions, but to become ''ladies'' and the ''fashionable'' wives of ''professional men.'' Note, for example, the ''Advice of Father to His Only Daughter'' in 1833: ''As your husband's success in his profession will depend upon his popularity, and as the manners of a wife have much influence in extending or lessening the respect and esteem of others for her husband, you should care to be affable and polite to the poorest as well as the richest.'' The measure of ''impudence'' that distinguished the ''professional man'' was not allowed his spouse.[14]

The exclusion of ''teachers'' from this domain seems somewhat more surprising. Unlike women and the poor, ''instructors'' in Winthrop's ''private'' and ''common schools'' displayed many of the features characteristic of the professions. Although there were some female ''teachers'' (often labeled ''mistress'' or ''instructress''), particularly in the summer-term common schools, the majority were expected to be and were male. Their efforts, too, were deemed ''headwork''; like other ''nonproducers'' they were accused of being ''lazy'' or ''above labor.'' ''Teachers'' also had some claim to being ''learned.'' It was they, after all, who equipped young men for the ''learned professions.'' Why, then, were they not also considered ''professional men''?[15]

First, educational careers had none of the exclusiveness that marked the professions. ''Masters'' in common schools were generally recruited from the neighborhood by an ''agent'' or committee of the district or by the district as a whole. There was a cursory ''examination'' of prospective ''candidates,'' but by most accounts, anyone with ''a smattering of Grammar and Arithmetic'' would receive a ''certificate'' to teach. The wording of the certificate and district rulings suggest that ''character'' and a willingness to work for the lowest possible pay were more important qualifications than intellect.[16]

Since, too, ''candidates'' were usually ''neighbors,'' residents were reluctant to disqualify any applicant. A parent explained: ''I have, on several occasions, after the examination of an unqualified teacher, heard such a remark as this, 'we may as well give him a Certificate; he *may* keep a good school; if we refuse him, we shall put the Agent to a good deal of trouble to procure another teacher, besides *hurting his feelings* and the feelings of his friends.' '' ''Instructors'' were very seldom "college" graduates, that is, "learned" in the same sense as "professional men," nor were they expected to be. They were usually themselves the products of common schools, the sons of local "farmers" looking for winter employment. They were often "minors" (i.e., persons under twenty-one years of age) and usually held only one-term appointments. A similar turnover and lack of distinction, though somewhat less severe, marked "private teachers," who could become "tutors" or establish a "singing school" merely by posting notice.[17]

Second, besides belonging to a less exclusive and "learned" class, "teachers" were assumed to be far less wealthy than "professional men." Despite, for example, steadily increasing public support during the period, "masters" of common schools never received more than about twenty dollars per month, and "mistresses" half that amount. Fringe benefits could include free schooling for the "instructor" 's children or board with the "lowest bidder" in the district. It should be recalled, moreover, that this support lasted only for the one- to four-month school term.[18]

By some indicators Winthrop education was well endowed. In 1850, for instance, the town's school support per child, $1.42, ranked it third among the twenty-nine towns in the county. Yet this figure seems to have reflected poorly on the other towns rather than well on Winthrop; many residents complained that Winthrop's educational support was dismal and that of others simply worse. Nevertheless, by any estimate, teaching was not, nor was it expected to be, a road to riches. Typically, a resident advised:

> The persons under whose instructions our youth are to be placed, should not be one who engages in teaching merely for his financial benefit — for the renumeration [*sic*], the "loaves and fishes," but one who feels an earnest solicitude for the best interest of the rising generation — one who will enlist with his whole soul in the arduous, but delightful task of teaching the "young idea to shoot," one who will repair to the schoolroom with the feelings of a benefactor — a philanthropist.[19]

Evidently the profit motive, which was to serve others so well, would somehow corrupt "the responsibility of his station." Thus, while the ''professional man'' was associated with wealth, the ''teacher'' was explicitly divorced from it.

These characteristics suggest an anomaly in the structure of occupational categories. On the one hand, ''teachers'' were not a sufficiently exclusive class, neither ''learned'' nor wealthy enough, to be judged ''professional men'': ''The occupation of the school-teacher is . . . looked upon as a stripling employment, beneath the dignity of a gentleman or a literary man.''[20] On the other hand, by the nature of their work, ''teachers'' were well recognized to be ''nonproducers'' and more like ''professional men'' than ''businessmen.'' Thus it remained unclear whether ''teachers'' properly contrasted with or were included among ''professional men,'' whether one category stood taxonomically beside or below the other. This might help to explain why residents treated teaching in such special terms, why, for example, ''financial benefits'' should be less relevant for ''teachers,'' or why, in general, ''teachers'' were so seldom compared to those in other occupations. ''School masters'' did not bear comparison because theirs was a kind of marginal employment; they did not fit in the occupational structure.

The anomaly also helps to explain some important inconsistencies in the data. In 1850, for example, though Winthrop supported at least a half-dozen private and twenty common school ''instructors,'' the census taker noted only one who would claim to be a ''teacher'' by vocation. One way to avoid the confusion, then, was simply to say that teaching was not an occupation.[21] Such an assertion could both reflect that teaching was generally not considered a predominant employment and render moot any questions about what type of employment it was — whether ''art,'' ''trade,'' or ''profession.''

Yet residents assigned their ''school masters'' great social responsibility. Their actual or ideal characteristics were issues of intense public debate. One would expect, then, some attempt to resolve the ''instructor'' 's anomalous occupational identity, evidence of cultural change that would place ''teacher'' more precisely in the structure of occupational categories. Specifically, one would expect changes in the ''teacher'' 's defining attributes so that he might be more properly included among ''professional men.''

Such changes were, indeed, part of a movement in Winthrop, as elsewhere, to "raise the Standard of Education." From 1807 on, town committees, dominated by reformers, worked to improve the district schools, posing an increasing challenge to local authority. Of course, there were many issues involved in this effort. Reformers emphasized the importance of good schoolhouses, textbooks, and equipment as well as the responsibility of parents and scholars for educational progress. But, above all, they stressed the need for a new kind of "teacher," one with "higher" qualifications who would receive greater rewards.[22] Not surprisingly, these ideals were precisely those that would make teaching a "profession," a more exclusive, respected, wealthy, and learned vocation. By their design "teachers" would be added to the ranks of "professional men."

Heading the list of higher qualifications was a more severe demand for teaching "method":

> Your [Superintending School] Committee would drop a word on the erroneous though common opinion, that almost any person is competent to teach young children. . . . Teachers who have perhaps a knowledge of the rudiments they undertake to teach, but yet are as ignorant of the art of teaching as the children, perhaps not knowing there is such an art. . . . In addition to their literary attainments, they ought to be capable of adopting the best methods of instruction.

This was more than a lofty ideal, for by the late 1830s districts were censoring and dismissing their "instructors" as well as denying certificates to new "candidates" on these very grounds. In the 1840s residents commonly vowed that not only every "good school master" but "every man worthy the name of *teacher*" would possess the most "advanced" or "scientific" classroom techniques. He would, for example, know how to use a blackboard, appeal to reason and common experience, tailor lessons to each child's capabilities, and introduce "improved" textbooks. As learning "by rote," by "parrot-like" recitation, declined in favor, the "instructor" 's responsibilities necessarily increased. As residents demanded a matching increase in "competence," they were limiting, making more exclusive, the class of men who could be designated "teachers."[23]

There was a simultaneous effort to increase the "honor" of their vocation: ''Winthrop has furnished a large number for the highly important, but by no means duly appreciated, occupation of teaching common schools.'' Residents began to argue that ''teachers'' who were ''worthy the name'' would display a ''gentlemanly'' manner, a ''*mixture of dignity and affability* . . . [that] will inspire . . . *love* and *fear*.''[24] They begged parents to show greater ''respect'' and children greater ''obedience'' to their ''school masters.''[25]

Ideally ''instructors'' were to receive better financial as well as honorary ''encouragement.'' The school committees repeatedly ''cautioned against the wasteful, insane practice of seeking such as could be obtained for a small compensation.'' In disgust a resident asked, ''Shall we continue to employ the *cheapest* teacher merely because he is so?'' Many proposed that longer school terms and higher salaries would make teaching more of a ''profession.''[26]

Some also called for special educational institutions that could make ''teachers'' more ''learned'' in the ''professional man'' 's sense. By the late 1830s residents were advocating a ''state teacher's seminary.'' Their hopes were not soon to be fulfilled, but over the next decade, annual ten-day ''teachers' institutes'' were founded to raise both the ''standard of education'' and the ''standing'' of ''instructors'' in the country.[27]

The promotion of ''institutes'' or ''seminaries'' as well as higher ''teacher'' qualifications and rewards indicate the beginning of precisely the kind of cultural change that the semantic analysis would suggest. The movement for ''educational reform'' was largely an effort to make ''school masters'' ''professional men'': ''Let school teaching be a distinct trade (or *profession* if you please), and let it be pursued as a regular business.''[28] Though this goal was hardly to be reached by 1850, reformers had successfully begun to resolve the anomalous components of the ''teacher'' 's public image; he was, indeed, becoming more of a ''professional man.''

Those who were already recognized as ''professional gentlemen'' were distinguished by the ''service'' they performed. They were ''men eminent in the practice of law, physic, or divinity.''[29] (See Figure 26.)

''Lawyers'' (or ''attorneys,'' ''(e)squires,'' or ''counselors at law'') were among the most honored of Winthrop's citizens. They gained wealth and respect in attending to a wide variety of community

FIGURE 26

A Paradigm of the "Professional Man" Domain: Service

Practice or Service		
Law	Medicine	Ministry
Lawyer	Doctor	Minister

affairs.[30] Anyone who dealt in civil or criminal disputes or contracts of any significance could be expected to engage an "attorney," thereby becoming his "client." Such transactions involved special procedures in a code that only an "attorney" was supposed to understand. The social world of "plaintiffs," "defendants," "executors," "assigns," "administrators," and "magistrates" was his exclusive domain. Even if the elements were familiar (e.g. "heir," "guardian," or "felon"), a lawyer could define them in a way that was unfamiliar to the rest of the community.[31] Thus, the rewards and social import of legal practice made it a desirable vocation. An ambitious "farmer" might advise, "Son, I am about to give you an extra education, and I expect you to become a Lawyer, for that profession is the high road to honor."[32]

There were, however, ample complaints about inferior "lawyers," so-called "pettifoggers." These were men who, in the pursuit of profit and the "sport" of legal argument, turned neighborly disputes into weighty litigation. To blame were both the "litigous spirit" of the public and the "moral irresponsibility of the legal profession." Residents questioned the virtue of "attorneys" who could easily argue both sides of a question or "charge a poor man five dollars for a few words of advice." Such behavior was an obvious temptation in a profession where a man was "dependent upon the misfortunes and vices of those around him for support." One resident charged that "quirks and quibbles constitute a Lawyer's religion."[33]

There was a more general concern for the great social and political power of "attorneys." In part their influence was considered evidence of “high” ambition and skill: “They derive it by their superior talents, their activity, their exertion to excel in eloquence and all the branches of education.” Yet the preponderance of “lawyers” in government was also considered a threat to the political system. Indeed, some declared that government was becoming the “lawyer” ’s monopoly:

> As matters are now arranged in our country, lawyers are the only tyrants of whom we have to complain; they get into all the seats of power; they give laws to the community and then set about executing them; they are invested with both the legislative and executive power [by?] such laws as they please; they sit in our Councils, are our Judges, our Justices, our Presidents, our Governors; they creep into every seat of power from the lowest grade till they reach the last goal of their ambition in the highest office in the gift of the people.[34]

Generally political ambitions were viewed with more suspicion than others. “Attorneys” were frequently accused of being “mere *office seekers*.” This label, as opposed to those of more neutral value such as “candidate” or “public servant,” implied a deplorable, “mercenary” lust for power. The Reverend Mr. Thurston, for example, urged voters to reject mere “*office seekers,* whose greatest qualification for office is their earnest desire of it, who are too proud or too indolent to procure sustenance for themselves and families without public employment.”[35]

Moreover, an association with politics could hardly benefit the reputation of any group. Although residents paid frequent homage to “American democracy” and selected “statesmen,” their references to “politicians” in general were critical or just plain hostile. “Politicians,” residents accused, were often “shameless demagogues,” sharing the voter’s interests only in preelection rhetoric. Among their supposed faults were ignorance, laziness, devotion to self and party above principle, “chicanery and corruption.” Even United States congressmen were portrayed as those “who have eight dollars a day to fight about nothing half the time.”[36]

Despite whatever damage to their public image, “attorneys” continued to run for office and the voters to elect them. “Esquires” Benson, May, and Fillebrown, for instance, won long tenures in public office, largely dominating Winthrop's political arena to 1850 and beyond. Possibly their popularity indicates a lack of alternative candidates, but possibly, too, it indicates the shallowness of opposition to the office-seeking "attorney." Indeed, if the remarks of Ezekiel Holmes were at all typical, harangues against "office seekers," "lawyers," and "politicians" may have simply been normal electioneering rhetoric. They may have been dismissed as just further evidence of "demagoguery." Dr. Holmes, for example, did not let his disavowal of "politicians" preclude his spending several terms in the Maine House of Representatives and the Senate nor his candidacy for governor in 1852–53.[37] It is thus unclear whether opposition was limited to the "politician" as symbol or whether it was actually extended to the people who could be so labeled. In any case, complaints about the legal profession's hold on government appear throughout the period. For better or worse, "lawyers" were associated with political power no less than with wealth and honor.

"Physicians" (or "doctors" or "practitioners") were also assumed to possess great influence. In addition to "high standing" and their own measure of political power, "doctors" were the keepers of their neighbors' health. At a time when threats to health were so profound, they had a truly great responsibility. The announcement of a single case of cholera or smallpox was cause for universal alarm. Residents could easily recall the terror of epidemics like those in 1814 and 1822, when disease claimed dozens of lives in but a few months. Even more ordinary medical problems were extremely severe by modern standards. It was common for an older man to recall two or three children who never lived to see twenty, and one or even two wives who died during their childbearing years. To handle such threats was the "doctor" 's noble calling; he practiced "the healing arts."

His special social position was also indicated by the control he exercised over those who hired his services. The relationship between "doctor" and "patient" (or "applicant") was largely defined by the "doctor." This contrasts notably with "workingmen" and "businessmen" who tended to treat their "customers" more like partners in each transaction. To some extent all of the "learned professions" differed from other occupations in this way. The exchange that would otherwise make a person a "customer" would make one a "client" to an ''attorney,'' a ''patient'' to a ''doctor,'' and a ''hearer'' (though in a slightly different sense) to a ''minister''; in other words, the consumer's relationship with a ''professional man'' was unlike any other. Yet in medicine this relationship was particularly important and unique. For a ''physician'' to assume full responsibility for his work, the ''applicant'' had to qualify. An ''applicant'' had to be deemed *his* ''patient,'' and the ''physician'' himself would make the final determination. If an ''applicant'' failed to devote sufficient time and money to a ''doctor,'' the ''physician'' could deny responsibility for the effect of his treatments, claiming, ''He (or she) is not really my patient.'' Dr. Clark, for instance, explained: ''I have only lost one patient [i.e., he died], though I can hardly call him mine as he had been tracked over by other physicians and I only saw him five times for three weeks or more. I only saw him when they sent for me as the pieces did not exist 'to make expense.' . . . No blame attached to me.''[39]

Residents generally assumed that the ''physician'' 's ''high standing'' and influence were well deserved. Because he was ''learned,'' he could be expected to show ''skill'' in practice. Regardless of his particular specialty, whether ''surgeon,'' ''cold waterite,'' ''dentist,'' or general ''physician,'' he was supposed an effective master of ''the healing arts.''[40]

His knowledge could inspire even greater confidence because it was ''scientific.'' ''Progress'' in the profession was often attributed to the advances in chemistry and physiology which were promoted in medical schools. Those who were less ''scientific,'' like the Indian ''doctress'' or traveling ''phrenologist,'' were liable to ridicule. The *Maine Farmer,* for example, reported with glee that the expert opinion of a ''phrenologist'' was not admissible in court. The judge preferred the ''physician'' 's ''science'' to the ''mere theory'' of *''Bumpology.''*[41]

Patients could also expect their ''doctors'' to be of sound ''character,'' to be dedicated, compassionate, and sensible. They would rush to the bedside of the sick and do their best, whatever the financial rewards.[42]

This combination of ''skill'' and ''character'' placed ''doctors'' firmly in the public trust. Those who were particularly experienced and effective would receive even greater respect. They might serve as ''counselors'' on difficult cases or advise the selectmen on public health policy. They would gain the celebrity and fortunes that signal ''success.'' As one such ''physician'' boasted, ''My practice is increasing and my patients of a higher and paying grade.''[43]

Yet medicine had its hazards and disappointments as well: ''The physician may be happy when his scientific skill enables him to relieve the pain and anguish of his patients. But his avocation is one of fatigue and exposure. He is obliged to contend with competition, ignorance and prejudices and . . . the scenes of misery and distress with which he is daily conversant but cannot relieve.'' Obviously, Winthrop's ''physicians'' were noted for neither jocularity nor longevity.[44]

There were, too, ample complaints about inferior ''doctors,'' those who failed to possess the expected degree of skill and virtue. Among these, of course, was the familiar ''dandy'':

> Who are the surgeons of the present day? Why, Sir, they are the darling boys of some anxious mothers, that were too lazy or too pretty to work and forsooth they were sent to school and grow up in the effeminacy of our large towns and villages and attend two courses of lectures, and get them a set of surgical instruments and sally forth into the world with a heart no bigger than a pea, and then hoist a sign of Dr. ———.[45]

Often the label ''quack'' was applied to distinguish a particularly unqualified ''physician.'' Unlike his supposedly ''scientific'' peers, a ''quack . . . administers medicine of which he knows neither the nature nor the effect.'' He was typically pictured charging inflated fees for harmless but ineffective ''doses of calomel and jalep.'' There were those, too, who felt that ''quacks'' actually harmed their ''applicants.'' In a fine example of local humor, one resident observed: ''It was said with much point and truth, by an old physician, that in all cases of illness there were three things to consider — the patient, the disease, and the doctor; and if any two of them pulled together, they would be able to beat the third. In the case I have been supposing, it is the disease and the doctor against the patient.''[46] Such cases, however, were considered rare. The ''quack'' was notable because he was an exception. By reputation ''physicians'' remained honorable and skillful, ''gentlemen'' truly worthy of their ''standing.''

A "clergyman" 's duties and standing were no less significant. He tended the all-important spiritual health of his "hearers," guiding them from birth to the hereafter. The rites that he administered marked each of the recognized turning points in human development. Although by 1820 the church was politically and economically independent of the town, "ministers" still touched nearly every aspect of community life.[47] Note, for example, the breadth of the Reverend David Thurston's activities in but a single year:

> During this year [1812], I have attended two meetings of association, two of societies, three of councils, three ordinations, two schools, four town-meetings, four days of fasting and prayer, seven meetings of trustees, eight marriages, ten funerals, thirteen singing schools, forty-seven conferences; heard nineteen sermons and preached 147; administered six baptisms, made eighty-three pastoral and fifty-two friendly visits, and 330 calls; have received ninety-three companies and 149 calls; have written twenty-two letters, and ridden 1464 miles out of town.

It would require pages just to list the associations in which he participated as Winthrop's Congregational "pastor" from 1807 to 1851.[48]

"Ministers" were considered of such universal importance that residents could fear for any community without one, whether in Maine or Tahiti. Those unable to procure a "preacher" were labeled "the destitute," a name that provided its own call for "benevolence." Citizens of Winthrop, like those elsewhere, spent much of their time and money to send traveling "preachers" or "missionaries" to "destitute regions" through an intricate network of "missionary societies."[49] It is significant that no analogous phenomena existed for those lacking the services of men in other vocations.

Supposedly what "the destitute" missed most was spiritual guidance, but "ministers" were assumed to perform other valuable services as well. One such service was their help in arbitrating conflicts within and outside the church, a valuable service, indeed. Between 1820 and 1850, there were intense rivalries between denominations and between factions within denominations. The Reverend Mr. Thurston, for example, was a principal, if not the initiator, in nearly all these disputes, and several times an "ecumenical council" recommended his removal to restore peace in the community. In order to retain their ''pastor'' in 1819, ''Congregationalists'' pleaded, ''He is viewed as a kind of ligament, by which the church and society are kept together; and it is very much feared that his dismission would dissolve the ties by which they have been so long united.'' His advice in disputes was so important that failure to heed it could be grounds for a member's dismissal from the church.[50]

A ''minister'' was also responsible for the community's moral leadership. There were, of course, great denominational and individual differences over the particular positions and sanctions that he should employ, but in any case his responsibility was great. By all accounts, a ''minister'' would at least ''strive to *be an example of believers* in word, in conversation, in charity, in spirit, in faith, in purity.'' Because he was such a moral authority, he could be called on to officially assess the ''private character'' of his neighbors.[51]

In many respects this authority was beyond reproach, a consideration which the Reverend Mr. Thurston exploited for nearly half a century. His calls for ''moral reform'' provide a veritable catalogue of early nineteenth-century ''benevolence.'' He promoted temperance, abolitionism, sabbath schools, common school reform, female education, missionary and Bible societies, vegetarianism, lyceums, and even scientific agriculture. Many of these positions were politically taboo in this solidly ''Whig'' community, but because he was a ''minister,'' many complained, he had to be tolerated. Only when Thurston pressed his demands that the church actually endorse a political slate was he dismissed.[52] Though his activism was unique, clearly ''ministers'' were allowed great social as well as spiritual influence.

For the most part, however, their position was considered a ''religious'' as opposed to an occupational appointment. Discussions of their qualifications and merits appear almost exclusively in contexts that identify their relationship to ''truth'' and ''doctrine'' rather than other employments. Moreover, this religious identity was at least as complicated as the denominational issues that have occupied historians and theologians since the Reformation. Residents were committed to a wide variety of Protestant positions. ''Congregationalists,'' ''Friends,'' ''Episcopal Methodists,'' ''Calvinist Baptists,'' and ''Universalists'' were represented in substantial number. There were, too, small or short-lived "Christian Band," "New Church," and "Free Will Baptist" congregations. The religious qualifications and responsibilities of Winthrop "preachers" were as diverse as the various doctrines.

Residents' expectations of their "ministers" varied too with a host of more local conditions, the economic and spiritual state of each church. For those who desired, the acquisition of a "settled minister" or "pastor" involved marshaling a large and generous parish as well as building or borrowing a sufficient house of worship. Add to this Winthrop's "ministerial fund controversy," a legacy of the separation of church and state lasting from 1798 to 1832, and the picture is complex indeed. "Preachers" could also be selected by their ability to occasion "revivals," a consideration that would vary in importance from year to year and as competing local "clergymen" enjoyed varying successes. In short, a "minister" 's religious identity was intricate and dynamic. Its analysis would be a major project in itself.[53]

Nevertheless, there were some very general common assumptions about pastoral service. While other men were judged by what they practiced or produced, a "minister" was usually judged by what he said and how he said it. His primary duty was to "instruct" and "convince" his "hearers"; he was "steward of the mysteries of God," "servant of Christ," "spiritual guide," and "messenger of salvation." In all he would promote the "truth" and its source, the Word, the Gospels, the Bible. Thus, a "pastor" 's public image was firmly tied to his most potent and personal discourse, the "sermon." Ideally he would preach "sound doctrine" with a "style and method" that would engage and deeply impress his "hearers." Elements of "style" were, indeed, crucial. Probably the most often cited mark of an unsatisfactory "preacher" was an audience of "drowsy hearers": "The design of the preacher is to convince, instruct, impress and persuade. . . . Let not ministers complain that their hearers sleep, when they themselves rock the cradle." Conversely, the mark of a superior "minister" was his ability "to urge the believer on to perfection." This, after all, was his ultimate purpose, to "prepare men for the world of glory." Thurston explained, "The best discharge of ministerial duties will ensure the salvation of all hearers."[54]

There were also more strictly occupational elements of the "clergyman'' 's reputation. Clearly ministry as much as law and medicine was considered a ''learned profession'' and its practitioners, ''professional men.'' The varying though generally increasing call for a ''learned ministry'' with ''stated salary'' was associated with the ''pastor'' 's professional as well as spiritual status. A ''minister,'' too, was subject to the usual grumbling about ''nonproducers''; for example, he was ''not one who feeds, but is fed by the flock.'' Nevertheless, his spiritual mission lent him almost unequaled respect. Though depending on ''workingmen'' for earthly sustenance, ''The minister of the gospel may delight to point the enquiring traveler to the pathway to Heaven.'' Few men could claim such a noble calling.[55]

In sum, residents considered ''professional men'' among their most important citizens. They were distinguished not only by their wealth and honor but also by the significance of their service. They tended the vital legal, medical, and spiritual prosperity of the community. They were entrusted, as well, with great moral and political authority. Though, like others, they were liable to charges of idleness or incompetence, they were commonly supposed ''gentlemen'' worthy of ''high standing'' and wide emulation. A ''professional man'' thus could enjoy by definition the ''success'' that ''workingmen'' might toil a lifetime to attain.

CHAPTER 10

Conclusion

The cultural constitution of occupations in Winthrop, between 1820 and 1850, was complex and changing. Each category is probably best understood in its relationship to those with which it contrasted. There is, I think necessarily, some distortion in considering the culture of work outside the contexts in which particular jobs were performed and discussed, outside, that is, the area on which ethnoscience justly focuses. With allowance for some distortion, however, it is possible to identify features that were sufficiently common and important to be considered characteristic of the occupational domain as a whole.

That residents could assume, for example, that anyone with an occupation was adult and male indicates two basic values, i.e., emphases on age and sex. In a period of lesser specialization, it was important, as well, to know which vocation dominated a man's time and energy, his "steady employment." These three factors — age, sex, and time — could be crucial to any occupational assignment.

The distinction between manual and nonmanual labor was no less significant. It could define the difference between "workingmen" and "nonproducers" or "gentlemen farmers" and "farmers" (proper). By stressing physical labor residents could also form expectations about their relative "standing," their wealth and honor.

Residents could base more specific label assignments on the products of a man's employment. For "workingmen," the vast majority of Winthrop workers, this meant a profound emphasis on things; they could be identified by what they made or raised. This component as well as the more general equation of wealth with ''success'' suggests an element of materialism in Winthrop culture.

Yet there were abundantly more human elements, too. Types of farm ''help'' could be distinguished by the procedures they followed, ''mechanics'' by the breadth of their responsibilities or independence, and ''professional men'' by the services they offered. Even a man's education could be crucial. It was largely a ''college'' education that made ''professional men'' ''learned'' and separated them from men in other vocations. All of these, then, were also basic values: emphases on skill, authority, independence, and education. There were likewise a number of discriminations based on ''character'' evaluations. One could tell a ''practical farmer'' from a ''book farmer'' by his sources of information or reasoning and his propensity to change. A man could be deemed a ''(true) gentleman,'' versus a ''dandy,'' because he was industrious, generous, trustworthy, refined, tasteful, polite, and temperate. A ''quack'' could be distinguished by his lack of compassion and dedication as well as effectiveness, a ''pettifogger'' by his selfishness. Since, too, ''quacks'' or the like were hardly admirable, these ''character'' considerations were doubly important. They could be emphasized to sort out not only the various types but the various qualities of people.

There were also a number of important connotations to each of the labels. Although not necessary to the definitions, they could affect the reputation of an entire group. They figured prominently in reference contexts, often portrayed as acceptable grounds for joining or avoiding an employment. Like the more strictly semantic components, they were often relevant in limited domains. Diversity, for example, may have been appealing only in agriculture, and intellect in the ''learned professions.''

Yet there were considerations that could affect the public image of nearly every vocation. One of the most important of these was ''standing''; the more an occupation was associated with wealth and honor, the ''higher'' the ''standing'' of its members. The supposed probability of enjoying such ''success'' as well as self-sufficiency and good health could be expected to influence a man's occupational goals. Residents could also evaluate vocations by their effect on the society as a whole, their contribution to the community's economic and moral well-being. Thus, for example, "farmers" could be recommended as "practical" or "productive" and "ministers" as models of "purity."

Such values could be applied to rate not only the occupational groups but also the individuals within those groups. These were the standards of performance associated with the various categories. Some of them, again, were unique to particular domains, but others appeared in nearly every domain. In addition, of course, to providing the product or service signified by his title, a man could be expected to work for "success" — for property and reputation. These two commodities could distinguish both the best of men and the best of innovations, those leading to "improvement" or "progress."

Probably the most widely touted means to these ends were industry and efficiency. Indeed, residents could assume that such "character" traits were a prerequisite for "success," that the two were indivisible. "Dandies" or other "idlers" might obtain the "exterior," the trappings of "success," but their indolence and folly could occasion wide disdain. Their eventual "embarrassment" or "failure" would be only predictable. Though less integral to "success," there were, too, other common standards of on-the-job morality. Ideally, men would be prompt, orderly, honest, and generally worthy the trust of their associates.

The study thus delineates some major aspects of the culture of occupational life in an American community. The various semantic and contextual features reveal values that the residents themselves may have applied to identify, evaluate, and perform their jobs. But this picture is more than a single-frame view; vantage is gained on the more dynamic as well as static aspects of employment.

First, there are the considerations that affected individual job development. During the course of his life a man could be expected to pass through an orderly series of identities. Residents could assume, for example, that a "farmer" was once a "hired hand" or "boy"; a "master mechanic" once an "apprentice"; a "merchant" once a "clerk"; and a "professional man" once a "graduate." The components that separated these identities were standards of mobility, of individual change in the community.

Second, there is the broader area of continuity and change in the culture itself. The study provides some clarification of the impact during the period, 1820 to 1850, of developments in the economy, ecology, technology, and society as a whole. It is notable, for instance, that these developments occasioned great change in the culture of farming, an employment traditionally identified with conservatism. The rise of a new ideal, the "scientific farmer," can be considered both a response and a stimulus to the revision of agricultural values. On the other hand, it is clear how little change appeared in the "mechanic" domain. The terminology was remarkably stable. Identity concepts in manufacturing were often so flexible, so tied to the product rather than technology, that they failed to reflect new industrial roles. For the emerging "factory girl" this failure proved a potent source of conflict. Traditional notions of "female employment" were inadequate in the face of new types of women, categories that defied the supposed division between the "mechanical" male and the "domestic" female. In the case of "school masters," a structural anomaly indicates not only a potential locus for cultural change but even the direction such a change might take. The analysis predicts (or, I suppose, "retrodicts") a demand for higher "teacher" qualifications and rewards, for features that would make them more like "professional men." These demands were indeed among mid-century proposals for educational reform.

A great deal is thereby discovered about the changing culture of this community, about occupational values in process. Here is the promised diachronic view of "standards for perceiving, believing, evaluating, and acting." Conclusions from this study might well be compared with those from others to gauge regional and temporal variations in the culture of work.

But far more is intended than just a cultural point estimate. In addition to portraying a single aspect of a lonely Maine town, I hope that I have demonstrated the general value of the approach, that ethnoscience in history is as productive in application as it is in theory.

There are, I believe, a host of questions about the American past that would benefit from a similar perspective. This study, for example, suggests some of the ways that women may have been excluded from occupational life. It would be interesting to examine the more inclusive aspects of female identity. What did it mean to be a "lady," "woman," "female," or "girl"? A "wife," "helpmeet," "daughter," or "mother"? What was the impact of the "female education movement" or the rise of "fashion"? A similar approach could guide inquiries into religion, government, the military, education, or the family, as well as communities of artists, reformers, or just plain "friends." Nor must application be limited to the study of naming or typing behavior. A whole array of methods has been introduced to examine events and decision making from an ethnoscience perspective.[1]

At the same time there is ample room for those more interested in quantitative methods. Structural models and the comparison of linguistic with other data are often best drawn through mathematics. Indeed, it may be argued that a study that combines the qualitative analysis of cognition and the statistical analysis of behavior would achieve better results than either analysis alone.[2] This, for example, could well be said of the relationship between this study and those typically in the so-called new urban history. Results could be more precise and culturally relevant if the approaches were united, if, for instance, equal attention were paid to standards of occupational mobility and the mobility actually observed in census records or the like.[3]

Ethnoscience, then, offers great promise to scholars of various persuasions. Its usefulness is hardly limited to the study of occupations or obscure Maine towns. There is, of course, much work to be done in further adapting the methodology to documentary research, but this merely indicates another fertile ground for the historian's attention.[4] For those frustrated by disciplinary boundaries, ethnoscience is a valuable alternative, one well suited to the description and analysis of cultures in the American past.

Notes

CHAPTER I: A THEORY OF DESCRIPTION

1. The most prominent interpretations of early nineteenth-century America include: Henry Adams, *History of the United States during the Administrations of Jefferson and Madison,* abridged with an introduction by George Dangerfield and Otey M. Scruggs (Englewood Cliffs: Prentice-Hall, 1963); Lee Benson, *The Concept of Jacksonian Democracy: New York as a Test Case* (New York: Atheneum, 1965); Rowland T. Berthoff, "Part 2: The Society of Individuals, 1775–1875," in *An Unsettled People: Social Order and Disorder in American History* (New York: Harper and Row, 1971), pp. 127–298; Daniel J. Boorstin, *The Americans: The National Experience* (New York: Random House, 1965); George Dangerfield, *The Awakening of American Nationalism, 1815–1828* (New York: Harper and Row, 1965); Marvin Meyers, *The Jacksonian Persuasion: Politics and Belief* (Stanford: Stanford University Press, 1969); Edward Pessen, *Jacksonian America: Society, Personality and Politics* (Homewood, Ill.: Dorsey, 1969); Arthur M. Schlesinger, Jr., *The Age of Jackson* (Boston: Little, Brown and Co., 1945); Charles S. Sydnor, *The Development of Southern Sectionalism 1819–1848,* (Baton Rouge: Louisiana State University, 1968); Alexis de Tocqueville, *Democracy in America,* 2 vols., with a critical appraisal of each volume by John Stuart Mill, trans. Henry Reeve (New York: Schocken Books, 1967); Frederick Jackson Turner, *Frontier and Section: Selected Essays of Frederick Jackson Turner,* with an introduction by Ray Allen Billington (Englewood Cliffs: Prentice-Hall, 1961); Glyndon G. Van Deusen, *The Jacksonian Era, 1828–1848* (New York: Harper and Row, 1963); and John W. Ward, *Andrew Jackson —Symbol for an Age* (New York: Oxford University Press, 1966). Excellent bibliographic surveys include: Boorstin, *The Americans,* pp. 433–95; Alfred A. Cave, *Jacksonian Democracy and the Historians,* University of Florida Monographs: Social Sciences no. 22 (Gainsville: University of Florida Press, 1964); and Pessen, *Jacksonian America,* pp. 352–93.
2. For a discussion of the relationship between perspective and fact in various disciplines, see: for science, Thomas S. Kuhn, *The Structure of Scientific Revolutions,* 2d ed., enl., *International Encyclopedia of Unified Science,* vol. 2, no. 2

(Chicago: University of Chicago Press, 1970); for sociology, Herbert Blumer, "Symbolic Interaction," in *Culture and Cognition: Rules, Maps, and Plans,* ed. James P. Spradley (San Francisco: Chandler, 1972), pp. 65–83; for anthropology, Irving A. Hallowell, "The Self and Its Behavioral Environment," in *Culture and Experience* (New York: Schocken Books, 1971), pp. 75–110; for philosophy, Herbert Spiegelberg, *The Phenomenological Movement: A Historical Introduction,* 2d ed. (The Hague: Martinas Nijhoff, 1969); for history, Murray G. Murphey, *Our Knowledge of the Historical Past* (New York: Bobbs-Merrill, 1972); for art, E. H. Gombrich, *Art and Illusion: A Study in the Psychology of Pictorial Representation,* A. W. Mellon Lectures in the Fine Arts, 1956, Bollingen Series 35 (5) (Princeton: Princeton University Press, 1969); for psychology, George A. Miller, Eugene Galanter, and Karl H. Pribram, "Plans," in *Culture and Cognition,* ed. Spradley, pp. 52–64; for musicology, Bruno Nettl, *Theory and Method in Ethnomusicology* (London: Collier-Macmillan, 1964), pp. 105–7; for linguistics, Benjamin Lee Whorf, *Language, Thought, and Reality: Selected Writings of Benjamin Lee Whorf,* ed. John B. Carroll (Cambridge: M.I.T. Press, 1964); for ethology, Donald R. Griffin, *The Question of Animal Awareness: Evolutionary Continuity of Mental Experience* (New York: Rockefeller University Press, 1976); and for political science, James C. Scott, *Political Ideology in Malaysia: Reality and the Beliefs of an Elite* (New Haven: Yale University Press, 1968). Since the problem of defining "facts" is not restricted to a single discipline, I do not hesitate to resort to several disciplines in seeking a solution. Ronald Cohen, "Generalizations in Ethnology," in *A Handbook of Method in Cultural Anthropology,* ed. Raoul Naroll and Ronald Cohen (New York: Columbia University Press, 1973), p. 46.

3. Peter L. Berger and Thomas Luckman, *The Social Construction of Reality* (Garden City: Doubleday, 1967). "What this means is that for any individual organism or organization there are no such things as 'facts.' There are only messages filtered through a changeable value system. . . . Part of our image of the world is the belief that this image is shared by other people like ourselves who are also part of our image of the world. . . . Science is a subculture among subcultures. It can claim to be useful. It may claim rather more dubiously to be good. It cannot claim to give validity. In summation, then, my theory might well be called an organic theory of knowledge. Its most fundamental proposition is that knowledge is what somebody or something knows, and that without a knower, knowledge is an absurdity." Kenneth E. Boulding, "The Image," in *Culture and Cognition,* ed. Spradley, pp. 48–50. For a less Platonic, more complex argument, see: Paul Feyerabend, *Against Method: Outline of an Anarchistic Theory of Knowledge* (London: NLB, 1975).

4. "In actuality not even the most concrete, objectively apparent physical objects can be identified apart from some culturally defined system of concepts." Charles O. Frake, "The Ethnographic Study of Cognitive Systems," in *Cognitive Anthropology,* ed. Stephen A. Tyler (New York: Holt, Rinehart, and Winston, 1969), p. 28. See also: Mary B. Black, "Eliciting Folk Taxonomy in Ojibwa," in *Cognitive Anthropology,* ed. Tyler, pp. 165–67; Blumer, "Symbolic Interaction," pp. 65–83; George Psathas, "Ethnoscience and Ethnomethodology," in *Culture and Cognition,* ed. Spradley, pp. 206–22.

5. Irving A. Hallowell, "Ojibwa Ontology, Behavior and World View," in *Culture in History: Essays in Honor of Paul Radin,* ed. Stanley Diamond (New York: Columbia University Press, 1960), pp. 19–52. "The study of social organization, defined as human relations of a certain kind, is perfectly intelligible as an objective approach to the study of this subject in any culture. But if, in the world view of a people, 'persons' as a class include entities other than human beings, then our objective approach is not adequate for presenting an accurate description of 'the way a man, in a particular society, sees himself in relation to all else.' A different perspective is required for this purpose. It may be argued, in fact, that a thoroughgoing 'objective' approach to the study of cultures cannot be achieved solely by projecting upon those cultures categorical abstractions derived from Western thought. For, in a broad sense, the latter are a reflection of our cultural subjectivity." Idem, p. 21.
6. This is, of course, an oversimplification. Neither sociologists nor Ojibwas have a monolithic conception of "persons." Members of both groups frequently disagree about what is or is not a "person." The breadth and consistency of disagreement, however, is clearly greater between the two groups than within them. In this sense analysts and their subjects hold two *sets* of perspectives rather than two perspectives.
7. Kenneth L. Pike develops the etic-emic distinction in *Language in Relation to a Unified Theory of the Structure of Human Behavior,* 2 vols. (Glendale: Summer Institute of Linguistics, 1954). See: Kenneth L. Pike, "Etic and Emic Standpoints for the Description of Behavior," in *Communication and Culture: Readings in the Codes of Human Interaction,* ed. Alfred G. Smith (New York: Holt, Rinehart, and Winston, 1966), pp. 152–63. Discussions and illustrations of the distinction also appear in: Alan Dundes, "From Etic to Emic Units in the Structural Study of Folktales," *Journal of American Folklore* 75 (1962): 95–105; Ward H. Goodenough, *Culture, Language and Society,* A McCaleb Module in Anthropology, Addison-Wesley Modular Publications (11560), vol. 2, module no. 7 (1971), pp. 6–8; Ward H. Goodenough, *Description and Comparison in Cultural Anthropology* (Chicago: Aldine, 1970), pp. 98–130; Pertti J. Pelto, *Anthropological Research: The Structure of Inquiry* (New York: Harper and Row, 1970); William C. Sturtevant, "Studies in Ethnoscience," in *Culture and Cognition,* ed. Spradley, p. 134; Oswald Werner and Joann Fenton, "Method and Theory in Ethnoscience or Ethnoepistemology," in *A Handbook of Method in Cultural Anthropology,* ed. Naroll and Cohen, p. 542; and Ibrahim Ag Youssouf, Allen D. Grimshaw, and Charles S. Bird, "Greetings in the Desert," *American Ethnologist* 3 (1976): 797–824.
8. These ten points appear in Pike's "Etic and Emic Standpoints," pp. 152–55.
9. Pike, *Language in Relation to a Unified Theory,* vol. 1, p. 8. "The description is an emic one to the extent that it is based on elements that are already components of that system; and the description is an etic one to the extent that it is based on conceptual elements that are not components of that system. The object of emic analysis is to arrive at a minimal set of conceptual components that can serve as the primitive points of reference for describing the rest of the content of the system. But this minimal set of conceptual components can only be described in etic terms, that is with reference to concepts that are extrinsic to the system being

described." Goodenough, *Culture, Language, and Society,* p. 7.

10. Pike, "Etic and Emic Standpoints," pp. 156–57.
11. Sturtevant, "Studies in Ethnoscience," p. 144.
12. Brent Berlin, "A Universalist-Evolutionary Approach in Ethnographic Semantics," *Bulletin of the American Anthropological Association* vol. 3, no. 3, pt. 2 (1970): 3–18. Harold C. Conklin, "Hanunóo Color Categories," *Southwestern Journal of Anthropology* 11 (1955): 339–44. Goodenough, *Description and Comparison,* pp. 98–130. Dell H. Hymes, "Directions in (ethno-) Linguistic Theory," *American Anthropologist* 66 (1964): 6–56. Paul Kay, "Some Theoretical Implications of Ethnographic Semantics," *Bulletin of the American Anthropological Association,* vol. 3, no. 3, pt. 2 (1970): 26-27. Sturtevant, "Studies in Ethnoscience," p. 134.
13. The distinction between the phenomenal order and the ideational order is popular in American anthropology, including ethnoscience. It is defined in: Ward H. Goodenough, "Introduction," in *Explorations in Cultural Anthropology,* ed. Goodenough (New York: McGraw-Hill, 1964), p. 11. See also: Kenneth E. Boulding, *The Image* (Ann Arbor: University of Michigan Press, 1969), p. 43. A sociologist put this quite directly: "Symbolic interactionism rests in the last analysis on three simple premises. The first premise is that human beings act toward things on the basis of the meanings that the things have for them. . . . The second premise is that the meanings of such things are derived from or arise out of the social interaction that one has with one's fellows. The third premise is that these meanings are handled in, and modified through, an interpretive process used by the persons in dealing with the things they encounter. . . . Behind the facade of the objectively perceived joint action the set of meanings that sustains the joint action has a life that the social scientist can ill afford to ignore." Blumer, "Symbolic Interaction," pp. 66–67, 81. See also: Kay, "Theoretical Implications," pp. 27–28; Miller, Galanter, and Pilbram, "Plans," pp. 52–60; and, for a materialist version, Bruce Kuklick, "Myth and Symbol in American Studies," *American Quarterly* 24 (1972): 435–50. These statements, like others, assume an opposition between mind, meaning, or idea and body, action, or fact. And there is something sensible there (if only for our dualist sensibility). We might talk of one as more observable, variable, factual, or even higher than the other. But I remain skeptical and move to a clearly opposing position when talk turns to separate orders or lives. It seems clear, for example, that the problems of being poor are only obscured if we assume that not having money and the idea or feeling of poverty are separable. What is to be gained by such an assumption? I would prefer to leave the issue open. It is only ironic that one of the easiest ways to discredit claims of "objectivity" (i.e., appeals to a true world independent of mind) is to play it out, to take the dualism seriously. See: Griffin, *Animal Awareness;* and Clifford Geertz, *The Interpretation of Cultures* (New York: Basic Books, 1973).
14. Philip K. Bock, "Foreword: On 'Culture Shock,' " in *Culture Shock: A Reader in Modern Cultural Anthropology,* ed. Bock (New York: Alfred A. Knopf, 1970), p. ix.
15. Ward H. Goodenough, "Cultural Anthropology and Linguistics," in *Report of the Seventh Annual Round Table Meeting on Linguistics and Language Study,* ed. Paul L. Garvin, George Washington University Monograph Series on Language

and Linguistics, no. 9 (Washington, D.C.: George Washington University Press, 1957), p. 167. Ward H. Goodenough, *Cooperation in Change* (New York: Russell Sage Foundation, 1963), p. 259. Goodenough, *Description and Comparison,* p. 104. "Culture" is, of course, defined in a wide variety of ways. Hundreds of these definitions are presented and discussed in Alfred L. Kroeber and Clyde Kluckhohn, *Culture: A Critical Review of Concepts and Definitions* (New York: Random House, 1952), see particularly p. 308. Culture is probably best conceived uniquely for each research purpose. It is, after all, an etic unit, only emic within the society of social analysts. As such it should be defined to suit the researcher. Hence, I intend to present, not the authoritative definition, but one that I believe most appropriate for this project. "Here, then, we shall reserve the term *culture* . . . for the things one needs to know in order to meet the standards of others." Goodenough, *Culture, Language, and Society,* p. 19. Presentations of a culture concept paralleling Goodenough's include: James P. Spradley and David W. McCurdy, "The Cultural Experience," in *The Cultural Experience: Ethnography in Complex Society,* ed. Spradley and McCurdy (Chicago: Science Research Associates, 1972), p. 8; Stephen A. Tyler, "Introduction: The Old and the New," in *Cognitive Anthropology,* ed. Tyler, p. 14; Anthony F. C. Wallace, "Culture and Cognition," in *Culture and Cognition,* ed. Spradley, pp. 111–13; and particularly Anthony F. C. Wallace, *Culture and Personality,* 2d ed. (New York: Random House, 1970), pp. 3–38. By this definition, "culture" includes *world view.* The world view of a people "is their picture of the way things in sheer actuality are, their concept of nature, of self, of society. It contains the most comprehensive ideas of order." Clifford Geertz, "Ethos, World-View and the Analysis of Sacred Symbols," in *Every Man His Way: Readings in Cultural Anthropology,* ed. Alan Dundes (Englewood Cliffs: Prentice-Hall, 1968), p. 303. See also: Black, "Eliciting Folk Taxonomy," p. 165; Geertz, *Interpretation of Cultures;* Hallowell, "Ojibwa Ontology, Behavior, and World View," p. 21; Hallowell, "The Self," pp. 91–92; Bronislaw Malinowski, *Argonauts of the Western Pacific* (London: George Routledge and Sons, 1922), p. 25; Jacques Maquet, "An African World View," in *Culture Shock,* ed. Bock, pp. 340–41; Miller, Galanter, and Pribram, "Plans," p. 61; and Whorf, *Language, Thought and Reality,* p. 214.

16. "The final goal, of which an Ethnographer should never lose sight . . . is, briefly, to grasp the native's point of view, his relation to life, to realise *his* vision of *his* world." Malinowski, *Argonauts,* p. 25. Exemplary versions of the definition and goals of emic ethnography include: Black, "Eliciting Folk Taxonomy," pp. 165–67; Charles O. Frake, "Struck By Speech," in *Culture and Cognition,* ed. Spradley, pp. 280–81; Charles O. Frake, "A Structural Description of Subanun 'Religious Behavior,' " in *Cognitive Anthropology,* ed. Tyler, pp. 123–24; Ward H. Goodenough, "Componential Analysis," in *Culture and Cognition,* ed. Spradley, p. 327; Goodenough, "Cultural Anthropology and Linguistics," p. 173; Psathas, "Ethnoscience and Ethnomethodology," pp. 208, 212; James P. Spradley, "Adaptive Strategies of Urban Nomads," in *Culture and Cognition,* ed. Spradley, pp. 237–41; Spradley and McCurdy, eds., *The Cultural Experience,* pp. 8–34; Wallace, "Culture and Cognition," pp. 113, 123; and Werner and Fenton, "Method and Theory," pp. 537–78.

17. "In essence, cognitive anthropology seeks to answer two questions: What material phenomena are significant for the people of some culture; and how do they organize these phenomena?" Tyler, "Introduction," p. 3.
18. Goodenough, *Culture, Language, and Society,* pp. 22–24. "The object of emic analysis is to arrive at a minimal set of conceptual components that can serve as the primitive points of reference for describing the rest of the content of the system," p. 7.
19. Jerome S. Bruner, Jacqueline J. Goodnow, and George A. Austin, "Categories and Cognition," in *Culture and Cognition,* ed. Spradley, pp. 169, 178–81. See also: Richard A. Watson and Patty Jo Watson, *Man and Nature: An Anthropological Essay in Human Ecology* (New York: Harcourt Brace Jovanovich, 1969), p. 3; and Robert B. Zajonc, "Cognitive Theories in Social Psychology," in *The Handbook of Social Psychology,* 2d ed., ed. Gardiner Lindzey and Elliot Aronson (Reading: Addison-Wesley, 1968), vol. 1, p. 332.
20. Probably the most noted such indictment comes from Marvin Harris in "Emics, Etics, and the New Ethnography," Chapter 20 of *The Rise of Anthropological Theory: A History of Theories of Culture* (New York: Thomas Y. Crowell, 1968), pp. 568–604. Although he admits that "in theory, an emic ethnography need be neither more nor less empirical, scientific, or intersubjective than an etic ethnography" (p. 576), he seems to reject emic ethnography largely on those very grounds. He says, "In larger perspective, however, the movement ["new" or emic ethnography] suffers from the accumulated liabilities of the past two hundred years of cultural-idealist thought. . . . For most human history we have no operational basis for getting inside people's heads in the manner proposed by Frake" (pp. 568, 604). Harris, however, rests much of his case on definitions of emic and etic that few ethnoscientists would accept. As Burling puts it, "I believe that Marvin Harris's recent work, which contrasts what he calls 'emic' and 'etic' points of view, seems to me to unnecessarily polarize our alternatives. . . . Harris's simplistic bifurcation into idealist 'emics' and materialist 'etics' is in danger of squeezing out the middle ground between them." Robbins Burling, "Linguistics and Ethnographic Description," *American Anthropologist* 71 (1969): 826n, 827n. I think it is Harris's rather than the new ethnographer's confusion that leads him to contrast "emic norms" with "etic events" or "etic reality." Harris, *The Rise of Anthropological Theory,* p. 592. See also: Henry A. Gleason, Jr., *An Introduction to Descriptive Linguistics,* rev. ed. (New York: Holt, Rinehart and Winston, 1961), pp. 12–13.
21. Gerald D. Berreman, "Anemic and Emetic Analysis in Social Anthropology," *American Anthropologist* 68 (1966): 349. "I too yearn for rigor in my research. I just urge that in my colleagues' search for scientific rigor, they not inadvertently succumb to scientific *rigor mortis*" (p. 353). It should be noted that I am using Berreman's remarks in support of the ethnoscientists he criticizes. Though apparently in agreement with their purposes, he decries their recent tendency toward oversimplification, rigidity, and triviality, particularly on the part of Frake. I hope this study will demonstrate that ethnoscience need not suffer these weaknesses.
22. Berreman, "Anemic and Emetic Analysis," pp. 346–47.
23. Berreman, "Anemic and Emetic Analysis," p. 349.
24. Ward H. Goodenough, "Yankee Kinship Terminology: A Problem in Componen-

tial Analysis," in *Cognitive Anthropology,* ed. Tyler, p. 285. Goodenough explains that componential analysis was originally his way of making explicit his intuitive "feel for Trukese kinship terminology" (pp. 257–58). "It forces us to be more precise and rigorous in stating what we think we know, thereby helping us to clarify to ourselves our knowledge and its limitation" (p. 285). See also: Gordon W. Allport, *The Use of Personal Documents in Psychological Science* (New York: Social Science Research Council, 1942); and Margaret Mead, "From Intuition to Analysis in Communication Research," *Semiotica* 1 (1969): 13–25.

25. Goodenough, *Culture, Language, and Society,* pp. 3–6. "The new ethnographer seeks. . . . to discover some part of the system of meanings by which people organize their world. The goal is raw cognition, if you will, but since the major realization of this cognition is the words people speak, semantics is considered an integral part of ethnography." Kay, "Theoretical Implications," p. 19.

26. Goodenough, "Componential Analysis," pp. 327–28. Many studies have argued that language has a broad influence on the cognitive aspects of human development. See, for example, the study based on American and Navaho data by John B. Carroll and Joseph B. Casagrande, "The Function of Language Classifications in Behavior," in *Communication and Culture,* ed. Smith, pp. 18–31. Also: Jean Piaget, *Psychology and Epistemology: Towards a Theory of Knowledge,* trans. Arnold Rosin (New York: Viking Press, 1971), p. 140; and Mary Sanches and Ben G. Blount, eds., *Sociocultural Dimensions of Language Use* (New York: Academic Press, 1975). The relationship between the semantic system and culture can, of course, be exaggerated. Sturtevant takes a rather extreme position in "Studies in Ethnoscience," pp. 130–31. Whorf's position is even more extreme: "We dissect nature along lines laid down by our native languages. . . . We cut nature up, organize it into concepts, and ascribe significances as we do, largely because we are parties to an agreement to organize it in this way — an agreement that holds throughout our speech community and is codified in the patterns of our language. The agreement is, of course, an implicit and unstated one, *but its terms are absolutely obligatory;* we cannot talk at all except by subscribing to the organization and classification of data which the agreement decrees." Whorf, *Language, Thought, and Reality,* p. 214.

Whorf's position seems too radical, for it fails to account adequately for individual variation or innovation or cultural change that precedes or is independent of linguistic change. It also implicitly excludes from culture such clearly cultural phenomena as extra-, para-, or body-linguistic communication (such as Amislan or gesture), context, and unnamed categories (covert or unlabeled taxa). See, for example: Ellen B. Basso, "Kalapalo Affinity: Its Cultural and Social Contexts," *American Ethnologist* 2 (1975): 207–28; Brent Berlin, Dennis E. Breedlove, and Peter H. Raven, "General Principles of Classification and Nomenclature in Folk Biology," *American Anthropologist* 75 (1973): 214–42; Cecil H. Brown, "Unique Beginners and Covert Categories in Folk Biological Taxonomies," *American Anthropologist* 76 (1974): 325–27; Brent Berlin, "Further Notes on Covert Categories and Folk Taxonomies: A Reply to Brown," *American Anthropologist* 76 (1974): 325–27; Brent Berlin, "Further Notes on Covert Categories and Folk Taxonomies: A Reply to Brown," *American Anthropologist* 76 (1974): 327–31; Ray L. Birdwhistell, *Kinesics and Context: Es-*

says on Body Motion Communication (Philadelphia: University of Pennsylvania Press, 1973); Jan-Petter Blom and John J. Gumperz, "Social Meaning in Linguistic Structures: Code-Switching in Norway," in *Directions in Sociolinguistics,* ed. John J. Gumperz and Dell Hymes (New York: Holt, Rinehart and Winston, 1972), p. 409; Peter M. Gardner, "Birds, Words, and a Requiem for the Omniscient Informant," *American Ethnologist* 3 (1976): 446–68; Terrence E. Hays, "An Empirical Method for the Identification of Covert Categories in Ethnobiology," *American Ethnologist* 3 (1976): 489–507; James Howe and Joel Sherzer, "Take and Tell: A Practical Classification from the San Blas Cuna," *American Ethnologist* 2 (1975): 435–60; Eugene Linden, *Apes, Men, and Language* (New York: Penguin Books, 1974); and Michael O. Watson, *Symbolic and Expressive Uses of Space: An Introduction to Proxemic Behavior,* A McCaleb Module in Anthropology, Addison-Wesley Modular Publications (11983), vol. 4 (1972), module no. 20. The relationship between language and culture in description is probably best restricted to that of the part (the semantic system) which implies much, yet hardly all, of the whole (culture).

27. "Whenever we finish talking to ourselves the world is as it should be. We renew it, we kindle it with life, we uphold it with our internal talk. Not only that, but we also choose our paths as we talk to ourselves. Thus we repeat the same choices over and over until the day we die, because we keep on repeating the same internal talk over and over until the day we die. A warrior is aware of this and strives to stop his talking." Don Juan, quoted in Carlos Castaneda, *A Separate Reality: Further Conversations with Don Juan* (New York: Simon and Schuster, 1971), p. 263. See also: David Silverman, *Reading Castaneda: A Prologue to the Social Sciences* (London: Routledge and Kegan Paul, 1975); Daniel C. Noel, *Seeing Castaneda: Reactions to the "Don Juan" Writings of Carlos Castaneda* (New York: Putnam, 1976); and Stan Wilk, "Castaneda: Coming of Age in Sonora," *American Anthropologist* 79(1) (1977): 84–91.

28. Frake, "Ethnographic Study of Cognitive Systems," p. 28.

29. The controversy often goes under Burling's rubric, "God's truth or hocus-pocus." Most of my discussion of validity in ethnoscience is derived from: Bruner, Goodnow, and Austin, "Categories and Cognition," pp. 183–88; Robbins Burling, "Cognition and Componential Analysis: God's Truth or Hocus-Pocus?" in *Cognitive Anthropology,* ed. Tyler, pp. 419–28; Burling, "Linguistics and Ethnographic Description," 817–27; Charles O. Frake, "Further Discussion of Burling," in *Cognitive Anthropology,* ed. Tyler, p. 432; Charles O. Frake, "Notes on Queries in Ethnography," in *Cognitive Anthropology,* ed. Tyler, pp. 123–37; Goodenough, "Componential Analysis," pp. 339–40; Goodenough, *Culture, Language and Society,* pp. 14–20; Goodenough, "Yankee Kinship Terminology," p. 286n; Dell H. Hymes, "Discussion of Burling's Paper," in *Cognitive Anthropology,* ed. Tyler, pp. 428–31; Floyd G. Lounsbury, "A Formal Account of the Crow- and Omaha-Type Kinship Terminologies," in *Cognitive Anthropology,* ed. Tyler, pp. 212–13; A. Kimball Romney and Roy G. D'Andrade, "Cognitive Aspects of English Kin Terms," in *Cognitive Anthropology,* ed. Tyler, pp. 369–96; Wallace, "Culture and Cognition," pp. 112–23; Wallace, *Culture and Personality,* pp. 3–38, 128–29; Anthony F. C. Wallace, "The Problem of the Psychological Validity of Componential Analyses," in

Cognitive Anthropology, ed. Tyler, pp. 396–418; Anthony F. C. Wallace and John Atkins, "The Meaning of Kinship Terms," in *Cognitive Anthropology,* ed. Tyler, pp. 345–69; and Murray J. Leaf, "The American English Kin Terminology as a Semantic System," paper delivered at the Seventy-first Annual Meeting of the American Anthropological Association, Toronto, 1972, pp. 2–3.

30. Wallace, "Psychological Validity of Componential Analyses," pp. 396–418. Wallace and Atkins, "The Meaning of Kinship Terms," pp. 345–69.
31. Goodenough, *Culture, Language, and Society,* p. 41; see pp. 38–42.
32. Frake, "Notes on Queries in Ethnography," p. 124.
33. Wallace, "Culture and Cognition," pp. 112–13.
34. One can, for instance, give a psychologically valid definition of "mother" without mentioning the Oedipus complex, whatever its "psychological" significance in other senses of the term: that is, "mother" may be distinguished from "non-mother" without resorting to the Oedipus complex.
35. Lounsbury, "Crow- and Omaha-Type Kinship Terminologies," pp. 212–13. The goal, in other words, is a minimal etic kit.
36. Wallace, "Psychological Validity of Componential Analyses," p. 417.
37. Lounsbury, "Crow- and Omaha-Type Kinship Terminologies," p. 212.
38. Wallace, "Psychological Validity of Componential Analyses," p. 416.
39. Excellent reviews and bibliographies of the literature in ethnoscience include: Benjamin N. Colby, "Ethnographic Semantics: A Preliminary Survey," *Current Anthropology* 7 (1966): 13–17; Harold C. Conklin, *Folk Classifications: A Topically Arranged Bibliography of Contemporary and Background References Through 1971* (New Haven: Yale University Department of Anthropology, 1972); Sturtevant, "Studies in Ethnoscience," pp. 129–67; Oswald Werner, "Ethnoscience 1972," *Annual Review of Anthropology,* ed. Bernard J. Siegel, vol. 1 (1972), pp. 271–308; and Marshal Durbin, "Cognitive Anthropology," in *Handbook of Social and Cultural Anthropology,* ed. John J. Honigmann (Chicago: Rand McNally, 1973), pp. 447–78.
40. Wilcomb E. Washburn, "Ethnohistory: History 'In the Round,' " Symposium on the Concept of Ethnohistory, *Ethnohistory* 8 (1961): 32, 45. Robert T. Anderson, *Traditional Europe: A Study in Anthropology and History* (Belmont, Calif.: Wadsworth, 1971), p. 7. Although I disagree with Anderson's (as well as Washburn's) characterization of history as chronology, his first chapter, "Anthropology and History," is an excellent discussion of the relationship between the two fields. Also see: Robert F. Berkhofer, Jr., *A Behavioral Approach to Historical Analysis* (New York: Free Press, 1969); Ben G. Blount and Mary Sanches, eds., *Sociocultural Dimensions of Language Change* (New York: Academic Press, 1976); Franz Boas, "History and Science in Anthropology: A Reply," *American Anthropologist* 38 (1936): 137–41; William Burton and Richard Lowenthal, "The First of the Mohegans," *American Ethnologist* (Special Issue: Uses of Ethnohistory in Ethnographic Analysis) 1 (1974): 589–99; William N. Fenton, "The Training of Historical Ethnologists in America," *American Anthropologist* 54 (1952): 328–30; E. J. Hobsbawm, "From Social History to the History of Societies," Historical Studies Today, *Daedalus* (Winter, 1971): 22–25; Alfred L. Kroeber, *An Anthropologist Looks at History* (Berkeley: University of California Press, 1963); Nancy O. Lurie, "Ethnohistory: An Ethnologi-

cal Point of View," Symposium on the Concept of Ethnohistory, *Ethnohistory* 8 (1961): 78–92; Murray G. Murphey, "An Approach to the Historical Study of National Character," *Context and Meaning in Cultural Anthropology,* ed. Melford E. Spiro (New York: Free Press, 1965), pp. 144–49; David C. Pitt, *Using Historical Sources in Anthropology and Sociology* (New York: Holt, Rinehart, and Winston, 1972); W. H. R. Rivers, "History and Ethnology," *History* 5 (1920): 65–80; Edward E. Saveth, ed., *American History and the Social Sciences* (New York: Free Press, 1964); Social Science Research Council, "The Social Sciences in Historical Study: A Report of the Committee on Historiography," *Social Science Research Council Bulletin* 64 (1954); Charles A. Valentine, "Symposium on the Concept of Ethnohistory — Comment," *Ethnohistory* 8 (1961): 271–80; Charles A. Valentine, "Uses of Ethnohistory in Acculturation Study," *Ethnohistory* 7 (1960): 1–27; Caroline F. Ware, ed., *The Cultural Approach to History* (New York: Columbia University Press, 1940).

41. Berkhofer, *Behavioral Approach to Historical Analysis,* pp. 109–17. Murphy, "Historical Study of National Character," pp. 144–49. Albert E. Stone, "Autobiography and American Culture," *American Studies* 11 (1972): 24–25.
42. Sturtevant, "Studies in Ethnoscience," p. 138. A notable precedent for the historical application of ethnosemantic methods is in Floyd G. Lounsbury, "A Semantic Analysis of the Pawnee Kinship Usage," *Language* 32 (1956): 158–94. I also make such an application in "Architecture and Culture: The Meaning of the Lowell Boarding House," *American Quarterly* 25 (1973): 64–82. It might actually be argued that any of the analyses that are based solely on field notes (i.e., without concurrent participant observation) are essentially historical uses of ethnoscience. Also see: John L. Caughey, "Simulating the Past: A Method for Using Ethnosemantics in Historical Research," *American Quarterly* 24 (1972): 616–42.
43. Caughey, "Simulating the Past," pp. 627, 632.

CHAPTER 2: METHODOLOGY

1. See Henry A. Gleason, Jr., *An Introduction to Descriptive Linguistics,* p. 54. Surveys of "meaning" in ethnoscience include: Einar Haugen, "The Semantics of Icelandic Orientation," in *Cognitive Anthropology,* ed. Tyler, pp. 330–42; Floyd G. Lounsbury, "A Semantic Analysis of the Pawnee Kinship Usage," pp. 188–90; Floyd G. Lounsbury, "The Structural Analysis of Kinship Semantics," in *Cognitive Anthropology,* ed. Tyler, p. 194; Floyd G. Lounsbury, "The Varieties of Meaning," in *Communication and Culture,* ed. Smith, pp. 158–64; Harvey B. Sarles, "An Examination of the Question-Response System in Language," *Semiotica* 2 (1970): 79–101; and Harold W. Scheffler, "Kinship Semantics," *Annual Review of Anthropology,* ed. Siegel, vol. 1, pp. 309–28.
2. Charles W. Morris, *Signs, Language, and Behavior* (New York: Prentice-Hall, 1946), pp. 17–20. For an earlier version, see: Charles W. Morris, *Foundations of the Theory of Signs, International Encyclopedia of Unified Science,* vol. 1, no. 2 (Chicago: University of Chicago Press, 1938), pp. 3–9, 21–27. Inasmuch as they can be distinguished from significata, I purposely overlook connotative aspects of reference. "An expression *connotes* other images or concepts that people associate with the expression's designatum, and from them people orient themselves

affectively and behaviorally; but these images or concepts are not themselves definitive attributes of the designated class." Ward H. Goodenough, "Componential Analysis," p. 329. Also see: John L. Caughey, "Simulating the Past," p. 633; and Lounsbury, "Structural Analysis of Kinship Semantics," p. 194.

3. Lounsbury, "Structural Analysis of Kinship Semantics," p. 194.
4. Irving I. Zaretsky, "The Language of Spiritualist Churches: A Study in Cognition and Social Organization," in *Culture and Cognition,* ed. Spradley, pp. 356–57.
5. Harold C. Conklin, "Lexicographical Treatment of Folk Taxonomies," in *Cognitive Anthropology,* ed. Tyler, pp. 43, 45. A label for a segregate is often termed a *lexeme*. See, for example, William C. Sturtevant, "Studies in Ethnoscience," pp. 137–38.
6. See: Sturtevant, "Studies in Ethnoscience," pp. 139–40. George Psathas says: "A segregate is a terminologically contrasted array of objects and a contrast set is a series of terminologically contrasted segregates." Psathas, "Ethnoscience and Ethnomethodology," p. 209.
7. Sturtevant, "Studies in Ethnoscience," p. 143.
8. James P. Spradley and David W. McCurdy, *Anthropology: The Cultural Perspective* (New York: John Wiley and Sons, 1975), pp. 86–94.
9. Football fans will recognize that the player argot is considerably broader than the one I have presented. I elaborate only one branch of properly a much larger taxonomy. I include only the terms for players in a standard-T offensive alignment.
10. Conklin, "Lexicographical Treatment of Folk Taxonomies," p. 49; Charles O. Frake, "The Ethnographic Study of Cognitive Systems," in *Cognitive Anthropology,* ed. Tyler, p. 34; Sturtevant, "Studies in Ethnoscience," p. 143; and Stephen A. Tyler, "Introduction," p. 7. For an explanation of taxonomy in terms of set theory, see: Oswald Werner and Joann Fenton, "Method and Theory in Ethnoscience or Ethnoepistemology," pp. 549–50, 561–62.
11. Frake, "Ethnographic Study of Cognitive Systems," p. 34. Stronger claims appear, for example, in: Sturtevant, "Studies in Ethnoscience," pp. 130–31; and Jay Miller, "Addendum on Ethno-Taxonomic Congresses," *American Anthropologist* 77 (1975): 887. I should add that there is some disagreement on the relevance of taxonomic systems to experience and hence their significance in cultural inference. Much of the controversy can be reduced to a materialist-idealist opposition which, I would argue, is not terribly useful. It is important, however, to remember that much of culture may have little to do with language. The relevance of taxonomy in describing those cultural processes is yet to be determined. (See chapter 1, note 26.) Other sources of conflict are the nontransitivity and cross-cutting principles evident in many taxonomies. There is reason to conclude that, inasmuch as taxonomies are appropriate models of experience, they are neither as expansive nor as clear-cut in practice as they are in theory. Otherwise, we may be led to logical but incorrect inferences, such as: "Strawberries are kinds of berries; berries are kinds of bushes; hence, strawberries are kinds of bushes." We, like Randall's informant, can only laugh and add, "Berries are *generally* bushes." Robert Randall, "How Tall is a Taxonomic Tree? Some Evidence for Dwarfism," *American Ethnologist* 3 (1976): 543–52. See also: Brent Berlin, "The Concept of Rank in Ethnobiological Classification: Some

Evidence from Aguaruna Folk Botany,'' *American Ethnologist* 3 (1976): 381–99; Cecil H. Brown, ''General Principles of Human Anatomical Partonomy and Speculations on the Growth of Partonomic Nomenclature,'' *American Ethnologist* 3 (1976): 400–24; Cecil H. Brown, John Kolar, Barbara J. Torrey, Tipawan Trưỡng-Quang, and Phillip Volkman, ''Some General Principles of Biological and Non-biological Folk Classification,'' *American Ethnologist* 3 (1976): 73–85; and Eugene Hunn, ''Toward a Perceptual Model of Folk Biological Classification,'' *American Ethnologist* 3 (1976): 508–24.

12. Keith H. Basso, ''Semantic Aspects of Linguistic Acculturation,'' in *Culture and Cognition,* ed. Spradley, pp. 348–49, see 350. Conklin, ''Lexicographical Treatment of Folk Taxonomies,'' p. 46. Peer Hage, ''Müchner Beer Categories,'' in *Culture and Cognition,* ed. Spradley, p. 264. Paul Kay, ''Some Theoretical Implications of Ethnographic Semantics,'' p. 24. Sturtevant, ''Studies in Ethnoscience,'' pp. 135, 140. Tyler, ''Introduction,'' p. 8.

13. Letter, David Thurston, to Asa Cummings, in *The Christian Mirror,* April 27, 1837, p. 149. See also: Resolution of the Church in Winthrop to the Kennebec Conference, in *The Christian Mirror,* October 8, 1835, p. 33. For discussions of relationships between ambiguities in the categorizing process and religion see the following articles in *Reader in Comparative Religion: An Anthropological Approach,* ed. William A. Lessa and Evon Z. Vogt (New York: Harper and Row, 1972): Mary Douglas, ''Pollution,'' pp. 196–202; Mary Douglas, ''The Abominations of Leviticus,'' pp. 202–5; and Edmund R. Leach, ''Anthropological Aspects of Language: Animal Categories and Verbal Abuse,'' pp. 206–20.

14. Lounsbury, ''Structural Analysis of Kinship Semantics,'' p. 193.

15. Please note that I will be using *paradigm* in a special sense, more loosely than some social scientists (e.g., Lounsbury) but more strictly than others (e.g., Kuhn). Harold C. Conklin, ''Ethnogenealogical Method,'' in *Cognitive Anthropology,* ed. Tyler, p. 107. Lounsbury, ''Structural Analysis of Kinship Semantics,'' pp. 193–94. Sturtevant, ''Studies in Ethnoscience,'' pp. 140–43. Stephen A. Tyler, ''Arrangements,'' in *Cognitive Anthropology,* ed. Tyler, p. 26. Werner and Fenton, ''Method and Theory,'' pp. 544–48. The notion of logical space is developed in Anthony F. C. Wallace, ''The Problem of the Psychological Validity of Componential Analyses,'' pp. 115–19; and Anthony F. C. Wallace and John Atkins, ''The Meaning of Kinship Terms,'' pp. 351–61. It should be emphasized that ethnoscientists use many semantic arrangements besides taxonomies and paradigms, including indexes, trees, keys, and typologies. Brief comparisons of these models appear in Conklin, ''Ethnogenealogical Method,'' pp. 106–8; and Paul Kay, ''Comments on Colby,'' in *Cognitive Anthropology,* ed. Tyler, pp. 78–90. I choose to use only the most standard models. As Werner and Fenton put it, ''To date, in ethnoscience, the cross-cultural universality of only two structures is fully recognized: taxonomies (in the strict sense) and paradigms (also in the strict sense).'' They continue, ''The word 'taxonomy' is used here in a technical sense strictly as Aristotelian class inclusion. . . . The word 'paradigm' is also used in a technical sense, to denote a special non-hierarchic intersection of classes.'' Werner and Fenton, ''Method and Theory,'' p. 544.

16. Frake, ''Ethnographic Study of Cognitive Systems,'' p. 36. Lounsbury, ''Struc-

tural Analysis of Kinship Semantics," pp. 193–94. Sturtevant, "Studies in Ethnoscience," p. 141. Psathas, "Ethnoscience and Ethnomethodology," pp. 210–11. Tyler, "Introduction," p. 8. Anthony F. C. Wallace, "Culture and Cognition," pp. 114–17. Wallace and Atkins, "Meaning of Kinship Terms," p. 347. Werner and Fenton, "Method and Theory," pp. 544, 546, 575.

17. Wallace and Atkins probably give the most concise outline of a componential analysis in its usual application, kinship terms: "The componential analysis of a kinship lexicon commonly consists of five steps: (1) the recording of a complete set (or a defined sub-set) of the terms of reference or address, using various boundary-setting criteria, such as constant syntactic context, a type of pragmatic situation, a common inclusion within the extension of a cover term for 'kinsmen'; (2) the definition of these terms in the traditional kin-type notation (i.e., as Fa, FaBr, DaHuBr [father, father's brother, daughter's husband's brother]); (3) the identification, in the principles of grouping of kin-types, of two or more conceptual dimensions each of whose values ('components') is signified (not connoted) by one or more terms; (4) the definition of each term, by means of symbolic notation, as a specific combination or set of combinations, of the components; (5) a statement of the semantic relationship among the terms and of the structural principles of the terminological system." Wallace and Atkins, "Meaning of Kinship Terms," p. 347. Ward H. Goodenough develops this method in: "Componential Analysis," pp. 327–43; "Componential Analysis and the Study of Meaning," *Language* 32 (1956): 195–216; "Rethinking 'Status' and 'Role': Toward a General Model of the Cultural Organization of Social Relationships," in *Cognitive Anthropology,* ed. Tyler, pp. 311–30; and "Yankee Kinship Terminology," pp. 255–88.

18. Romney and D'Andrade equate *sememes* (semantic components) of kin terms with *discriminative stimuli* in psychological function: "Our equation . . . is based on the fact that the test data presented above indicate that individuals make differential responses to the components of kin terms, not just to the unique term. . . . *The sememes are learned as discriminative stimuli through precisely the same set of operations which allow the analyst to uncover components*. . . . What both the individuals who use the native system and the analyst do is learn the set of contrasts which signal a difference (although the reinforcement for the analyst may be only a neat system, while the reinforcements for the individual in the system are approval and understanding)." A. Kimball Romney and Roy G. D'Andrade, "Cognitive Aspects of English Kin Terms," pp. 394–95.

19. Wallace and Atkins, "Meaning of Kinship Terms," pp. 346–50. Romney and D'Andrade, "Cognitive Aspects of English Kin Terms," pp. 369–96.

20. Wallace, "Psychological Validity of Componential Analyses," p. 403. "Psychologically real dimensions may be hypothesized from a knowledge of the social structure of the society, features of its language, themes and principles of discrimination which are operative in many contexts. . . . But the acid test is to impose a task in which given criteria must be matched with terms." Idem, p. 411.

21. *Reckoning* is intended in Wallace's sense of the term. In his proposal for testing the psychological validity of an analysis, he says, "The test must require the native speaker to display — verbally, in writing, or in visible manipulation — procedures which he employs. This reckoning procedure, or calculus, involves

three stages: first, the selection of sufficient relevant information about the reference object; second, the organization of the data so as to define the object's class or relationship; and third, the choice of the term appropriate to that class. We are chiefly interested in the first two stages of the process which involve respectively the dimensions and logical operations required for the solution of the problem." Wallace, "Psychological Validity of Componential Analyses," p. 403.

22. To construct this typology I first read a sample of documents, selecting statements that seemed to explain naming. I then abstracted criteria that would model my intuitive process. In returning to the source material, I found that the typology correctly glosses the procedure I applied in assembling clear evidence of feature-category relationships in cognition. I make these criteria explicit in order, first, to assure that I recognize evidence consistently, whatever the consequences for any hypothesis, and second, to promote reproducible (and thus somewhat testable) results. It should be noted, however, that I give the typology a fairly broad interpretation. Any clear componential explanation is recorded, even if its form is not entirely obvious. A common example is what might be termed *incomplete reckoning,* statements of insufficient information for label assignment (e.g., "I don't know if Bill is a carpenter, since I don't know if he works with wood"). They appear in a wide variety of logical forms that fit the typology only by implication. They are nonetheless considered valuable evidence. It should also be noted that *statement* has a contextual rather than a grammatical definition. The term is not limited to sentences or even paragraphs. As long as an explanation deals with what is in the subject's terms a single scene or pragmatic situation, it may be considered a statement.

23. More precisely: "Values, positive and negative, are (1) elements in the effective definition of the situation of action that designate desirable and undesirable modes, means, and ends of action, i.e., normative orientations related in varying ways to cognitive and affective processes; (2) may be explicit, i.e., given directly in value judgments or inferred from verbal and non-verbal behaviors that involve approval, blame, praise, reward, punishment, support, and suppression; (3) are persistent through time and manifest directionally, i.e., there is observable consistency of response to recurrent situations; and (4) are interrelated as elements in culturally or individually distinctive patterns or systems, i.e., as differentiated but interdependent parts of a whole." Ethel M. Albert, "The Classification of Values: A Method and Illustration," *American Anthropologist* 58 (1956): 221–22. Albert's definition is an elaboration of Kluckhohn's classic statement: "A value is a conception, explicit or implicit, distinctive of an individual or characteristic of a group, of the desirable modes, means, and ends of action." Clyde Kluckhohn, "Values and Value Orientations in the Theory of Action," in *Toward a General Theory of Action,* ed. Talcott Parsons and Edward A. Shills (Cambridge: Harvard University Press, 1951), p. 375. See also: Robin M. Williams, Jr., *American Society: A Sociological Interpretation* (New York: Alfred A. Knopf, 1951), pp. 381–82, see p. 4; Kenneth E. Boulding, "The Image," p. 46; Clyde Kluckhohn "Toward a Comparison of Value Emphases in Different Cultures," in *The State of the Social Sciences,* ed. Leonard D. White (Chicago: University of Chicago Press, 1956), pp. 116–32; Florence R. Kluckhohn and Fred L. Strodtbeck, *Variations in Value Orientations: A Theory Tested in Five Cultures* (Evanston: Row,

Peterson and Co., 1961); Charles W. Morris, *Varieties of Human Value* (Chicago: University of Chicago Press, 1956), pp. 10–12; Evon Z. Vogt and Ethel M. Albert, "The Comparative Study of Values in Five Cultures," in *Peoples of Rimrock: A Study of Five Cultures,* ed. Vogt and Albert (Cambridge: Harvard University Press, 1966), pp. 1–33; and Anthony F. C. Wallace, "Identity Processes in Personality and in Culture," in *Cognition, Personality, and Clinical Psychology,* ed. Richard Jerson and Seymour Fesbach (San Francisco: Jossey Bass, 1967), pp. 67–71.

24. The description thus focuses upon what Goodenough terms *social identity* in "Rethinking 'Status' and 'Role,' " pp. 311–13. See also: Philip K. Bock, *Culture Shock,* p. 67; Irving A. Hallowell "Ojibwa Ontology, Behavior, and World View," p. 48; and Orrin E. Klapp, *Heroes, Villains, and Fools: The Changing American Character* (Englewood Cliffs: Prentice-Hall, 1962).

CHAPTER 3: APPLICATION

1. For a discussion of the problem of cultural unity versus diversity in the United States, see for example: John Gillin, "National and Regional Cultural Values in the United States," *Social Forces* 34 (1955): 107–23; Robin M. Williams, Jr., *American Society,* pp. 382–85; Francis L. K. Hsu, "American Core Values and National Character," in *Psychological Anthropology,* ed. Hsu (Cambridge: Schenkman Publishing Co., 1972), pp. 241–62; and L. B. Cebik, "Identity: An Existential Fallacy?," *Georgia Review* 23 (1969): 484–500.
2. See: Robert Redfield, *The Little Community/Peasant Society and Culture* (Chicago: University of Chicago Press, 1971), pp. 1–182; Ward H. Goodenough, *Culture, Language, and Society,* p. 2; Donald R. McCoy, "Underdeveloped Sources of Understanding in American History," *Journal of American History* 54 (1967): 225–70; Gerald M. Platt, "The Sociological Endeavor and Psychoanalytic Thought," *American Quarterly* 28 (1976): 357–59; Paul Diesing, *Patterns of Discovery in the Social Sciences* (Chicago: Aldine-Atherton, 1971), part 2; Solon T. Kimball and Conrad M. Arensberg, *Culture and Community* (New York: Harcourt, Brace and World, 1965). For a bibliography of community studies accenting sociological approaches and rural America, see Raymond Payne and Wilfrid C. Bailey, comps., *The Community: A Classified, Annotated Bibliography* (Athens: University of Georgia Press, 1967).
3. Redfield, *The Little Community,* p. 2, and see pp. 1–182.
4. Michael Agar, *Ripping and Running: A Formal Ethnography of Urban Heroin Addicts* (New York: Seminar Press, 1973), p. 130. See: John J. Gumperz, "Linguistic and Social Interaction in Two Communities," *American Anthropologist* 66 (1964): 137–53.
5. For an introduction to Winthrop history, see: David Thurston, *A Brief History of Winthrop from 1764 to October, 1855* (Portland: Brown Thurston, 1855); Everett S. Stackpole, *History of Winthrop, Maine with Genealogical Notes* (Auburn, Maine: Merrill and Webber, 1925); and Charles I. Foster, ed., *History of Winthrop: Evolution of a Maine Community, 1771–1971* (Augusta: Kennebec Journal, 1971).
6. Another way to view the distinction is in terms of data definition. The

significational analysis works with individual statements, one sentence or paragraph at a time. The denotional analysis, however, works with denotata assembled from many statements at once. Only the denotational analysis, then, allows one to link different statements, to see, for example, if Mr. Smith, who is called a "shepherd" in the newspaper, is called a "farmer" in the census. The denotional analysis is particularly useful in dealing with intracultural variation and the so-called *usage objection*. See, for example: Michael Agar, "Selecting a Dealer," *American Ethnologist* 2 (1975): 47–60; Ellen B. Basso, "Kalapalo Affinity, 207–28; Jan-Petter Blom and John J. Gumperz, "Social Meaning in Linguistic Structures," p. 409; Ronald W. Casson, "The Semantics of Kin Term Usage," *American Ethnologist* 2 (1975): 229–38; Peter D. Dwyer, "An Analysis of Rofaifo Mammal Taxonomy," *American Ethnologist* 3 (1976): 425–45; Peter M. Gardner, "Birds, Words, and a Requiem for the Omniscient Informant," pp. 446–68; Terence E. Hays, "An Empirical Method for the Identification of Covert Categories in Ethnobiology," pp. 489–507; and James Howe and Joel Sherzer, "Take and Tell," pp. 435–60.

7. See: Cecil H. Brown, "Psychological, Semantic, and Structural Aspects of American English Kinship Terms," *American Ethnologist* 1 (1973): 415–36.
8. See, for example: Ward H. Goodenough, "Rethinking 'Status' and 'Role,' " pp. 311–13; and Agar, *Ripping and Running*.

CHAPTER 4: FARMERS

1. U.S., Bureau of the Census, *Fourth Census of the United States, 1820: Population,* vol. 4, p. 643.
2. For a survey of Winthrop's role in Maine farming, see: Clarence A. Day, *A History of Maine Agriculture, 1604–1860,* University of Maine Studies, second series, no. 68 (Orono: University of Maine Press, 1954), pp. 115–298; Whitney Hodgkins and Clarence A. Day, "Agriculture in Early Winthrop," in *History of Winthrop,* ed. Charles I. Foster (Augusta: Kennebec Journal, 1971), pp. 29–32.
3. U.S., *Fourth Census, 1820: Population,* vol. 4, p. 643; *Sixth Census, 1840: Population,* vol.3, p. 367; *Seventh Census, 1850: Population,* vol.8, pp. 35–87.
4. In a letter to the editor, one "plain farmer" of Winthrop put the turning point more precisely in the year 1828. *Maine Farmer,* April 23, 1842, p. 2. Talk of "hard times" appears in the Winthrop newspaper from its first publication in 1833. See such editorials as: "Cold Weather and Hard Times," *Maine Farmer,* May 2, 1837, p. 89; and "Hard Times," *Maine Farmer,* June 13, 1840, p. 177. For a sample complaint about emigration, see: *Maine Farmer,* July 29, 1839, p. 213.
5. In Winthrop in 1850 there were about three hundred "farmers," mostly owners and their sons, on 204 farms with an average cash value of $1,084. U.S., *Seventh Census, 1850: Population,* vol. 8, pp. 35–87; *Agriculture,* vol. 129, pp. 378–85.
6. U.S., *Fourth Census, 1820: Manufacturing,* p. 50. *Seventh Census, 1850: Agriculture,* vol. 129, pp. 378–85.
7. "Report of the Committee for the Payment of the Bounty on Wheat," State of Maine, *Public Documents: 1838,* no. 41, p. 7. U.S., *Seventh Census, 1850: Agriculture,* vol. 129, pp. 378–85.

8. Ezekiel Holmes, Editorial, *Maine Farmer,* August 27, 1842, p. 1. Samuel P. Benson, "Historic Address of Honorable S. P. Benson," in *An Account of the Centennial Celebration at Winthrop, Maine, May 20, 1871* (Augusta: Sprague, Owen, and Nash, 1871), p. 40.
9. Winthrop's Ezekiel Holmes documented the climatic disasters in many of his editorials in the *Maine Farmer*. See: August 27, 1842, p. 1; June 24, 1836, p. 161; November 13, 1838, p. 313; May 2, 1837, p. 89; May 8, 1841, p. 136; August 27, 1842, p. 1; and February 22, 1849, p. 2. In the 1849 article Holmes came to the discouraging conclusion that Maine winters must be getting colder. See also: "Report of the Corresponding Secretary of the Kennebec County Agricultural Society," *Maine Farmer,* February 21, 1837, p. 9; Hodgkins and Day, "Agriculture in Early Winthrop," p. 31.
10. *Maine Farmer,* February 5, 1839, p. 414.
11. Only the winter of 1838–39 received significant positive note. See: " 'Fine Weather, Sir,' " *Maine Farmer,* January 16, 1838, p. 385; and *Maine Farmer,* May 18, 1839, p. 130.
12. Ezekiel Holmes, *The Northern Shepherd* (Winthrop: William Noyes, 1835), p. 10. *Maine Farmer,* February 28, 1837, p. 17. Hodgkins and Day, "Agriculture in Early Winthrop," pp. 31–32.
13. *Maine Farmer,* December 2, 1836, p. 350.
14. *Maine Farmer,* August 27, 1842, p. 1: November 13, 1838, p. 313; June 20, 1837, p. 145; February 28, 1837, p. 17.
15. *Maine Farmer,* June 13, 1840, p. 177. See also August 26, 1843, p. 1.
16. *Maine Farmer,* January 1, 1842, p. 404. See also: *Maine Farmer,* January 11, 1840, p. 1.
17. Cited in: Nathaniel T. True, "Biographical Sketch of Ezekiel Holmes, M.D.," *Agriculture of Maine,* Tenth Annual Report of the Secretary of the Maine Board of Agriculture: 1865 (Augusta: Stevens and Sayward, 1865), p. 222. For other biographies of Dr. Holmes, see also: Samuel L. Boardman, *Agricultural Bibliography of Maine* (Augusta: the author, 1893), pp. 44–46; Clarence A. Day, *Ezekiel Holmes, Father of Maine Agriculture,* University of Maine Studies, Second series, no. 86 (Orono: University of Maine Press, 1968); and Lawrence M. Sturtevant, "Ezekiel Holmes and His Influence, 1801–1865," M.A. thesis, University of Maine at Orono, 1948.
18. Benson, "Historic Address," p. 40. David Thurston, *A Brief History of Winthrop, from 1764 to October, 1855,* p. 158. Though previously in existence, the society was incorporated in 1829 by the state legislature, "for the promotion of agriculture, the mechanic arts, and manufacture." *Maine Acts and Resolves: 1829* (Portland: Day and Fraser, 1829), p. 76. In order to qualify for state subsidies, it changed its name to the Kennebec County Agricultural Society in 1832. *Maine Acts and Resolves: 1832* (Augusta: I. Berry and Co., 1832), p. 425. True, "Ezekiel Holmes," p. 214. See also: *Maine Farmer,* September 9, 1836, p. 249.
19. Holmes, *Northern Shepherd.*
20. See, for example: "Cattle Show and Fair of the Kennebec County Agricultural Society held in Winthrop on Wednesday, October 3, 1832," *Maine Farmer,* January 21, p. 1. Winners were awarded cash prizes or subscriptions to the *Maine Farmer*. See, for example: *Maine Farmer,* March 6, 1841, p. 66.

21. This group met annually for several years to elect officers and formulate policy. The *Maine Farmer* did not, however, publish any reports of the effect of their policies. See, for example: *Maine Farmer,* June 24, 1833, pp. 178–79.
22. For a brief history of the *Maine Farmer,* see: "The Maine Farmer, Semi-Centennial Number," *Maine Farmer,* November 23, 1882, p. 1; Day, *History of Maine Agriculture,* pp. 240–47; Day, *Ezekiel Holmes,* pp. 57–73, 120–21; and of course, the *Maine Farmer* itself, which has been microfilmed through 1852 by the American Periodical Series, no. 1000, reels 422–27. The film includes Clarence A. Day's three-volume index, "Vital Statistics from the Paper Maine Farmer for the period 1833–1852." The *Maine Farmer* was published in Winthrop, Hallowell, or Augusta until 1924, when it merged with the *Portland Press Herald.*
23. See the list of subscribers published for several months, beginning on January 22, 1839, p. 395. See also a letter by Samuel P. Collins or "Scrutator," *Maine Farmer,* June 27, 1840, p. 194. It is but one in an emotionally charged series between him and Nathan Foster or "O. S. M." that appeared in print.
24. *Maine Farmer,* April 2, 1842, p. 3; July 16, 1842, p. 1; February 20, 1835, p. 17.
25. *Maine Farmer,* March 4, 1833, p. 152; March 25, 1833, p. 78; February 6, 1836, p. 1.
26. *Maine Farmer,* December 21, 1833, p. 386. Holmes included "mechanics" in his intended readership, but they apparently showed less interest in the paper than did farmers. Nevertheless, he continued his efforts to appeal to all types of workingmen. *Maine Farmer,* September 16, 1836, p. 262; September 30, 1836, p. 273; November 13, 1841, p. 353. For a nice poem on the contents and purposes of the *Maine Farmer,* see: *Maine Farmer,* February 9, 1839, p. 8.
27. *Maine Farmer,* April 30, 1846, p. 2.
28. Ezekiel Holmes, "Commencement of the Volume and Commencement of the Year," *Maine Farmer,* January 3, 1850, p. 2. *Maine Farmer,* January 7, 1847, p. 1.
29. The details of these developments appear in Day's *History of Maine Agriculture.* Winthrop reactions are documented in the pages of the *Maine Farmer,* February 16, 1839, p. 3; August 21, 1838, p. 217; November 21, 1844, p. 1; May 20, 1845, p. 2; August 28, 1838, p. 225.
30. Samuel W. Cole, *The American Fruit Book* (Boston: John P. Jewett, 1850), pp. 104, 108, 110, 111. Day, *History of Maine Agriculture,* p. 215.
31. "Hints upon Grain Growing," *Maine Farmer,* October 10, 1837, p. 273.
32. "Rev. John Todd's Address Delivered before the Agricultural Society at Northampton, October 7, 1835," *Maine Farmer,* December 4, 1835, p. 349.
33. "Address Delivered by Isaac Hill before the Kennebec County Agricultural Society," *Maine Farmer,* November 13, 1841, p. 356. See also a letter from "a plough boy" who "contracted with a gentleman farmer to take charge of his farm." *Maine Farmer,* April 29, 1833, p. 115.
34. Henry Colman, "An Address Delivered before the Hampshire, Franklin, and Hampden Agricultural Societies, October 23, 1833," *Maine Farmer,* February 14, 1834, p. 33.
35. Colman, "Address," p. 33.
36. *Maine Farmer,* October 10, 1837, p. 273; April 15, 1833, p. 99; July 15, 1833, p. 202; March 20, 1835, p. 52; January 23, 1841, p. 18; October 3, 1840, p. 305;

June 5, 1841, p. 169; October 3, 1840, p. 305. The above refer to only the most explicit of innumerable statements, generally in the form: "Every farmer is (or does, or has, or wants) . . ."

37. See: *Maine Farmer,* December 9, 1843, p. 2; June 17, 1833, p. 170; October 16, 1835, p. 150; January 13, 1837, p. 393; and Ezekiel Holmes, *Report of an Exploration and Survey of the Territory on the Aroostook River* (Augusta: Smith and Robinson, 1839), p. 77. Most often "Yankee" denoted a man from the North whose character typified these qualities. It was used in contrast to "foreigners" and, more commonly, "nullifiers," "duellists," or other "southern bullies." See, for example: *Maine Farmer,* March 23, 1839, p. 56.
38. See, for example: Ezekiel Holmes, Private Journal, October 2, 1834, in *Home Farm,* November 20, 1884, p. 2.
39. "Decisions of Character," *Maine Farmer,* October 3, 1840, p. 305. See also: *Maine Farmer,* March 23, 1839, p. 52; June 5, 1841, p. 169.
40. James Fillebrown, Private Journal, August 10, 1826, in *Genealogy of the Fillebrown Family with Biographical Sketches,* Charles B. Fillebrown (Boston: the author, 1910), p. 64.
41. A. B., Letter to the Editor, *Maine Farmer,* April 15, 1833, p. 99. B. F. Robbins, "Farewell," *Maine Farmer,* January 23, 1841, p. 17.
42. *Maine Farmer,* March 11, 1833, p. 58. See: Ezekiel Holmes, "Twelve Letters to a Shepherd Being Directions for Managing Sheep in Every Month of the Year," in *Northern Shepherd,* pp. 33–65.
43. For good examples of the use of these labels, see: *Maine Farmer,* July 20, 1839, p. 2; February 11, 1833, p. 28; September 14, 1833, p. 274; November 16, 1833, p. 345; November 2, 1833, p. 331; June 24, 1833, p. 179; September 21, 1833, p. 285; February 18, 1833, p. 33; November 9, 1833, p. 341; September 9, 1836, p. 255; June 19, 1835, p. 154; March 11, 1833, p. 58; January 21, 1833, p. 3. It is interesting that the term "dairy farmer" does not appear until the 1840s. Instead, we find only "cow [or cattle] keeper." See: "Dairy Farmer," *Maine Farmer,* April 8, 1843, p. 1.
44. *Maine Farmer,* May 20, 1833, p. 139; May 13, 1833, p. 133; November 23, 1833, p. 360; March 25, 1833, pp. 74, 75; March 4, 1833, p. 55; November 27, 1835, p. 339. Thurston, *Brief History of Winthrop,* pp. 158–59. Holmes, *Report of an Exploration,* p. 78. New members were "proposed" and "elected" to the Agricultural Society by the membership. They were thereafter sustained by paying the one-dollar annual "assessment" required by state subsidy laws. *Maine Farmer,* May 22, 1841, p. 153; August 28, 1835, p. 239.
45. *Maine Farmer,* January 28, 1833, p. 12; January 21, 1833, p. 3.
46. See, for example, *Maine Farmer,* April 15, 1833, p. 99.
47. *Maine Farmer,* November 21, 1837, p. 320; January 28, 1833, p. 12.
48. *Maine Farmer,* January 28, 1833, p. 12. Ezekiel Holmes, "Thinks I to Myself," *Maine Farmer,* December 5, 1837, p. 337. The latter piece is an excellent, point-by-point explanation of what Holmes "sees" when he thinks that a man is "not a good farmer."
49. *Maine Farmer,* June 26, 1835, p. 164. See also: *Maine Farmer,* February 6, 1835, p. 1; December 25, 1835, p. 371; June 3, 1833, p. 154.
50. Ezekiel Holmes borrowed this definition from the *Geneese Farmer*. He used it to

denounce the "prejudice" against "book farmers." *Maine Farmer,* February 6, 1835, p. 1.

51. *Maine Farmer,* November 25, 1836, p. 341; February 27, 1841, p. 59; October 5, 1833, p. 302. See also: *Maine Farmer,* February 4, 1833, p. 20; November 30, 1833, p. 367; December 5, 1834, p. 364.
52. Types of "authorities" or "men of science" were usually designated by Latinate labels with the suffix "-ist" (e.g., "horticulturalist"). Holmes apparently folowed this rule in making facetious reference to an "onionist" in "Onions, Scullions, and Onion Worms," *Maine Farmer,* July 24, 1841, p. 224. See: *Maine Farmer,* August 5, 1833, p. 229; May 20, 1836, p. 123; August 17, 1833, p. 248; August 31, 1833, p. 257; July 22, 1833, p. 212.
53. "Meeting of the Friends of Agriculture at the State House," *Maine Farmer,* February 27, 1841, p. 59.
54. *Maine Farmer,* May 20, 1833, p. 140. For a good example of positive reckoning, see a letter to the editor, signed by a "plough jogger," *Maine Farmer,* May 20, 1833, p. 141. See also: *Maine Farmer,* June 3, 1833, p. 154; June 19, 1841, p. 188; June 26, 1835, p. 164; and Ezekiel Holmes, Letter to the Editor of the *American Farmer* at Baltimore, Maryland, September 15, 1825, in *Home Farm,* July 17, 1884, p. 1.
55. *Maine Farmer,* March 23, 1839, p. 52; June 26, 1835, p. 164.
56. *Maine Farmer,* June 5, 1841, p. 169; February 9, 1839, p. 2.
57. See, for example: *Maine Farmer,* March 4, 1833, p. 50; May 20, 1833, p. 140; November 2, 1833, p. 337.
58. Rev. David Thurston, "Address Delivered before the Kennebec County Agricultural Society at their Annual Fair and Cattle Show at Winthrop, September 18, 1834," *Maine Farmer,* December 5, 1834, p. 364. See also: *Maine Farmer,* February 6, 1835, p. 1; November 30, 1833, p. 367; February 4, 1833, p. 20.
59. See, for example: *Maine Farmer,* March 20, 1835, p. 52; February 11, 1833, p. 28.
60. *Maine Farmer,* May 20, 1833, p. 140; February 4, 1833, p. 19.
61. *Maine Farmer,* February 9, 1839, p. 2.
62. *Maine Farmer,* February 4, 1833, p. 19.
63. *Maine Farmer,* December 25, 1835, p. 371; February 6, 1835, p. 1.
64. *Maine Farmer,* February 6, 1835, p. 1.
65. See, for example: *Maine Farmer,* November 30, 1833, p. 367; July 10, 1838, p. 172.
66. *Maine Farmer,* January 23, 1841, p. 17.

CHAPTER 5: FARM HELP

1. *Maine Farmer,* June 5, 1835, p. 144; September 7, 1833, p. 265; September 28, 1833, p. 291; April 17, 1835, p. 87.
2. *Maine Farmer,* October 5, 1833, p. 302. William H. Parlin, *Reminiscences of East Winthrop,* reprinted from the *Winthrop Banner,* 1882 (East Winthrop: Banner Publishing Co., 1891), p. 85. *Maine Farmer,* May 13, 1836, p. 115.
3. "Ladies Department," *Maine Farmer,* February 18, 1833, p. 40. W. A. A., "Should Females be Employed in Cookery," from the *American Ladies Magazine, Maine Farmer,* December 2, 1834, p. 372.

4. Parlin, *Reminiscences of East Winthrop,* pp. 85–86, 89. *Maine Farmer,* July 25, 1834, p. 217.
5. *Maine Farmer,* August 31, 1833, p. 250. See also: *Maine Farmer,* October 19, 1833, p. 217.
6. *Maine Farmer,* April 22, 1833, p. 107; September 23, 1836, p. 267; July 15, 1833, p. 208. "Dairy women" were also called "butter makers." *Maine Farmer,* November 18, 1836, p. 330.
7. Rev. J. Todd, "Female Education," *Maine Farmer,* December 18, 1835, p. 364.
8. See, for example: *Maine Farmer,* March 25, 1833, p. 74; August 7, 1835, p. 215; September 28, 1833, p. 291; June 12, 1835, p. 151.
9. "Hired Labor or Wages," *Maine Farmer,* August 1, 1840, p. 233.
10. See such "hired hand" want ads as: *Maine Farmer,* June 12, 1835, p. 151; March 13, 1838, p. 47; May 1, 1835, p. 103. And a letter from Ezekiel Holmes, Gardiner, to John Hare Powell, Philadelphia, January, 1828, in *Home Farm,* August 14, 1884, p. 4.
11. David Thurston, *A Sermon Delivered by David Thurston, Pastor of a Church in Winthrop, Maine, at the Third Annual Meeting of the American Missionary Association at Boston, Mass., September 25, 1849* (New York: American Missionary Association, 1849), p. 8. *Maine Farmer,* March 25, 1833, p. 74; March 6, 1841, p. 69.
12. *Maine Farmer,* August 7, 1835, p. 215. *Maine Farmer,* June 26, 1835, p. 163.
13. *Maine Farmer,* June 26, 1835, p. 163.
14. "Hired Help," *Maine Farmer,* April 9, 1842, p. 1. See: "To Hired Men," *Maine Farmer,* July 31, 1841, p. 234.
15. *Maine Farmer,* March 13, 1835, p. 47.
16. "Hired Help," *Maine Farmer,* April 9, 1842, p. 1. See also: "To Hired Men," *Maine Farmer,* July 31, 1841, p. 234.
17. See: Letter, Ezekiel Holmes, Gardiner, to John Hare Powell, Philadelphia, January 1828, in *Home Farm,* August 14, 1884, p. 4; and "To Hired Men," *Maine Farmer,* July 31, 1841, p. 234.
18. See: "Pruning Trees," *Maine Farmer,* April 8, 1833, p. 84; and *Maine Farmer,* April 11, 1834, p. 98; October 19, 1839, p. 314.
19. See: *Maine Farmer,* July 25, 1834, pp. 217–18; May 13, 1833, p. 132; August 24, 1833, pp. 250–51; August 21, 1838, p. 217; August 17, 1833, p. 244; January 11, 1834, p. 234. "Gatherer" and "binder" were sometimes used synonymously.
20. See: *Maine Farmer,* May 13, 1833, p. 132; August 24, 1833, pp. 250–51; July 25, 1834, p. 218.
21. *Maine Farmer,* July 25, 1834, pp. 217–18; August 24, 1833, pp. 250–51; May 13, 1833, p. 132.

CHAPTER 6: MECHANICS

1. For a survey of Winthrop's industrial growth, see: David Thurston, *A Brief History of Winthrop from 1764 to October, 1855,* pp. 24–25, 85–89; Everett S. Stackpole, *History of Winthrop, Maine with Genalogical Notes,* pp. 189–209; Charles I. Foster, ed., *History of Winthrop,* pp. 54–65, 80–85.

2. Foster, *History of Winthrop,* pp. 54–56.
3. Foster, *History of Winthrop,* pp. 58–59. Stackpole, *History of Winthrop,* pp. 190–94. "Winthrop Factory," *Maine Farmer,* April 30, 1842, p. 1. Thurston, *Brief History of Winthrop,* p. 88. U.S., Bureau of the Census, *Fourth Census of the United States, 1820: Manufacturing,* p. 48. U.S., Department of the Treasury, *Documents Relative to the Manufactures in the United States Collected and Transmitted to the House of Representatives in Compliance With a Resolution of January 19, 1832 by the Secretary of the Treasury* (Washington: Duff Green, 1833), vol. 1, pp. 3–4. The credit problems of Little, Wood, and Company from 1841 to 1843 are detailed in the correspondence of Josiah Little in the Little Family Collection at the New York Public Library.
4. G. E. N. [George E. Newman?], "My Boyhood Days," *Winthrop Weekly Budget,* April 22 [?], 1822. Foster, *History of Winthrop,* p. 55.
5. Foster, *History of Winthrop,* pp. 64, 120. Stackpole, *History of Winthrop,* p. 197. Thurston, *Brief History of Winthrop,* p. 88.
6. Winthrop Town Records, vol. 4, April 18, 1826, p. 122; March 13, 1828, p. 182; April 6, 1829, p. 208; February, 1832, pp. 283–84. Foster, *History of Winthrop,* p. 120.
7. U.S., *Fourth Census, 1820: Manufacturing,* p. 48. *Maine Farmer,* April 16, 1842, p. 3; September 10, 1842, pp. 1–2; August 26, 1843, p. 1.
8. *Maine Farmer,* January 21, 1833, p. 4; September 16, 1836, p. 262; September 30, 1836, p. 273; November 13, 1841, pp. 353, 359; September 16, 1836, p. 263; December 4, 1838, p. 343.
9. *Maine Farmer,* November 11, 1836, p. 323.
10. See, for example: Foster, *History of Winthrop,* pp. 56–57.
11. See: U.S., *Fourth Census, 1820: Manufacturing,* p. 50. *Seventh Census, 1850: Population,* vol. 8, pp. 35–87; *Industry,* vol. 132, pp. 161–64.
12. Foster, *History of Winthrop,* pp. 56–57. U.S., *Seventh Census, 1850: Population,* vol. 8, pp. 35–87; *Industry,* vol. 132, pp. 161–64.
13. Foster, *History of Winthrop,* p. 62. U.S., *Seventh Census, 1850: Industry,* vol. 132, p. 161. See the biography of Moses Bailey by his second wife which quotes extensively from his papers, letters, and diary: Hannah J. Bailey, *Reminiscences of a Christian Life* (Portland: Hoyt, Fogg and Donham, 1884).
14. *United States, Patent Office,* Records, patent nos. X-8362, 542, 1728, 3497. *Maine Farmer,* August 21, 1838, p. 217; May 27, 1843, p. 2; June 3, 1843, p. 1; June 24, 1843, p. 2; July 15, 1843, p. 3; July 25, 1840, p. 231; August 1, 1840, p. 239; August 15, 1840, pp. 255–56; August 29, 1840, pp. 270–71; September 12, 1840, p. 287; September 19, 1840, pp. 289, 295–96; September 26, 1840, p. 303; November 21, 1844, p. 1; May 20, 1845, p. 2. Foster, *History of Winthrop,* pp. 32, 60–62. Thurston, *Brief History of Winthrop,* p. 89.
15. "Winthrop Factory," *Maine Farmer,* April 30, 1842, p. 1. Foster, *History of Winthrop,* p. 59. Stackpole, *History of Winthrop,* p. 193. Treasury, *Documents Relative to the Manufactures in the United States,* pp. 3–4. U.S. *Seventh Census, 1850: Industry,* vol. 132, pp. 161–64. In 1832 the mill operated more than thirteen hours a day (one hour less in the winter), twelve months a year.
16. U.S., *Fourth Census, 1820: Manufacturing,* p. 50. *Seventh Census, 1850: Population,* vol. 8, pp. 35–87; *Industry,* vol. 132, pp. 161–64. *Maine Farmer,* De-

cember 16, 1847, p. 2; September 28, 1848, p. 2; October 5, 1848, p. 2. According to the 1850 industrial statistics, Horace Parlin and Company produced more shoes than the entire town thirty years earlier, and it was but one of ten footwear factories.

17. See: *Maine Farmer,* October 5, 1848, p. 2.
18. U.S., *Fourth Census, 1820: Population,* vol. 4, p. 643. *Seventh Census, 1850: Population,* vol. 8, pp. 35–87.
19. See an anonymous address delivered to the Winthrop Lyceum in 1844, "On the Subject of War and Peace," p. 2, in manuscript at the Charles M. Bailey Public Library; and *Maine Farmer,* November 11, 1836, p. 323.
20. Letter, Josiah Little, Jr., Winthrop, to Josiah Little, Esq., Newbury, Mass., September 27, 1841. See: *Maine Farmer,* April 29, 1836, p. 104; June 24, 1833, p. 179; and U.S., *Fourth Census, 1820: Manufacturing,* p. 48.
21. See: Letter, Samuel L. Clark, Augusta, to Miller Clark, February 10, 1833; Letter, N. M. Whitman, Waterville, to Samuel L. Clark, Winthrop, June 13, 1837. These letters involve Samuel Clark's efforts to interest his sons in running his Winthrop tannery.
22. See: *Maine Farmer,* September 28, 1833, p. 290; July 15, 1833, p. 202; August 24, 1833, p. 256.
23. See, for example: *Maine Farmer,* November 23, 1833, p. 356; November 20, 1835, p. 332.
24. See: *Maine Farmer,* March 18, 1833, p. 70; January 28, 1833, p. 11; September 14, 1833, p. 278; July 24, 1835, p. 195; November 11, 1836, p. 328.
25. See, for example: *Maine Farmer,* November 11, 1836, p. 328; October 12, 1833, p. 311; December 16, 1847, p. 2.
26. See: *Maine Farmer,* July 17, 1835, p. 19; October 28, 1836, p. 305; November 27, 1835, p. 339.
27. *Maine Farmer,* June 8, 1839, p. 162; December 28, 1833, p. 399.
28. *Maine Farmer,* August 15, 1840, p. 256; July 29, 1836, p. 206; September 2, 1836, p. 246; May 25, 1839, p. 143; January 28, 1833, p. 15; August 7, 1835, p. 215.
29. David Thurston, *Letters from a Father to a Son, An Apprentice,* comp. Brown Thurston (Portland: Hezekiah Packard, 1858), pp. 7, 127, 13–19. See also pp. 45, 84–86, 119–23, 107, 115–16.
30. Thurston, *Letters from a Father,* p. 58. See p. 107 and *Maine Farmer,* June 8, 1839, p. 162.
31. *Maine Farmer,* May 27, 1833, p. 150; July 1, 1833, p. 190; December 28, 1833, p. 399; July 29, 1836, p. 206.
32. *Maine Farmer,* June 8, 1839, p. 162. See also: *Maine Farmer,* February 25, 1833, p. 46; July 22, 1833, p. 216; August 5, 1833, p. 230.
33. Ezekiel Holmes, "To Mechanics," *Maine Farmer,* January 7, 1843, p. 2. See also: *Maine Farmer,* August 24, 1833, p. 256; September 21, 1833, p. 288.
34. "The American Mechanic," *Maine Farmer,* August 19, 1836, p. 230. See: *Maine Farmer,* August 5, 1833, p. 230; November 28, 1834, p. 356; and the discourse by "a libertyman" in the *Winthrop Emulator,* February 6, 1845, p. 12. The *Emulator* was produced each week in longhand by the members of the Winthrop Lyceum.

35. "Mechanics," *Maine Farmer,* February 5, 1842, p. 2. *Maine Farmer,* September 28, 1833, pp. 289–90.
36. *Maine Farmer,* October 28, 1842, p. 4; April 10, 1835, p. 80; March 13, 1835, p. 42; October 28, 1842, p. 4.
37. *Maine Farmer,* March 25, 1833, p. 78; "Memoirs of the Life of Eli Whitney," *Maine Farmer,* November 30, 1833, p. 365. *Maine Farmer,* November 27, 1838, p. 336; September 28, 1833, p. 289.
38. "Necessity of Knowledge to Insure the Health of the Mechanic," from the *Boston Mechanic, Maine Farmer,* February 26, 1836, pp. 28–29. "Interesting to Mechanics," *Maine Farmer,* April 29, 1833, p. 117. See: *Maine Farmer,* March 4, 1833, p. 54.
39. *Maine Farmer,* November 23, 1833, p. 356. See: *Maine Farmer,* March 4, 1836, pp. 37–38.
40. See, for example: *Maine Farmer,* December 7, 1833, p. 375; November 21, 1837, p. 327; November 27, 1838, p. 336; March 11, 1833, p. 63; November 20, 1835, p. 332.
41. *Maine Farmer,* March 18, 1833, p. 70; May 27, 1833, p. 150; February 13, 1838, p. 1; January 21, 1847, p. 2; November 30, 1835, p. 332. See, particularly: "Great Invention for Boot Makers: Tucker's Boot Crimping Machine," *Maine Farmer,* December 16, 1847, p. 2.
42. Thurston, *Letters from a Father,* p. 16. *Maine Farmer,* July 15, 1833, p. 203. See: *Maine Farmer,* November 20, 1835, p. 332; November 21, 1837, p. 327; August 15, 1840, p. 256; and Letter, Samuel L. Clark, Augusta, to Miller Clark, February 10, 1833.
43. *Maine Farmer,* July 22, 1833, p. 216; July 15, 1833, p. 203.
44. The taxonomic and componential definitions come from references too numerous to mention, but mainly from the *Maine Farmer* and the U.S. census. I do not cover the various coastal tradesmen, such as "ship builders" or "caulkers," both because references are exceedingly rare and because the contexts are so limited.
45. See, for example: *Maine Farmer,* June 19, 1833, p. 155.
46. See: *Maine Farmer,* September 28, 1833, p. 290; July 15, 1833, pp. 202, 216; January 11, 1834, p. 411; October 31, 1834, p. 327; November 28, 1834, p. 356; August 19, 1836, p. 230; and Thurston, *Brief History of Winthrop,* pp. 85–87.
47. See: *Maine Farmer,* November 20, 1835, p. 332; January 11, 1834, p. 411; and U.S., *Seventh Census, 1850: Population,* vol. 8, pp. 35–87; *Industry,* vol. 132, pp. 161–64.
48. See: Thurston, *Brief History of Winthrop,* pp. 86–87. For examples of denotata, see: *Maine Farmer,* April 8, 1833, p. 95; November 21, 1837, p. 327; and U.S., *Seventh Census, 1850: Population,* vol. 8, pp. 35–87.
49. Z. E. B., "Correspondence," *Maine Farmer,* November 11, 1836, p. 328.
50. Treasury, *Documents Relative to the Manufactures in the United States,* p. 3. See also: U.S., *Seventh Census, 1850: Industry,* vol. 132, p. 162.
51. "Cattle Show and Fair," *Maine Farmer,* September 28, 1833, p. 289. See also: Benjamin Tappan, *A Sermon Delivered in Winthrop, September 25, 1822, before the Kennebec Missionary Society at Their First Annual Meeting* (Hallowell: Goodale, Glazier and Co., 1822), pp. 19–20.
52. See, for example: *Maine Farmer,* July 24, 1835, p. 195; December 21, 1833, p.

391; January 28, 1833, p. 11; July 8, 1833, p. 198; May 25, 1839, p. 143; August 5, 1833, p. 227; August 19, 1836, p. 231; July 24, 1835, p. 195.

53. Letter, Josiah Little, Jr., to Josiah Little, Esq., February 24, 1841. See: *Maine Farmer,* August 19, 1836, p. 231; January 30, 1841, p. 30.
54. *Maine Farmer,* December 7, 1833, p. 375. See also: *Maine Farmer,* July 24, 1835, p. 195; May 27, 1843, p. 4.
55. *Maine Farmer,* July 24, 1835, p. 195; November 14, 1834, p. 344; June 6, 1840, p. 170; November 4, 1836, p. 314. See particularly: M. L. Weems, "The Bachelors — Bliss of Matrimony," *Maine Farmer,* November 4, 1836, p. 320.
56. See: *Maine Farmer,* May 13, 1833, p. 135; August 19, 1836, p. 231; July 24, 1835, p. 195; David Thurston, *A Sermon Delivered by David Thurston, Pastor of a Church in Winthrop, at the Third Annual Meeting of the American Missionary Association at Boston, Mass., September 25, 1849* (New York: American Missionary Association, 1849), p. 8; and William H. Parlin, *Reminiscences of East Winthrop,* p. 8.
56. "Taking in Work" from the *Portland Tribune, Maine Farmer,* January 15, 1842, p. 2. See also: *Maine Farmer,* July 24, 1835, p. 195; March 5, 1841, p. 72.
58. Thurston, *A Sermon . . . at the Third Annual Meeting of the American Missionary Association,* p. 8. See also: *Maine Farmer,* March 5, 1841, p. 72.
59. H. C., "Value of Female Labor," *Maine Farmer,* July 24, 1835, p. 195.
60. These points were part of the fairly consistent editorial policy of the *Maine Farmer* from 1833 to 1850.
61. Letter, Samuel L. Clark and Susanna Clark to Dr. Samuel L. Clark, Bangor, November 10, 1844.
62. *Maine Farmer,* March 5, 1841, p. 72. See also: *Maine Farmer,* January 30, 1841, p. 30.
63. For an excellent summary of this position, see: H. C., "Value of Female Labor," *Maine Farmer,* July 24, 1835, p. 195.
64. *Maine Farmer,* July 24, 1835, p. 195.
65. Mary, "Song of the Factory Girl," *Maine Farmer,* May 27, 1843, p. 4.

CHAPTER 7: WORKINGMEN AND GENTLEMEN

1. Letter to the Editor, *Maine Farmer,* January 13, 1837, p. 393. See also: *Maine Farmer,* February 5, 1842, p. 2; July 15, 1833, p. 202.
2. See: *Maine Farmer,* December 14, 1839, p. 377; March 18, 1833, p. 70; April 22, 1833, pp. 107, 113. Though there is a disappointing lack of evidence, those who had relatively manual occupations but were not "laborers," "farmers," or "mechanics" were probably also counted among the "producers." This would include "drovers," "drivers" (or "teamsters" or "wagoners"), "innkeepers" (or "innholders," "landlords," or "victualers"), "publishers," and "watchmen." For example, David Thurston discusses "innholders" in the section titled "Manufactures and Mechanics," in *A Brief History of Winthrop from 1764 to October, 1855,* pp. 85–89. See also: *Maine Farmer,* September 16, 1836, p. 261; April 3, 1835, p. 70; September 28, 1833, p. 290; July 29, 1836, p. 206; August 17, 1833, p. 242; March 18, 1833, p. 70; February 20, 1835, p. 23; June 17, 1833, p. 176; Letters, Josiah Little, Jr., to Josiah Little, Esq., February 24, 1841,

and June 22, 1841; [Samuel G. Goodrich], *Peter Parley's Spelling Book with Engravings* (Philadelphia: Henry F. Anners, 1834), p. 142.

3. *Maine Farmer,* July 15, 1833, p. 202.
4. "Mechanics," *Maine Farmer,* February 5, 1842, p. 2.
5. "Do Non-Producers Rule the Producers?" *Maine Farmer,* December 14, 1839, p. 377. See also: *Maine Farmer,* March 18, 1833, p. 70; February 5, 1842, p. 2; July 15, 1833, p. 202.
6. Amicus, Poem, *Maine Farmer,* May 20, 1833, p. 144. *Maine Farmer,* February 5, 1842, p. 2; December 14, 1839, p. 377. "Self-Made Men," *Maine Farmer,* August 19, 1847, p. 2. Francis Southworth and S. W. Davis, *Lives of Distinguished Shoemakers* (Portland: Thurston and Co., 1849).
7. For an example of one of the few references that is even remotely clear, see: *Maine Farmer,* August 31, 1833, p. 264. Even here most of the semantic questions remain unanswered.
8. *Maine Farmer,* September 26, 1833, p. 290. See also: *Maine Farmer,* June 3, 1833, p. 160; June 13, 1840, p. 180.
9. U.S., Bureau of the Census, *Seventh Census of the United States, 1850: Population,* vol. 8, p. 48. See: *Maine Farmer,* September 7, 1833, p. 272; October 10, 1834, p. 304; September 16, 1836, p. 268. Roswell C. Smith, *Practical and Mental Arithmetic,* rev. ed. (Hallowell: Glazier, Masters and Smith, 1843), p. 241. Benjamin Tappan, *A Sermon Delivered in Winthrop, September 25, 1822, before the Kennebec Missionary Society at Their First Annual Meeting,* pp. 18–19.
10. See: *Maine Farmer,* October 19, 1833, p. 316; January 4, 1834, p. 408; and [Goodrich], *Peter Parley's Spelling Book,* p. 74.
11. Nathan Foster, Letter to the Editor, *Maine Farmer,* June 13, 1840, p. 180.
12. Smith, *Practical and Mental Arithmetic,* p. 241. Tappan, *Sermon Delivered in Winthrop, September 25, 1822,* p. 19. *Maine Farmer,* September 26, 1844, p. 2; September 4, 1838, p. 233; February 19, 1842, p. 1; March 26, 1842, p. 1; November 7, 1834, p. 336; June 13, 1840, p. 180; October 19, 1833, p. 316; September 7, 1833, p. 271; June 24, 1836, p. 163; August 26, 1836, p. 240; May 27, 1836, p. 135; June 3, 1833, p. 160.
13. *Maine Farmer,* September 4, 1838, p. 233; November 7, 1834, p. 336.
14. *Maine Farmer,* September 26, 1844, p. 2; September 4, 1838, p. 233; October 5, 1839, p. 302.
15. "What Constitutes a Gentleman?" *Maine Farmer,* October 14, 1847, p. 2. "The Fop," *Maine Farmer,* August 29, 1844, p. 2.
16. T. G. Fessenden, Poem, *Maine Farmer,* October 10, 1834, p. 304. *Maine Farmer,* August 1, 1840, p. 233. See: *Maine Farmer,* September 4, 1838, p. 233; June 27, 1837, p. 153; April 23, 1842, p. 1.
17. *Maine Farmer,* August 1, 1840, p. 233; September 7, 1833, p. 271.
18. "New Land," Letter to the Editor, *Maine Farmer,* April 23, 1842, p. 1. "Observor," Letter to the Editor, *Maine Farmer,* September 7, 1833, p. 272.
19. G. G., "Eccentricities," *Maine Farmer,* April 20, 1839, p. 88. *Maine Farmer,* June 24, 1836, p. 163; September 7, 1833, p. 272; September 4, 1838, p. 233; April 20, 1839, p. 88; September 26, 1844, p. 2.
20. T. G. Fessenden, Poem, *Maine Farmer,* October 10, 1834, p. 304. G. G.,

"Eccentricities," *Maine Farmer,* April 20, 1839, p. 88. *Maine Farmer,* November 7, 1834, p. 336.

21. *Maine Farmer,* May 27, 1836, p. 135.
22. *Maine Farmer,* November 7, 1834, p. 336.

CHAPTER 8: BUSINESSMEN

1. For a survey of Winthrop's commercial history, see: David Thurston, *A Brief History of Winthrop, from 1764 to October, 1855,* pp. 34–35, 89; Everett S. Stackpole, *History of Winthrop, Maine with Genealogical Notes,* pp. 189–211, 235–41; Charles I. Foster, ed., *History of Winthrop,* pp. 26–28, 70–75. U.S., Bureau of the Census, *Fourth Census of the United States, 1820: Population,* vol. 4, p. 643; *Sixth Census, 1840: Population,* vol. 3, p. 367; *Seventh Census, 1850: Population,* vol. 8, pp. 35–87.
2. See, for example, the Clark Family Papers (1816–55) in the private possession of Laurence and Ruth Foster in Winthrop, and the Letters of Little, Wood and Company (1841–43) in the Little Family Collection at the New York Public Library.
3. Stackpole, *History of Winthrop,* pp. 221–24; Foster, *History of Winthrop,* p. 28.
4. Thurston, *Brief History of Winthrop,* pp. 34–35; Stackpole, *History of Winthrop,* pp. 57–74; Foster, *History of Winthrop,* pp. 26–29. See also: Winthrop Town Records, 1820–50.
5. Foster, *History of Winthrop,* p. 26. See, for example, a report on a Winthrop meeting of a canal association, August 14, 1835: *Maine Farmer,* August 21, 1835, p. 225.
6. For an excellent historical survey of the Maine railway, see: Edward E. Chase, *Maine Railroads: A History of the Development of the Maine Railroad System* (Portland: A. J. Huston, 1926).
7. *Maine Farmer,* December 17, 1846, p. 3. Samuel P. Benson, "Historic Address of Honorable S. P. Benson," p. 43. Chase, *Maine Railroads,* pp. 20–23. *Maine Farmer,* March 11, 1847, p. 2.
8. C., Letter to the *Boston Courier,* September 25, 1848, in *Maine Farmer,* October 5, 1848, p. 2.
9. *Maine Farmer,* July 5, 1849, p. 2; July 12, 1849, p. 2. Chase, *Maine Railroads,* pp. 21–23. Foster, *History of Winthrop,* pp. 70–71.
10. *Maine Farmer,* July 5, 1849, p. 2; August 23, 1849, p. 2. See: Charles Hotham, "Vacationland," in *History of Winthrop,* ed. Foster, pp. 90–93.
11. "Railroad Frolics," *Maine Farmer,* December 27, 1849, p. 2.
12. The frequency of accidents in the area probably encouraged the railroad company to hire local help. For example, a derailment occurred in Winthrop less than four months after the line opened. *Maine Farmer,* November 8, 1849, p. 2.
13. Ezekiel Holmes, "Opening of the Railroads," *Maine Farmer,* July 12, 1849, p. 2.
14. *Maine Farmer,* August 9, 1849, p. 2. Thurston, *Brief History of Winthrop,* p. 89.
15. See, for example: "The Business Men's Party," *Maine Farmer,* April 22, 1843, p. 2.
16. See, for example: *Maine Farmer,* February 5, 1842, p. 2; Roswell C. Smith,

Practical and Mental Arithmetic, pp. 36, 69–70, 177; Enoch Plummer, Due Notice to Samuel L. Clark of Winthrop, no date, in the Clark Family Papers, in the possession of Laurence and Ruth Foster, Winthrop. "Merchant" may also include "pedlar," a man in the rare position of doing retail trade outside a "shop." See: *Maine Farmer,* October 30, 1835, p. 310; and *Winthrop Emulator,* vol. 2, no. 6 (1846), p. 5.

17. Rev. J. Todd, "Female Education: Address Delivered at the Opening of the Northampton Female Seminary, November, 1835," *Maine Farmer,* December 18, 1835, p. 364.
18. *Maine Farmer,* August 19, 1836, p. 230. "Hints to Capitalists," *Maine Farmer,* April 17, 1841, p. 117. See also: *Maine Farmer,* January 4, 1834, p. 40; November 16, 1833, p. 352.
19. See, for example: *Maine Farmer,* January 4, 1834, p. 40; November 16, 1833, p. 352; April 17, 1841, p. 117.
20. *Maine Farmer,* April 17, 1841, p. 117; February 4, 1833, p. 24. "Speculation in Western Lands," *Maine Farmer,* January 27, 1837, p. 414. "Internal Improvements," *Maine Farmer,* November 7, 1834, p. 330. See also: *Maine Farmer,* January 13, 1837, p. 394; November 16, 1833, p. 352; June 24, 1833, p. 179; and David Thurston, *Letters from a Father to a Son, An Apprentice,* p. 30.
21. See, for example: *Maine Farmer,* July 15, 1833, p. 203; November 14, 1834, p. 340.
22. Riddle, *Maine Farmer,* March 14, 1834, p. 72. *Maine Farmer,* January 13, 1837, p. 394. See also: *Maine Farmer,* September 7, 1833, pp. 272–73.
23. Thurston, *Brief History of Winthrop,* pp. 146–53. *Maine Farmer,* May 9, 1834, p. 130; June 26, 1841, p. 193; February 19, 1842, p. 3; February 26, 1842, pp. 2–3; May 23, 1840, p. 155. Henry D. Kingsbury and Simeon Deyo, *Illustrated History of Kennebec County, Maine, 1799–1892* (New York: H. W. Blake and Co., 1892), vol. 2, p. 832. Samuel L. Boardman, *The Agriculture and Industry of the County of Kennebec,* p. 157. Records of the Church of Christ in Winthrop, Maine, vol. 2: May 13, 1835; December 17, 1840; April 24, 1847. Winthrop Town Records, vol. 3, pp. 237–38 (April 6, 1830), p. 275 (April 4, 1836).
24. *Maine Farmer,* May 23, 1840, p. 155. Thurston, *Brief History of Winthrop,* pp. 146–53.
25. David Thurston, *A Sermon Delivered by David Thurston, Pastor of a Church in Winthrop, Maine, at the Third Annual Meeting of the American Missionary Association at Boston, Mass., September 25, 1849,* p. 8. See also: Thurston, *Brief History of Winthrop,* p. 16.
26. *Maine Farmer,* June 24, 1833, p. 178. Note that "agent" could also properly designate those who represented the business interests of any "establishment" or association. "Agents," for example, advertised goods or services for sale, managed mills, or even announced meetings of missionary societies. See, for instance: *Maine Farmer,* November 25, 1836, p. 343; February 18, 1833, p. 39; December 11, 1835, p. 356; and Letter, Josiah Little, Jr., Winthrop, to Josiah Little, Esq., Newbury, Mass., September 4, 1843.
27. David Thurston, Letter, *Maine Farmer,* November 28, 1834, p. 356. *Maine Farmer,* June 24, 1833, p. 179; February 22, 1840, p. 49.

28. *Maine Farmer,* June 24, 1833, pp. 178–79; June 10, 1833, p. 162; April 24, 1835, p. 90.
29. *Maine Farmer,* June 20, 1837, p. 145. See also: *Maine Farmer,* March 25, 1833, p. 74; January 13, 1837, p. 394.
30. *Maine Farmer,* November 14, 1834, p. 340. See also: *Winthrop Emulator,* February 6, 1845, pp. 3–4.
31. Letter, Samuel L. Clark, Winthrop, to Dr. Bezer Snell, Wheeler Springs, Charlotte County, Va., August 26, 1826. Letter, Samuel L. Clark, Augusta, to Miller Clark, February 10, 1833. Letter, N. M. Whitman, Waterville, to Samuel L. Clark, Winthrop, June 13, 1837. Letter, Dr. Bezer Snell, Charlotte County, Va., to Samuel L. Clark, Winthrop, December 17, 1827.
32. *Maine Farmer,* July 15, 1833, p. 203.
33. See: "The Aspirant to be a Merchant," from the *Hartford Patriot, Maine Farmer,* February 29, 1840, p. 64. Letter from Observor, *Maine Farmer,* September 7, 1833, p. 272. Smith, *Practical and Mental Arithmetic,* pp. 237–38. The role of "cashier" may have served a similar purpose in banking. See, for example: Thurston, *Brief History of Winthrop,* p. 89.
34. *Winthrop Emulator,* February 6, 1845, p. 3. See: Letters, Josiah Little, Jr., to Josiah Little, Esq., November 29, 1841, and December 15, 1841; *Maine Farmer,* December 21, 1839, p. 393; and Smith, *Practical and Mental Arithmetic,* pp. 30, 36, 71, 194.
35. *Maine Farmer,* October 1, 1842, p. 3; September 7, 1833, p. 273; April 15, 1833, p. 104. Thurston, *Brief History of Winthrop,* p. 63. Smith, *Practical and Mental Arithmetic,* pp. 69, 215, 229.
36. Letter, Ezekiel Holmes, Starks, to Asaph Holmes, February 1, 1830, excerpted in *Home Farm,* August 28, 1884, p. 4. Ezekiel Holmes, Private Journal, February 12, 1835, in *Home Farm,* December 11, 1884, p. 3. See: Thurston, *A Sermon Delivered . . . at the Third Annual Meeting of the American Missionary Association,* p. 8.
37. *Maine Farmer,* May 27, 1833, p. 151. See: Thurston, *Letters from a Father,* pp. 30, 65; "Owe No Man," *Maine Farmer,* December 26, 1834, p. 392; Methodist Episcopal Church, *The Doctrines and Discipline of the Methodist Episcopal Church* (New York: T. Mason and G. Lane, 1836), pp. 44–45; and Church of Christ, Winthrop, Maine, Records, vol. 2: January 19, 1829–March 15, 1860.
38. *Maine Farmer,* July 15, 1833, p. 203.
39. See, for example: *Maine Farmer,* May 27, 1833, p. 149; April 22, 1836, p. 89; February 25, 1833, p. 44; November 23, 1833, p. 360; December 23, 1836, p. 374; November 27, 1835, p. 342; September 7, 1833, p. 272; July 15, 1833, p. 203; Letter, Little, Wood and Co. [probably to Josiah Little, Esq., in mid-1841]; *Winthrop Emulator,* February 6, 1845, pp. 3–4.
40. *Maine Farmer,* November 23, 1833, p. 360. "How to Judge Customers," *Maine Farmer,* November 27, 1835, p. 342. See also: Letter, Little, Wood and Co. [probably to Josiah Little, Esq., in mid-1841].
41. *Maine Farmer,* January 13, 1837, p. 394. "If I Was He," *Maine Farmer,* September 18, 1835, p. 264. See also: *Maine Farmer,* November 23, 1833, p. 360; and Thurston, *Letters from a Father,* p. 30.

42. See, for example: *Maine Farmer,* November 2, 1833, p. 329; November 14, 1834, p. 340; November 28, 1834, p. 356; February 29, 1840, p. 64; February 5, 1842, p. 2; *Winthrop Emulator,* February 6, 1845, pp. 3–4; and Letter, N. M. Whitman, Waterville, to Samuel L. Clark, Winthrop, June 13, 1837.

CHAPTER 9: PROFESSIONAL MEN

1. U.S., Bureau of the Census, *Sixth Census of the United States, 1840: Population,* vol. 3, p. 367. *Seventh Census, 1850: Population,* vol. 8, pp. 35–87.
2. David Thurston, *A Brief History of Winthrop from 1764 to October, 1855,* pp. 98–109.
3. *Maine Farmer,* April 18, 1834, p. 112. See, for example: *Maine Farmer,* January 6, 1836, p. 390.
4. "Dialogue between Nathan and Solomon on the Comparative Advantages of the Learned Professions," *Maine Farmer,* July 10, 1841, p. 209. *Maine Farmer,* November 23, 1833, p. 356.
5. "Wrong Estimate of the Professions," from the *Saturday Courier, Maine Farmer,* September 16, 1836, p. 268. *Maine Farmer,* July 10, 1841, p. 209; September 28, 1833, p. 289; November 16, 1833, p. 348.
6. *Maine Farmer,* July 8, 1833, p. 202. See also: *Maine Farmer,* September 28, 1833, p. 289; April 29, 1833, p. 113.
7. Letter by J. H. J., Peru, *Maine Farmer,* March 11, 1836, p. 41. The letter probably refers to S. P. B. [Samuel P. Benson], a Winthrop "attorney" interested in scientific agriculture. See also: *Maine Farmer,* November 13, 1838, p. 315.
8. *Maine Farmer,* September 16, 1836, p. 268. See also: *Maine Farmer,* November 23, 1833, p. 350.
9. *Maine Farmer,* March 11, 1836, p. 41.
10. For a survey of the history of education in Maine, see: Charles A. Snow, *The History of the Development of Public School Supervision in the State of Maine,* University of Maine Studies, second series, no. 46 (Orono: University of Maine Press, 1939). For an excellent historical survey of education in Winthrop, see: Mary Oatway, "Education in Early Winthrop," in *History of Winthrop, Evolution of a Maine Community, 1771–1971,* ed. Foster, pp. 46–53. Also: Thurston, *Brief History of Winthrop,* pp. 91–94; the annual reports of the School Committee in the *Maine Farmer* and Winthrop Town Records, vols. 3–4, 1815–38; Record of School District No. 7, 1837–77, at the Charles M. Bailey Public Library, Winthrop; and District Book for District No. 3 in Winthrop, Maine, 1815–49, in the possession of Mary Oatway, East Winthrop. See particularly the 1828–36 Day Book of George C. Whitney, in the Charles M. Bailey Public Library. The Day Book covers Whitney's activities as a "farmer" as well as a "private" and "common school teacher" in Winthrop. It also gives the names and numbers of specific texts used in the schools.
11. *Maine Farmer,* September 19, 1834, p. 382. See: *Maine Farmer,* July 10, 1841, p. 209; March 18, 1836, p. 55; and Thurston, *Brief History of Winthrop,* pp. 97–109.
12. *Maine Farmer,* July 10, 1841, p. 209.
13. See, for example: *Maine Farmer,* December 21, 1833, p. 392; December 18,

1835, p. 364; March 18, 1836, p. 55; and Thomas N. Lord, *An Address Delivered at Winthrop, before the Sewing Circle and Ladies' Benevolent Society, September 20, 1833* (Winthrop: William Noyes and Co., 1833), pp. 3–4.

14. Oatway, "Education in Early Winthrop," pp. 50–53. *Maine Farmer,* March 18, 1835, p. 55. "Education — Female Habits," from the *New York Cultivator, Maine Farmer,* September 9, 1836, p. 253. *Maine Farmer,* December 21, 1833, p. 392.
15. Oatway, "Education in Early Winthrop," pp. 46–53. State of Maine, Board of Education, *Fourth Report of the Board of Education of the State of Maine, 1850* (Augusta: William T. Johnson, 1850), pp. 78, 88, 98. State of Maine, "Abstract from the Returns of Common Schools Made by the Several Cities, Towns, and Plantations in Maine for the Year 1838," *Public Documents* (Augusta: Smith and Robinson, 1839), vol. 2, p. 18. U.S., *Seventh Census, 1850: Social Statistics,* vol. 133, pp. 341–43. *Maine Farmer,* June 10, 1833, p. 162. L. P. P., "Short Essays on Common Schools," *Maine Farmer,* March 9, 1839, p. 34. See also: Record of School District No. 7, 1837–77; and *Maine Farmer,* October 12, 1833, p. 312.
16. Oatway, "Education in Early Winthrop," pp. 46–53. L. P. P., "Short Essays on Common Schools," *Maine Farmer,* March 9, 1839, p. 34. See: Record of School District No. 7, 1837–77; District Book for District No. 3, 1815–49; and Ezekiel Holmes, Private Journal, December 12, 1834, in *Home Farm,* November 27, 1884, p. 1.
17. L. P. P., "Common Schools," *Maine Farmer,* January 15, 1839, p. 386. *Maine Farmer,* August 5, 1833, p. 231. See: Oatway, "Education in Early Winthrop," pp. 46–53.
18. Maine Board of Education, *Fourth Report,* pp. 78, 88, 98. State of Maine, "Abstracts from the Returns of Common Schools," *Public Documents,* vol. 2, p. 18. U.S., *Seventh Census, 1850: Social Statistics,* vol. 133, pp. 341–43. L. P. P., "Common Schools," *Maine Farmer,* January 15, 1839, p. 386. See also: Oatway, "Education in Early Winthrop," pp. 48–50; Thurston, *Brief History of Winthrop,* pp. 91–94; Winthrop Town Records, vols. 3–4, 1815–38.
19. O. P. Q., East Winthrop, "Common Schools," *Maine Farmer,* December 25, 1838, p. 362.
20. B. P. W., *Maine Farmer,* June 13, 1839, p. 179.
21. Maine Board of Education, *Fourth Report,* pp. 78, 88, 98. U.S., *Seventh Census, 1850: Social Statistics,* vol. 133, pp. 341–43.
22. See: *Maine Farmer,* December 18, 1838, p. 354; December 25, 1838, p. 362; January 25, 1839, pp. 20–21; February 22, 1840, p. 53; March 28, 1849, p. 96; and Thurston, *Brief History of Winthrop,* pp. 93–94.
23. Winthrop, Superintending School Committee, "Report of the Superintending School Committee," Winthrop Town Records, vol. 4, April 2, 1827, pp. 153–54. See: "Review of the Report of the Superintending School Committee of the Town of Winthrop, 1838," *Maine Farmer,* June 19, 1838, pp. 148–49, and July 24, 1838, pp. 188–89; O. P. Q., East Winthrop, "Common Schools," *Maine Farmer,* December 25, 1838, p. 362; L. P. P., "Common Schools, *Maine Farmer,* January 8, 1839, p. 378, and January 15, 1839, p. 386; "Questions for School Teachers," *Maine Farmer,* January 2, 1841, p. 411; L. P. P., "The

Qualifications of Teachers,'' *Maine Farmer,* January 29, 1839, p. 408, and February 16, 1839, p. 10; O. P. Q., *Maine Farmer,* March 28, 1849, p. 96; O. S. M. of Winthrop, *Maine Farmer,* January 25, 1840, pp. 20–21. Also: Record of School District No. 7, 1837–77; and District Book for District No. 3, 1815–49.

24. Thurston, *Brief History of Winthrop,* p. 97. L. P. P., ''The Qualifications of Teachers,'' *Maine Farmer,* February 16, 1839, p. 10. See also: ''Report of School Committee,'' *Maine Farmer,* April 17, 1845, p. 2; Superintending School Committee, ''Report,'' Winthrop Town Records, vol. 4, April 2, 1827, pp. 154–55; B. F. W., *Maine Farmer,* June 13, 1839, p. 179; O. P. Q., ''Common Schools,'' *Maine Farmer,* December 25, 1838, p. 362; L. P. P., ''Common Schools,'' *Maine Farmer,* January 8, 1839, p. 378.
25. See, for example: O. P. Q., ''Common Schools,'' *Maine Farmer,* December 25, 1838, pp. 361–62; or L. P. P., ''Common Schools,'' *Maine Farmer,* January 8, 1839, p. 378.
26. Thurston, *Brief History of Winthrop,* p. 95. L. P. P., ''Short Essays on Common Schools,'' *Maine Farmer,* March 9, 1839, p. 34. See: Agricola, *Maine Farmer,* December 18, 1838, p. 354; and L. P. P., ''Common Schools,'' *Maine Farmer,* January 8, 1839, p. 378, and January 15, 1839, p. 386.
27. L. P. P., ''Short Essays on Common Schools,'' *Maine Farmer,* March 9, 1839, p. 34. ''Kennebec Teachers' Institute at Winthrop,'' *Maine Farmer,* November 21, 1850, p. 2. Oatway, ''Education in Early Winthrop,'' p. 50.
28. L. P. P., ''Short Essays on Common Schools,'' *Maine Farmer,* March 9, 1839, p. 34. See also an article by Agricola, *Maine Farmer,* December 18, 1838, p. 354.
29. *Maine Farmer,* May 20, 1833, p. 140. See also: *Maine Farmer,* February 4, 1833, p. 20; February 11, 1833, pp. 25–26; April 29, 1833, p. 140; July 8, 1833, p. 202.
30. Thurston, *Brief History of Winthrop,* pp. 104–7. See also: *Maine Farmer,* June 24, 1833, p. 184; and August 10, 1833, pp. 238, 239; Letter, Samuel P. Benson to Bowdoin College, November 3, 1855, in Bowdoin College Special Collections; Letter in verse, Samuel E. Benjamin to John Benjamin, Winthrop, 1845, in Fogler Library Special Collections; and Nehemiah Cleaveland, *History of Bowdoin College with Biographical Sketches of Its Graduates from 1806 to 1879, Inclusive,* edited and completed by Alpheus S. Packard (Boston: James Ripley Osgood and Co., 1882), p. 291.
31. See, for example: *Maine Farmer,* February 11, 1833, p. 26; July 22, 1833, p. 216; June 17, 1833, pp. 174–75; March 11, 1833, p. 62; or the host of legal manuscripts in: Clark Family Papers, 1816–55, in the possession of Laurence and Ruth Foster, Winthrop; Packard Family Papers, 1801–57; and Foster Family Notes, the latter two in the collections of the Maine Historical Society. In recognition of common ignorance, the *Maine Farmer* ran a series of articles in 1837 and 1838 to explain law and its jargon to the public. See, for example: ''Explanation of Legal Terms,'' *Maine Farmer,* January 30, 1838, p. 404.
32. Observo, ''Education of Farmers' Sons,'' *Maine Farmer,* April 4, 1834, p. 91. See also: *Maine Farmer,* November 14, 1834, p. 340; February 11, 1833, pp. 25–26.
33. ''Mechanics Settle Their Own Differences,'' *Maine Farmer,* January 15, 1842, p.

2. "If I Was He," *Maine Farmer,* September 18, 1835, p. 264. *Maine Farmer,* November 14, 1834, p. 340. T. W., Letter, *Maine Farmer,* June 19, 1841, p. 186. See also: *Maine Farmer,* March 11, 1833, p. 62; May 20, 1833, p. 144; May 27, 1833, p. 151; June 24, 1833, p. 184.

34. *Maine Farmer,* March 25, 1833, p. 78. See also: *Maine Farmer,* August 10, 1839, p. 237.

35. David Thurston, *A Sermon Delivered at Winthrop, April 7, 1825, at the Annual Fast in Maine* (Augusta: Eaton and Severance, 1825), p. 7. See: *Maine Farmer,* June 10, 1833, p. 164; December 21, 1833, p. 386; "American Society," from the *Knickerbocker, Maine Farmer,* September 9, 1836, p. 252.

36. *Winthrop Emulator,* February 6, 1845, p. 5. See, in the *Maine Farmer:* February 11, 1833, p. 30; October 26, 1833, p. 324; December 21, 1833, p. 386; January 11, 1834, p. 410; October 2, 1835, p. 274; December 25, 1835, p. 371; September 9, 1836, p. 252; October 30, 1841, p. 342; September 3, 1842, p. 1; January 21, 1843, p. 1. Also: Ezekiel Holmes, Private Journal, January 9, 1835, in *Home Farm,* December 11, 1884, p. 2; and Thurston, *Sermon Delivered at Winthrop . . . at the Annual Fast in Maine,* pp. 4–7.

37. Thurston, *Brief History of Winthrop,* pp. 36–51, 77–82. See: Everett S. Stackpole, *History of Winthrop, Maine with Genealogical Notes,* pp. 242–46, 281–85, 500–4, 366–67; Charles B. Fillebrown, *Genealogy of the Fillebrown Family with Biographical Sketches,* pp. 24–39, 58–70; "Death of Dr. Holmes," *Maine Farmer,* February 16, 1865, p. 1; Nathaniel T. True, "Biographical Sketch of Ezekiel Holmes, M.D.," pp. 207–26.

38. See: Thurston, *Brief History of Winthrop,* pp. 98–104, 168, 170–71; Stackpole, *History of Winthrop,* p. 154; Winthrop Town Records, vol. 4, July 7, 1832, p. 302; and *Maine Farmer,* August 31, 1833, p. 262; September 7, 1833, p. 271; February 29, 1840, p. 62; August 2, 1849, p. 2. See also: Letters, Samuel L. Clark, Winthrop, to Susanna Clark, Middleborough, Mass., July 27, 1832, August 13, 1832, and September 6, 1832; and Letter, Samuel L. Clark, Bangor, to the Clark family, Winthrop, November 11, 1849.

39. Letter, Samuel L. Clark, Bangor, to Elias M. Clark, Winthrop, October 9, 1846. See also: Letter, A. Blake, Monmouth, to Dr. Lewis Clark, Winthrop, April 24, 1840; and "Maine Insane Hospital," *Maine Farmer,* February 20, 1841, p. 49.

40. Thurston, *Brief History of Winthrop,* pp. 98–103, 168. David Thurston, *A Sermon Preached May 10, 1826, at the Ordination of the Rev. Josiah Tucker over the Congregational Church and Society in Madison* (Hallowell: Glazier and Co., 1826), p. 7. *Maine Farmer,* August 17, 1833, p. 247; June 24, 1833, pp. 177, 183; November 14, 1834, p. 340; July 11, 1840, p. 208. In regard to the distinct qualifications of a military "surgeon," see: Letters, Samuel L. Clark, Philadelphia, to Elias M. Clark, Winthrop, August 7, 1842, and August 26, 1843.

41. "Mary, An Indian Doctress," *Maine Farmer,* July 1, 1833, p. 192. *Maine Farmer,* November 21, 1834, p. 351. See: *Maine Farmer,* February 12, 1842, p. 3; August 17, 1833, p. 242; and Thurston, *Brief History of Winthrop,* p. 101.

42. Thurston, *Brief History of Winthrop,* p. 101. *Maine Farmer,* May 20, 1833, p. 144; February 11, 1833, pp. 25–26. Thomas J. Lee, *The Primary Class Book: A Selection of Easy Lessons in Reading, for the Younger Classes in Common Schools* (Hallowell: Glazier, Masters and Co., 1827), pp. 172–76.

43. Letter, Samuel L. Clark, Bangor, to Elias M. Clark, Winthrop, October 9, 1846. See: Thurston, *Brief History of Winthrop,* pp. 98–102, 168; and William H. Parlin, *Reminiscences of East Winthrop,* p. 53.
44. *Maine Farmer,* November 14, 1834, p. 340. See also: Letter, John Mitchel, Bangor, to Samuel L. Clark, Winthrop, May 8, 1833, which questions the prospects a Dr. Snell should expect if he were to practice in Winthrop.
45. *Maine Farmer,* November 19, 1842, p. 1.
46. "Annual Report of the Trustees of the Kennebec County Agricultural Society," *Maine Farmer,* April 29, 1833, p. 113. *Maine Farmer,* September 18, 1835, p. 264. *Maine Farmer,* November 14, 1833, p. 342. See: *Maine Farmer,* June 3, 1833, p. 153; Letter, Samuel L. Clark, Bangor, to Elias M. Clark, Winthrop, May 31, 1847; and Thurston, *Sermon Preached . . . at the Ordination of the Rev. Josiah Tucker,* p. 7.
47. For a survey of the religious history of Winthrop, see: Thurston, *Brief History of Winthrop,* pp. 110–42; Stackpole, *History of Winthrop,* pp. 80–116; Foster, *History of Winthrop,* pp. 39–43, 115–17; as well as the standard denominational histories.
48. David Thurston, Journal, excerpted in *In Memoriam: A Sketch of the Life of David Thurston,* written for the *Congregational Quarterly,* Rev. Thomas Adams (Portland: B. Thurston and Co., 1867), p. 18. Adams's *In Memoriam* provides a good biography and partial bibliography of the Reverend Mr. Thurston. It includes extensive quotations from his journal and correspondence. Additional biographical material and journal excerpts appear in Brown Thurston, comp., *Thurston Genealogies, 1635–1880* (Portland: B. Thurston and Hoyt, Fogg and Donham, 1880), pp. 89–102. See also: Calvin M. Clark, *American Slavery and Maine Congregationalists: A Chapter in the History of the Development of Anti-Slavery Sentiment in the Protestant Churches of the North* (Bangor: the author, 1940). It is dedicated to Thurston's memory.
49. Benjamin Tappan, *A Sermon Delivered in Winthrop, September 25, 1822, before the Kennebec Missionary Society, at Their First Annual Meeting,* p. 14. David Thurston, *A Sermon Delivered in Saco, June 26, 1816, before the Maine Missionary Society at Their Ninth Annual Meeting* (Hallowell: N. Cheever, 1816), pp. 4–7, 11. John Smith, *A Sermon, Delivered in Winthrop, June 23, 1830, before the Maine Missionary Society, at Their Twenty-Third Anniversary* (Portland: Shirley, Hyde and Co., 1830), pp. 9, 20. Thurston, *Brief History of Winthrop,* p. 101. Manuscripts covering Winthrop's missionary activities include: Minutes of the Maine Baptist Missionary Society, 1805–44, in the Convention Library of the American Baptist Churches of Maine, Augusta; Account Book of the Bowdoinham Missionary Society, 1811–1907, in the possession of Mary Oatway, East Winthrop; and Winthrop Correspondence, 1820–50, in the Archives of the American Missionary Association and American Home Missionary Society, Amistad Research Center, Dillard University, New Orleans.
50. Records of the Church of Christ in Winthrop, Maine, vol. 1, June 21, 1819; see also vol. 2, April 13, 1843.
51. David Thurston, *A Sermon Preached at the Ordination of the Rev. David Starret, over the Congregational Church and Society in Weld, September 26, 1821* (Hallowell: Goodale, Glazier and Co., 1821), p. 7; see also pp. 7–11. See: Letter,

Peyton Bradshaw, Exeter, to Samuel L. Clark, Winthrop, August 1, 1828.

52. Thurston, *Sermon Delivered . . . before the Maine Missionary Society,* p. 7 Letter, David Thurston, Winthrop, to Thomas Adams, Ohio, January 25, 1850, in Adams, *In Memoriam,* p. 25. David Thurston, Journal, n.d., in Thurston, *Thurston Genealogies,* p. 99. See also the political correspondence of Samuel L. Clark, Bangor, to the Clark family, Winthrop, 1840–50.

53. The "ministerial fund controversy" was mainly fought by "Congregationalists" and "Methodists" over the dispensation of a substantial income which had accrued from Winthrop's "ministerial lot," a piece of land dedicated to church support by Plymouth Colony. It was unclear whether the money in the "ministerial fund" properly belonged to the church which had been recognized by the Massachusetts legislature, to each of the several churches in town in proportion to their memberships at a given time, or to the town and the churches according to some more complicated formula. After more than thirty years of bitterness and litigation, a settlement was reached whereby the fund, in effect, went to support the town's schools. In addition to the surveys of Winthrop's religious history, see: Winthrop Methodist Church, *One Hundred Fifty Years of History, 1811–1961,* souvenir pamphlet (Winthrop: Winthrop Methodist Church, 1961); and the various editions of Methodist Episcopal Church, *The Doctrines and Discipline of the Methodist Episcopal Church,* beginning with the 20th edition (New York: N. Bangs and T. Mason, 1820). See also: Records and History of the Methodist Episcopal Church in Winthrop, vol. 1, 1793–1875, in possession of the Methodist Episcopal Church in Winthrop; Minutes of the First Parish in Winthrop, 1831–1857; and Records of the Church of Christ in Winthrop, Maine, vols. 1–2, 1776–1860, both in the possession of the Congregational Church in Winthrop; and in the Maine Historical Society: Leeds Monthly Meeting of Friends, Men's Meeting Minutes, vols. 1–3, 1813–52; Leeds Monthly Meeting of Friends, Women's Meeting Minutes, vols. 1–2, 1813–41; and Litchfield Monthly Meeting of Friends, Book of Records: Births, Deaths, Marriages, Certificates, 1813–72. Note that the name of the monthly meeting that Winthrop Friends attended changed from Leeds to Litchfield in 1839.

54. "A Short Sermon on Long Ones," *Maine Farmer,* December 12, 1834, p. 371. Thurston, *Sermon Preached at the Ordination of Rev. David Starret,* p. 15, and see pp. 3, 7–19. See: David Thurston, *Letters from A Father to a Son, An Apprentice,* pp. 122–23; David Thurston, *Causes of an Unsuccessful Ministry, A Sermon Preached at the Installation of the Rev. Henry Sewall, over the Church and Society in Bethel (West Parish), January 20, 1819* (Hallowell: E. Goodale, 1819), p. 9; Thurston, *Sermon Preached . . . at the Ordination of the Rev. Josiah Tucker,* pp. 4–14; David Thurston, *A Sermon Preached, August 9, 1826, at the Ordination of the Rev. Stephen Thurston over the Congregational Church and Society in Prospect* (Hallowell: Glazier and Co., 1826), p. 16; Smith, *Sermon Delivered . . . before the Maine Missionary Society,* pp. 6, 13–20; Stephen Chapin, *The Superior Glory of Gospel Worship: A Sermon Delivered November 19, 1823, at the Dedication of the Baptist Meeting House in Winthrop, Maine* (Waterville: William Hastings, 1823), p. 33; Records of the Church of Christ in Winthrop, Maine, vol. 2, July 28 and October 28, 1838; Parlin, *Reminiscences of East Winthrop,* pp. 20–27; Robert Page, Jr., "What Has Been Done for the

Instruction of the Slaves in the West Indias?,'' dissertation read before the Society of Inquiry at Andover Theological Seminary, c. 1814, in the possession of the Andover Newton Theological School; and *Maine Farmer,* February 11, 1833, pp. 25–26; November 14, 1834, p. 340.

55. David Thurston, *A Discourse Preached in Winthrop, April 3, 1823, at the Annual Fast in Maine* (Hallowell: Goodale, Glazier and Co., 1823), p. 21. ''Modern Meaning to Old Words,'' *Maine Farmer,* May 6, 1836, p. 110. *Maine Farmer,* November 14, 1834, p. 340. See also: *Maine Farmer,* February 11, 1833, pp. 25–26; Amicus, Poem, *Maine Farmer,* May 20, 1833, p. 144; and Thurston, *Sermon Preached . . . at the Ordination of the Rev. Josiah Tucker,* p. 12.

CHAPTER 10: CONCLUSION

1. For a survey of some of the more recent work, see: Naomi Quinn, ''Decision Models of Social Structure,'' *American Ethnologist* 2 (1975): 19–45. A fine example of such work on an American subject is Michael Agar's *Ripping and Running: A Formal Ethnography of Urban Heroin Addicts.* See also: Michael Agar, ''Selecting a Dealer,'' pp. 47–60; Stephen M. Fjellman, ''Talking about Talking about Residence: An Akamba Case,'' *American Ethnologist* 3 (1976): 671–82; James Howe and Joel Sherzer, ''Take and Tell,'' pp. 435–60; James P. Spradley and Brenda J. Mann, *The Cocktail Waitress: Woman's Work in a Man's World* (New York: John Wiley and Sons, 1975); and James P. Spradley and Michael A. Rynkiewich, eds., *The Nacirema: Readings on American Culture* (Boston: Little, Brown and Co., 1975).
2. See, for example: Oswald Werner, ''Ethnoscience 1972,'' *Annual Review of Anthropology* (ed. Bernard J. Siegel) 1 (1972): 271–308. An article that presents a convincing argument for the use of both cognitive models and behavioral statistics is: Allen Johnson, ''Ethnoecology and Planting Practices in a Swidden Agricultural System,'' *American Ethnologist* 1 (1974): 87–101.
3. Prominent examples of the new urban history include: Stephen Thernstrom, *Poverty and Progress: Social Mobility in a Nineteenth Century City* (New York: Atheneum, 1970); and Stephen Thernstrom and Richard Sennett, eds., *Nineteenth Century Cities: Essays in the New Urban History* (New Haven: Yale University Press, 1970). See also: Peter M. Blau and Otis D. Duncan, *The American Occupational Structure* (New York: John Wiley and Sons, 1967). I would only add that the analysis of folk categories should *precede* quantification. In other words, variables should first be defined in the subjects' terms and then related to the analyst's, not vice versa. The alternative runs a greater risk of uncovering trends that are an artifact of the analyst's, not the subjects', experience. At the very least, I hope that I have shown that this is a tricky business. Unpacking the meaning of statements like ''I am a carpenter,'' made to a local census-taker, even with rigorous analysis, is neither a simple nor a terribly precise endeavor. Since (1) mobility may be a function of change in such statements over time, and (2) the meaning of such statements is variably, contextually, and imprecisely defined, there are severe limits to the precision quantification can achieve. Ethnoscience in history is one way to probe those limits. I, like Thernstrom, am looking to ''provide information essential to arranging harder data in meaningful categories;

for instance, instead of imposing an occupational classification scheme derived from research by contemporary sociologists, one may . . . develop a scheme more appropriate to the context.'' Stephen Thernstrom, ''Reflections on the Urban History,'' *Daedalus* 100 (1971): p. 371.

4. See: John L. Caughey, ''Simulating the Past,'' pp. 626–42.

Bibliography

A. Methodological References

Agar, Michael. *Ripping and Running: A Formal Ethnography of Urban Heroin Addicts*. New York: Seminar Press, 1973.

———. "Selecting a Dealer." *American Ethnologist* 2 (1975): 47–60.

Albert, Ethel M. "The Classification of Values: A Method and Illustration." *American Anthropologist* 58 (1956): 221–48.

Allport, Gordon W. *The Use of Personal Documents in Psychological Science*. New York: Social Science Research Council, 1942.

Anderson, Robert T. *Traditional Europe: A Study in Anthropology and History*. Belmont, Calif.: Wadsworth, 1971.

Basso, Ellen B. "Kalapalo Affinity: Its Cultural and Social Contexts." *American Ethnologist* 2 (1975): 207–28.

Berger, Peter L., and Thomas Luckman. *The Social Construction of Reality*. Garden City: Doubleday, 1967.

Berkhofer, Robert F., Jr. *A Behavioral Approach to Historical Analysis*. New York: Free Press, 1969.

Berlin, Brent. "The Concept of Rank in Ethnobiological Classification: Some Evidence from Aguaruna Folk Botany." *American Ethnologist* 3 (1976): 381–99.

———. "Further Notes on Covert Categories and Folk Taxonomies: A Reply to Brown." *American Anthropologist* 76 (1974): 327–31.

———. "A Universalist-Evolutionary Approach in Ethnographic Semantics." *Bulletin of the American Anthropological Association,* vol. 3, no. 3, pt. 2 (1970): 3–18.

Berlin, Brent, Dennis E. Breedlove, and Peter H. Raven. "Covert Categories and Folk Taxonomies." *American Anthropologist* 70 (1968): 290–99.

———. "General Principles of Classification and Nomenclature in Folk Biology." *American Anthropologist* 75 (1973): 214–42.

Berreman, Gerald D. "Anemic and Emetic Analysis in Social Anthropology." *American Anthropologist* 68 (1966): 346–54.

Birdwhistell, Ray L. *Kinesics and Context: Essays on Body Motion Communication*. Philadelphia: University of Pennsylvania Press, 1973.

Blau, Peter M., and Otis D. Duncan. *The American Occupational Structure*. New York: John Wiley and Sons, 1967.

Blount, Ben G., and Mary Sanches, eds. *Sociocultural Dimensions of Language Change*. New York: Academic Press, 1976.

Boas, Franz. "History and Science in Anthropology: A Reply." *American Anthropologist* 38 (1936): 137–41.

Bock, Philip K., ed. *Culture Shock: A Reader in Modern Cultural Anthropology*. New York: Alfred A. Knopf, 1970.

Bornstein, Marc H. "The Influence of Visual Perception on Culture." *American Anthropologist* 77 (1975): 774–98.

Boulding, Kenneth E. *The Image*. Ann Arbor: University of Michigan Press, 1969.

Brown, Cecil H. "General Principles of Human Anatomical Partonomy and Speculations on the Growth of Partonomic Nomenclature." *American Ethnologist* 3 (1976): 400–24.

———. "Psychological, Semantic, and Structural Aspects of American English Kinship Terms." *American Ethnologist* 1 (1973): 415–36.

———. "Unique Beginners and Covert Categories in Folk Biological Taxonomies." *American Anthropologist* 76 (1974): 325–27.

Brown, Cecil H., John Kolar, Barbara J. Torrey, Tipawan Trưởng-Quang, and Philip Volkman. "Some General Principles of Biological and Non-Biological Folk Classification." *American Ethnologist* 3 (1976): 73–85.

Burling, Robbins. "Linguistics and Ethnographic Description." *American Anthropologist* 71 (1969): 817–27.

Burton, William, and Richard Lowenthal. "The First of the Mohegans." *American Ethnologist* (Special Issue: Uses of Ethnohistory in Ethnographic Analysis) 1 (1974): 589–99.

Casson, Ronald W. "The Semantics of Kin Term Usage." *American Ethnologist* 2 (1975): 229–38.

Castaneda, Carlos. *A Separate Reality: Further Conversations with Don Juan*. New York: Simon and Schuster, 1971.

Caughey, John L. "Simulating the Past: A Method for Using Ethnosemantics in Historical Research." *American Quarterly* 24 (1972): 626–42.

Cebik, L. B. "Identity: An Existential Fallacy?" *Georgia Review* 23 (1969): 484–500.

Colby, Benjamin N. "Ethnographic Semantics: A Preliminary Survey." *Current Anthropology* 7 (1966): 13–17.

Conklin, Harold C. *Folk Classifications: A Topically Arranged Bibliography of Contemporary and Background References through 1971*. New Haven: Yale University Department of Anthropology, 1972.

———. "Hanunóo Color Categories." *Southwestern Journal of Anthropology* 11 (1955): 339–44.

Diamond, Stanley, ed. *Culture in History: Essays in Honor of Paul Radin*. New York: Columbia University Press, 1960.

Diesing, Paul. *Patterns of Discovery in the Social Sciences*. Chicago: Aldine-Atherton, 1971.

Dundes, Alan. "From Etic to Emic Units in the Structural Study of Folktales." *Journal of American Folklore* 75 (1962): 95–105.

Dundes, Alan, ed. *Every Man His Way: Readings in Cultural Anthropology*. Englewood Cliffs: Prentice-Hall, 1968.

Dwyer, Peter D. "An Analysis of Rofaifo Mammal Taxonomy. *American Ethnologist* 3 (1976): 425–45.

Fenton, William N. "The Training of Historical Ethnologists in America." *American Anthropologist* 54 (1952): 328–39.

Feyerabend, Paul. *Against Method: Outline of an Anarchistic Theory of Knowledge*. London: NLB, 1975.

Fjellman, Stephen M. "Talking about Talking about Residence: An Akamba Case." *American Ethnologist* 3 (1976): 671–82.

Gardner, Peter M. "Birds, Words, and a Requiem for the Omniscient Informant." *American Ethnologist* 3 (1976): 446–68.

Garvin, Paul L., ed. *Report of the Seventh Annual Round Table Meeting on Linguistics and Language Study*. George Washington University Monograph Series on Language and Linguistics, no. 9. Washington: George Washington University Press, 1957.

Geertz, Clifford, *The Interpretation of Cultures*. New York: Basic Books, 1973.

Geoghegan, William H. "Polytypy in Folk Biological Taxonomies." *American Ethnologist* 3 (1976): 469–80.

Gillin, John. "National and Regional Cultural Values in the United States." *Social Forces* 34 (1955): 107–23.

Gleason, Henry A., Jr. *An Introduction to Descriptive Linguistics*. Rev. ed. New York: Holt, Rinehart and Winston, 1961.

Gombrich, E. H. *Art and Illusion: A Study in the Psychology of Pictorial Representation*. A. W. Mellon Lectures in the Fine Arts, 1956, Bollingen Series 35 (5). Princeton: Princeton University Press, 1969.

Goodenough, Ward H. "Componential Analysis and the Study of Meaning." *Language* 32 (1956): 195–216.

———. *Cooperation in Change*. New York: Russell Sage Foundation, 1963.

———. *Culture, Language and Society*. A McCaleb Module in Anthropology. Addison-Wesley Modular Publications (11560), vol. 2 (1971), module no. 7.

———. *Description and Comparison in Cultural Anthropology*. Chicago: Aldine, 1970.

Goodenough, Ward H., ed. *Explorations in Cultural Anthropology*. New York: McGraw-Hill, 1964.

Griffin, Donald R. *The Question of Animal Awareness: Evolutionary Continuity of Mental Experience*. New York: Rockefeller University Press, 1976.

Gumperz, John J. "Linguistic and Social Interaction in Two Communities." *American Anthropologist* 66 (1964): 137–53.

Gumperz, John J., and Dell Hymes, eds. *Directions in Sociolinguistics*. New York: Holt, Rinehart and Winston, 1972.

Hall, Edward T. *The Silent Language*. Garden City: Doubleday, 1959.

Hallowell, Irving A. *Culture and Experience*. New York: Schocken Books, 1971.

Harris, Marvin. *The Rise of Anthropological Theory: A History of Theories of Culture*. New York: Thomas Y. Crowell, 1968.

Hays, Terence E. "An Empirical Method for the Identification of Covert Categories in Ethnobiology." *American Ethnologist* 3 (1976): 489–507.

Hobsbawm, E. J. "From Social History to the History of Societies." Historical Studies Today. *Daedalus* (Winter, 1971): 20–45.

Honingmann, John J., ed. *Handbook of Social and Cultural Anthropology*. Chicago: Rand McNally, 1973.

Horwitz, Richard P. "Architecture and Culture: The Meaning of the Lowell Boarding House." *American Quarterly* 25 (1973): 64–82.

Howe, James, and Joel Sherzer. "Take and Tell: A Practical Classification from the San Blas Cuna." *American Ethnologist* 2 (1975): 435–60.

Hsu, Francis L. K., ed. *Psychological Anthropology*. Cambridge, Mass.: Schenkman Publishing Co., 1972.

Hunn, Eugene. "Toward a Perceptual Model of Folk Biological Classification." *American Ethnologist* 3 (1976): 508–24.

Hymes, Dell H. "Directions in (ethno-) Linguistic Theory." *American Anthropologist* 66 (1964): 6–56.

Jerson, Richard, and Seymour Fesbach, eds. *Cognition, Personality, and Clinical Psychology*. San Francisco: Jossey Bass, 1967.

Johnson, Allen. "Ethnoecology and Planting Practices in a Swidden Agricultural System." *American Ethnologist* 1 (1974): 87–101.

Kay, Paul. "Some Theoretical Implications of Ethnographic Semantics." *Bulletin of the American Anthropological Association,* vol. 3, no. 3, pt. 2 (1970): 19–31.

Kimball, Solon T., and Conrad M. Arensberg. *Culture and Community*. New York: Harcourt, Brace and World, 1965.

Klapp, Orrin E. *Heroes, Villians, and Fools: The Changing American Character*. Englewood Cliffs: Prentice-Hall, 1962.

Kluckhohn, Florence R., and Fred L. Strodtbeck. *Variations in Value Orientations: A Theory Tested in Five Cultures*. Evanston: Row, Peterson and Co., 1961.

Kroeber, Alfred L. *An Anthropologist Looks at History*. Berkeley: University of California Press, 1963.

Kroeber, Alfred L., and Clyde Kluckhohn. *Culture: A Critical Review of Concepts and Definitions*. New York: Random House, 1952.

Kuhn, Thomas S. *The Structure of Scientific Revolutions*. 2d ed., enl. *International Encyclopedia of Unified Science,* vol. 2, no. 2. Chicago: University of Chicago Press, 1970.

Kuklick, Bruce. "Myth and Symbol in American Studies." *American Quarterly* 24 (1972): 435–50.

Leaf, Murray J. "The American English Kin Terminology as a Semantic System." Paper delivered at the Seventy-first Annual Meeting of the American Anthropological Association. Toronto, 1972.

Lessa, William A., and Evon Z. Vogt, eds. *Reader in Comparative Religion: An Anthropological Approach*. New York: Harper and Row, 1972.

Linden, Eugene. *Apes, Men, and Language*. New York: Penguin Books, 1974.

Lindzey, Gardiner, and Elliot Aronson, eds. *The Handbook of Social Psychology*. 2d ed. Reading: Addison-Wesley, 1968.

Lounsbury, Floyd G. "A Semantic Analysis of the Pawnee Kinship Usage." *Language* 32 (1956): 158–94.

Lurie, Nancy D. "Ethnohistory: An Ethnological Point of View." Symposium on the Concept of Ethnohistory. *Ethnohistory* 8 (1961): 78–92.

Malinowski, Bronislaw. *Argonauts of the Western Pacific*. London: George Routledge and Sons, 1922.

McCoy, Donald R. "Underdeveloped Sources of Understanding in American History." *Journal of American History* 54 (1967): 255–70.

Mead, Margaret. "From Intuition to Analysis in Communication Research." *Semiotica* 1 (1969): 13–25.

Miller, Jay. "Addendum on Ethno-Taxonomic Congresses." *American Anthropologist* 77 (1975): 887.

Morris, Charles W. *Foundations of the Theory of Signs. International Encyclopedia of Unified Science*, vol. 1, no. 2. Chicago: University of Chicago Press, 1938.

———. *Signs, Language, and Behavior*. New York: Prentice-Hall, 1946.

———. *Varieties of Human Value*. Chicago: University of Chicago Press, 1956.

Murphey, Murray G. *Our Knowledge of the Historical Past*. New York: Bobbs-Merrill, 1972.

Naroll, Raoul, and Ronald Cohen, eds. *A Handbook of Method In Cultural Anthropology*. New York: Columbia University Press, 1973.

Nettl, Bruno. *Theory and Method in Ethnomusicology*. London: Collier-Macmillan, 1964.

Noel, Daniel C. *Seeing Castaneda: Reactions to the "Don Juan" Writings of Carlos Castaneda*. New York: Putnam, 1976.

Parsons, Talcott, and Edward A. Shills, eds. *Toward a General Theory of Action*. Cambridge: Harvard University Press, 1951.

Payne, Raymond, and Wilfrid C. Bailey, comps. *The Community: A Classified, Annotated Bibliography*. Athens: University of Georgia Press, 1967.

Pelto, Pertti J. *Anthropological Research: The Structure of Inquiry*. New York: Harper and Row, 1970.

Piaget, Jean. *Psychology and Epistemology: Towards a Theory of Knowledge*. Translated by Arnold Rosin. New York: Viking Press. 1971.

Pike, Kenneth L. *Language in Relation to a Unified Theory of the Structure of Human Behavior*. 2 vols. Glendale: Summer Institute of Linguistics, 1954.

Pitt, David C. *Using Historical Sources in Anthropology and Sociology*. New York: Holt, Rinehart and Winston, 1972.

Platt, Gerald M. "The Sociological Endeavor and Psychoanalytic Thought." *American Quarterly* 28 (1976): 345–59.

Quinn, Naomi. "Decision Models of Social Structure." *American Ethnologist* 2 (1975): 19–45.

Randall, Robert A. "How Tall is a Taxonomic Tree? Some Evidence for Dwarfism." *American Ethnologist* 3 (1976): 543–52.

Redfield, Robert. *The Little Community/Peasant Society and Culture*. Chicago: University of Chicago Press, 1971.

Rivers, W. H. R. "History and Ethnology." *History* 5 (1920): 65–80.

Sanches, Mary, and Ben G. Blount, eds. *Sociocultural Dimensions of Language Use*. New York: Academic Press, 1975.

Sarles, Harvey B. "An Examination of the Question-Response System in Language." *Semiotica* 2 (1970): 79–101.

Saveth, Edward E., ed. *American History and the Social Sciences*. New York: Free Press, 1964.

Scheffler, Harold W. "Kinship Semantics." *Annual Review of Anthropology* (edited by Bernard J. Siegel) 1 (1972): 309–28.

Scott, James C. *Political Ideology in Malaysia: Reality and the Beliefs of an Elite.* New Haven: Yale University Press, 1968.

Silverman, David. *Reading Castaneda: A Prologue to the Social Sciences.* London: Routledge and Kegan Paul, 1975.

Smith, Alfred G., ed. *Communication and Culture: Readings in the Codes of Human Interaction.* New York: Holt, Rinehart, and Winston, 1966.

Social Science Research Council. "The Social Sciences in Historical Study: A Report of the Committee on Historiography." *Social Science Research Council Bulletin* 64 (1954).

Spiegelberg, Herbert. *The Phenomenological Movement: A Historical Introduction.* 2d ed. The Hague: Martinas Nijhoff, 1969.

Spiro, Melford E., ed. *Context and Meaning in Cultural Anthropology.* New York: Free Press, 1965.

Spradley, James P., ed. *Culture and Cognition: Rules, Maps and Plans.* San Francisco: Chandler, 1972.

Spradley, James P., and Brenda J. Mann. *The Cocktail Waitress: Woman's Work in a Man's World.* New York: John Wiley and Sons, 1975.

Spradley, James P., and David W. McCurdy. *Anthropology: The Cultural Perspective.* New York: John Wiley and Sons, 1975.

Spradley, James P., and David W. McCurdy, eds. *The Cultural Experience: Ethnography in Complex Society.* Chicago: Science Research Associates, 1972.

Spradley, James P., and Michael A. Rynkiewich. *The Nacirema: Readings on American Culture.* Boston: Little, Brown and Co., 1975.

Stone, Albert E. "Autobiography and American Culture." *American Studies* 11 (1972): 22–36.

Thernstrom, Stephen. "Reflections on the New Urban History." *Daedalus* 100 (1971): 359–75.

Tyler, Stephen A., ed. *Cognitive Anthropology.* New York: Holt, Rinehart, and Winston, 1969.

Valentine, Charles A. "Symposium on the Concept of Ethnohistory — Comment." *Ethnohistory* 8 (1961): 271–80.

Vogt, Evon Z., and Ethel M. Albert, eds. *Peoples of Rimrock: A Study of Five Cultures.* Cambridge: Harvard University Press, 1966.

Wallace, Anthony F. C. *Culture and Personality.* 2d ed. New York: Random House, 1970.

Ware, Caroline F., ed. *The Cultural Approach to History.* New York: Columbia University Press, 1940.

Washburn, Wilcomb E. "Ethnohistory 'In the Round.' " Symposium on the Concept of Ethnohistory. *Ethnohistory* 8 (1961): 31–45.

Watson, O. Michael. *Symbolic and Expressive Uses of Space: An Introduction to Proxemic Behavior.* A McCaleb Module in Anthropology. Addison-Wesley Modular Publications (11983), vol. 4 (1972), module no. 20.

Watson, Richard A., and Patty Jo Watson. *Man and Nature: An Anthropological Essay in Human Ecology.* New York: Harcourt Brace Jovanovich, 1969.

Werner, Oswald. "Ethnoscience 1972." *Annual Review of Anthropology* (edited by Bernard J. Siegel) 1 (1972): 271–308.

White, Leonard D., ed. *The State of the Social Sciences*. Chicago: University of Chicago Press, 1956.

Whorf, Benjamin Lee. *Language, Thought, and Reality: Selected Writings of Benjamin Lee Whorf*. Edited by John B. Carroll. Cambridge: M. I. T. Press, 1964.

Wilk, Stan. "Castaneda: Coming of Age in Sonora." *American Anthropologist* 79 (1) (1977): 84–91.

Williams, Robin M., Jr. *American Society: A Sociological Interpretation*. New York: Alfred A. Knopf, 1951.

Youssouf, Ibrahim Ag, Allen D. Grimshaw, and Charles S. Bird. "Greetings in the Desert." *American Ethnologist* 3 (1976): 797–824.

B. Primary Historical Sources

(The following includes all available material identifiably written or read in Winthrop, 1820–50. The list also includes secondary sources that cite primary material no longer available in original form.)

Adams, Thomas. *In Memoriam: A Sketch of the Life of David Thurston*. Written for the *Congregational Quarterly*. Portland: B. Thurston, 1867.

The Advocate of Freedom. Brunswick, Augusta, and Hallowell, 1838–41.

American Antislavery Society. *Proceedings of the Antislavery Convention Assembled at Philadelphia, December 4, 5, and 6, 1833*. New York: Dorr and Butterfield, 1833.

American Baptist Magazine and Mission Intelligencer. Boston, 1824.

American Home Missionary Society. Correspondence, 1828–32. In American Home Missionary Society Archives, Amistad Research Center, Dillard University.

American Missionary Association. Correspondence, 1847–50. In American Missionary Association Archives, Amistad Research Center, Dillard University.

Bailey, Hannah Johnson. *Reminiscences of a Christian Life*. Portland: Hoyt, Fogg and Donham, 1884.

Benjamin, Samuel E. Letter in verse, Samuel E. Benjamin to John Benjamin, Winthrop, 1845. In Special Collections of Fogler Library, University of Maine.

Bowdoin College. Papers and correspondence of students, officers, and alumni, 1820–50. In Special Collections of Bowdoin College Library.

Bowdoinham Association. *Minutes of the Bowdoinham Association; Held in Winthrop, September 26 and 27, 1827; Together with their Circular and Corresponding Letters*. Winthrop: Bowdoinham Association, 1827.

———. *Minutes of the Fiftieth Anniversary of the Bowdoinham Association, Holden at Winthrop, Wednesday and Thursday, September 28th, 29th, 1836*. Winthrop: Bowdoinham Association, 1836.

Bowdoinham Missionary Society. Account Book, 1811–1907. In possession of Mary Oatway, East Winthrop.

Butler, John. *Definitions and Explanations in Geography and Astronomy by John*

Butler, Pastor of the Baptist Church at Winthrop, Maine and Principal of the Female Academy in that Place. Hallowell: Glazier and Co., 1825.

———. *Friendly Letters to a Lady; In Which Several Important Doctrines of the Gospel are Explained and Vindicated*. Boston: James Loring, 1830.

Chapin, Stephen. *The Superior Glory of Gospel Worship: A Sermon Delivered November 19, 1823, at the Dedication of the Baptist Meeting-House in Winthrop, Maine*. Waterville: William Hastings, 1823.

Christian Mirror. Portland, 1826–56.

Church of Christ in Winthrop. Records of the Church of Christ in Winthrop, Maine. Vols. 1–2, 1776–1860. In possession of the Congregational Church, Winthrop.

Clark Family Papers. 1816–55. In possession of Laurence and Ruth Foster, Winthrop.

Cobb Family Papers. 1848–1900. In possession of Marion Cobb, Winthrop.

Cole, Samuel W. *The American Fruit Book; Containing Directions for Raising, Propagating, and Managing Fruit Trees, Shrubs, and Plants; With a Description of the Best Varieties of Fruit Including New and Valuable Kinds*. Boston: John P. Jewett, 1850.

Cushman, Andrew. "A Brief Narrative of Andrew Cushman's Life Furnished by Himself, December 12, 1843." 1843. In collections of Maine Historical Society.

Day, Clarence A., supervisor. "Vital Statistics from the Paper 'Maine Farmer' for the Period 1833–1852." 3 vols. Orono: University of Maine Press, n.d. Typescript in Maine State Library. Also appears on American Periodical Series 1000, reel 427, along with vols. 17 and 18 of the *Maine Farmer*.

District Book for District No. 3 in Winthrop, Maine. 1815–49. In possession of Mary Oatway, East Winthrop.

Emmons, Chansonetta S., ed. "Reminiscences of Capt. Nathaniel Fairbanks of Winthrop Maine." Typescript prepared for the Col. Asa Whitcomb Chapter of the Daughters of the American Revolution. Kingfield, 1931. In Maine State Library.

"Ezekiel Holmes. Memorials, Journals and Correspondence." *The Home Farm*, vols. 4–5, 1884.

Fillebrown, Charles B. *Genealogy of the Fillebrown Family with Biographical Sketches*. Boston: the author, 1910.

First Parish in Winthrop. Minutes, 1831–57. In possession of Congregational Church, Winthrop.

Foster, Charles I., ed. *History of Winthrop: Evolution of a Maine Community, 1771–1971*. Augusta: Kennebec Journal, 1971.

Foster Family Notes. N.d. In collections of Maine Historical Society.

The Free Soil Republican. Hallowell, 1848–49.

General Conference of the Congregational Churches of Maine. *A Manual of Congregationalism*. Prepared for the General Conference of the Congregational Churches of Maine and recommended by that body to the consideration of the churches. Portland: Hyde and Lord, 1848.

Gillet, Eliphalet. *Blessedness of the Pious Dead. A Sermon Preached in Winthrop, at the Interment of Mrs. Elizabeth Fillebrown, Consort of the Hon. Thomas Fillebrown, Who Departed Life October 23, 1817, Aged 46*. Hallowell: N. Cheever, 1817.

———. *A Sermon on Infant Baptism, Preached at Winthrop, November 4, 1804, at the Baptism of Rev. Mr. Belden's Child, to Which is Subjoined the Rev. Mr. Fisher's Hymn on Infant Dedication.* Hallowell: S. K. Gilman, 1820.

[Goodrich, Samuel G.] *Peter Parley's Common School History.* Philadelphia: Marshal, Williams and Butler, 1840.

———. *Peter Parley's Geography for Children. With Nine Maps and Seventy-five Engravings.* New York: F. J. Huntington, 1838.

———. *Peter Parley's Spelling Book with Engravings.* Philadelphia: Henry F. Anners, 1834.

Holmes, Ezekiel. Correspondence, 1845–47. In Aaron Young, Jr. Papers, Library of the American Philosophical Society.

———. *The Northern Shepherd, Being a Report of a Committee of the Kennebec County Agricultural Society, upon the Diseases and Management of Sheep.* Winthrop: William Noyes, 1835.

———. Papers, 1827–1909. In Special Collections of Fogler Library, University of Maine.

———. *Report of an Exploration and Survey of the Territory on the Aroostook River, during the Spring and Autumn of 1838.* Augusta: Smith and Robinson, 1839.

Howard Family Papers. 1838–1900. In possession of Marion Cobb, Winthrop.

Howard, Oakes. Justice Record Book, 1838–46. In possession of Marion Cobb, Winthrop.

Lee, Thomas J. *The First Book; or Spelling Lessons for Primary Schools.* Boston: Munroe and Francis, 1841.

———. *The Primary Class Book: A Selection of Easy Lessons in Reading, for the Younger Classes in Common Schools.* Hallowell: Glazier, Masters, and Co., 1827.

Lee, Thomas J., comp. *The National Class Book: A Selection of Exercises in Reading, for the Use of the Higher Classes in Common Schools.* Hallowell: Glazier, Masters, and Co., 1830.

Leeds Monthly Meeting of Friends. Men's Meeting Minutes. Vols. 1–3, 1813–52. In collections of Maine Historical Society.

———. Women's Meeting Minutes. Vols. 1–2, 1813–41. In collections of Maine Historical Society.

A Letter to the Rev. John Butler, Containing a Review of His "Friendly Letters to a Lady" Together with a General Outline of the Doctrine of the Freewill Baptists. By a Freewill Baptist. Limerick: Silas Curtis, 1832.

Liberty Standard. Hallowell, 1841–48.

The Life of George Washington; Maps and Subscribers' Names. Philadelphia: C. P. Wayne, 1807.

Litchfield Monthly Meeting of Friends. Book of Records: Births, Deaths, Marriages, Certificates, 1813–72. In collections of Maine Historical Society.

Little Family Papers. 1841–43. In the Little Family Collection, New York Public Library.

Lord, Daniel W. Correspondence, 1838. In Lord Collection, Maine Historical Society.

Lord, Thomas N. *An Address, Delivered at Winthrop, before the Sewing Circle and Ladies' Benevolent Society, September 20, 1833.* Winthrop: William Noyes, 1833.

———. "Centennial Address," *Centennial of the Congregational Church in Winthrop, Maine, September 4, 1876*. Portland: B. Thurston, 1876.

McKeen, Silas. *The Triumph of Christ's Enemies No Cause of Discouragement. A Sermon Delivered at Winthrop, June 21, 1830, on the Evening Previous to the Meeting of the General Conference of Maine*. Portland: Shirley, Hyde, and Co., 1830.

Maine Baptist Convention. *A Pamphlet Containing the Doings of the Late Baptist Convention, Holden at Winthrop, Maine, June 23, 1824, with an Appendix to the Question: Why God Employs Feeble Means to Produce Great Effects*. Waterville: William Hastings, 1824.

———. *Twenty-first Anniversary. Minutes of the Maine Baptist Convention, Held at East Winthrop, June 17, 1845*. Portland: Charles Day, 1845.

Maine Baptist Missionary Society. Minutes, 1805–44. In the Convention Library of the American Baptist Churches of Maine, Augusta.

Maine Evangelist. Lewiston, 1859.

Maine Farmer. Winthrop, 1833–43; Augusta, 1844–82.

Methodist Episcopal Church. *The Doctrines and Disciplines of the Methodist Episcopal Church*. New York, 1820–50.

Methodist Episcopal Church in Winthrop. Records and History of the Methodist Episcopal Church in Winthrop. Vol. 1, 1793–1875. In possession of the Winthrop Methodist Episcopal Church.

Murray, Lindley. *An Abridgement of Murray's English Grammar with an Appendix, Containing Exercises in Orthography, in Passing in Punctuation, and in Prosody. Designed for the Younger Classes of Learners*. 3d Hallowell ed. Hallowell: E. Goodale, 1815.

———. *English Grammar. Adapted to the Different Classes of Learners, with an Appendix Containing Rules and Observations, for Assisting the More Advanced Students to Write with Perspicuity and Accuracy*. 3d Hallowell ed. Hallowell: E. Goodale and S. K. Gilman, 1819.

———. *The English Reader; or Pieces in Prose and Poetry. Selected from the Best Writers Designed to Assist Young Persons to Read with Propriety and Effect; to Improve their Language and Sentiments; and to Inculcate Some of the Most Important Principles of Piety and Virtue. With a Few Preliminary Observations on the Principles of Good Reading*. Brunswick: J. Griffin, 1823.

"On the Subject of War and Peace." Address by unknown author delivered to a lyceum in Winthrop, 1844. In Charles M. Bailey Public Library.

Packard Family Papers. 1801–57. In collections of the Maine Historical Society.

Page, Robert, comp. Biographical sketches of members of the Bowdoin College Class of 1810 for a meeting of survivors in 1852. In Special Collections of Bowdoin College Library.

Parish, Elijah. *A Sermon Preached at the Ordination of the Rev. David Thurston, over the Church of Christ in Winthrop, February 18, 1807*. Augusta: Peter Edes, 1807.

Parlin, William H. *Reminiscences of East Winthrop*. Reprinted from the *Winthrop Banner*, 1882. East Winthrop: Banner Publishing Co., 1891.

Pope, Alexander. *An Essay on Man; In Four Epistles to H. St. John, Lord*

Bolingbroke. To Which Is Added, the Universal Prayer. Hallowell: S. K. Gilman, 1819.

Record of School District No. 7. 1837–77. In Charles M. Bailey Public Library.

Robbins, Benjamin. Account of the Death of Ann Orpha Robbins Thomas, September 10, 1857. In collections of Maine Historical Society.

———. Diary, 1810–16. 3 vols. In collections of Maine Historical Society.

Smith, John. *A Sermon, Delivered in Winthrop, June 23, 1830, before the Maine Missionary Society, at Their Twenty-third Anniversary.* Portland: Shirley, Hyde and Co., 1830.

Smith, Roswell C. *Practical and Mental Arithmetic, on a New Plan, in Which Mental Arithmetic Is Combined with the Use of the Slate; Containing a Complete System for All Practical Purposes, Being in Dollars and Cents. To Which Is Added, Practical System of Book-keeping.* Rev. ed. Hallowell: Glazier, Masters and Smith, 1843.

Southworth, Francis, and S. W. Davis. *Lives of Distinguished Shoemakers.* Portland: Thurston, 1849.

Stackpole, Everett S. *History of Winthrop, Maine with Genealogical Notes.* Auburn: Merrill and Webber, 1925.

State of Maine. Board of Education. *Fourth Report of the Board of Education of the State of Maine, 1850.* Augusta: William T. Johnson, 1850.

State of Maine. *Public Documents.* Augusta, 1820–50.

Tappan, Benjamin. *A Sermon Delivered in Winthrop, September 25, 1822, before the Kennebec Missionary Society, at Their First Annual Meeting.* Hallowell: Goodale, Glazier and Co., 1822.

Temple Lodge No. 25 of Winthrop. Papers, 1817–65. In possession of the Office of Grand Secretary, Maine Freemasons, Portland.

Thurston, Brown, comp. *Thurston Genealogies, 1635–1880.* Portland: B. Thurston, 1880.

Thurston, David. *An Address Delivered before the Kennebec Bible Society, at Their Annual Meeting, in Augusta, June 5, 1822.* Hallowell: Goodale, Glazier and Co., 1823.

———. *A Brief History of Winthrop from 1764 to October, 1855.* Portland: Brown Thurston, 1855.

———. *Causes of an Unsuccessful Ministry. A Sermon, Preached at the Installation of the Rev. Henry Sewall, over the Church and Society in Bethel (West Parish), January 20, 1819.* Hallowell: E. Goodale, 1819.

———. *A Discourse Preached in Winthrop, April 3, 1823: At the Annual Fast in Maine.* Hallowell: Goodale, Glazier and Co., 1823.

———. *Discourse Preached in Winthrop, April 12, 1821, at the Annual Fast in Maine.* Hallowell: Goodale, Glazier and Co., 1821.

———. *Letters from a Father to a Son, An Apprentice.* Compiled by Brown Thurston. Portland: Hezekiah Packard, 1858.

———. *A Sermon at the Funeral of Rev. Isaac Case Who Died at Readfield, November 3, 1852, in the Ninety-second Year of His Age.* Portland: Brown Thurston, 1852.

———. *A Sermon Delivered at Winthrop, April 7, 1825, at the Annual Fast in Maine.*

Augusta: Eaton and Severance, 1825.

———. *A Sermon Delivered before the Somerset Association for the Reformation of Morals at Their Annual Meeting in Norridgewock, February 17, 1819*. Hallowell: E. Goodale, 1819.

———. *A Sermon Delivered by David Thurston, Pastor of a Church in Winthrop, Maine, at the Third Annual Meeting of the American Missionary Association at Boston, Mass., September 25, 1849*. New York: American Missionary Association, 1849.

———. *A Sermon Delivered in Saco, June 26, 1816, before the Maine Missionary Society, at Their Ninth Annual Meeting*. Hallowell: N. Cheever, 1816.

———. *A Sermon Preached at the Ordination of the Rev. David Starret, over the Congregational Church and Society in Weld, September 26, 1821*. Hallowell: Goodale, Glazier and Co., 1821.

———. *A Sermon Preached, August 9, 1826, at the Ordination of the Rev. Stephen Thurston over the Congregational Church and Society in Prospect*. Hallowell: Glazier and Co., 1826.

———. *Sermon Preached, March 8, 1826, at the Ordination of the Rev. Joseph Underwood over the Congregational Church and Society in New Sharon*. Hallowell: Glazier and Co., 1826.

———. *A Sermon Preached, May 10, 1826, at the Ordination of the Rev. Josiah Tucker over the Congregational Church and Society in Madison*. Hallowell: Glazier and Co., 1826.

Transactions of the Agricultural Societies in the State of Maine for 1853. Augusta: William T. Johnson, 1854.

United States. Bureau of the Census. *Fourth Census of the United States, 1820: Population,* vol. 4; *Manufacturing* (for New England States).

———. *Fifth Census of the United States, 1830: Population,* vols. 7–10.

———. *Sixth Census of the United States, 1840: Population,* vol. 3.

———. *Seventh Census of the United States, 1850: Population,* vol. 8; *Agriculture,* vol. 129; *Industry,* vol. 132; *Social Statistics,* vol. 133. Original Schedules in Maine State Archives.

United States. Department of the Treasury. *Documents Relative to the Manufactures in the United States Collected and Transmitted to the House of Representatives in Compliance with a Resolution of January 19, 1832 by the Secretary of the Treasury*. Vol. 1. Washington: Duff Green, 1833.

United States. Patent Office. Records, 1834–44.

Vaughan Family Papers. N.d. In Library of the American Philosophical Society.

Whitney, George C. Day Book, 1828–38. In Charles M. Bailey Public Library, Winthrop.

Winthrop Emulator. Winthrop, 1845–46. In Charles M. Bailey Public Library, Winthrop.

Winthrop Moral, Tract and Sabbath School Society. Constitution. N.d. In collections of Maine Historical Society.

Winthrop Social Library. *By-laws of the Social Library in Winthrop; Established February 10, 1823; with a Catalogue of Books in the Library*. Hallowell: Glazier, Masters and Co., 1829.

Winthrop Town Records. Vols. 3–5, 1815–58. In possession of the town of Winthrop.

Wood, Samuel. "History of Temple Lodge No. 25 from 1817 to 1860." Documentary history of the lodge prepared in 1862. In possession of the Office of Grand Secretary, Maine Freemasons, Portland.

Zion's Advocate and Eastern Baptist. Portland, 1841–45.

C. Secondary Historical Sources.

An Account of the Centennial Celebration at Winthrop, Maine, May 20, 1871, Embracing the Historic Address and Poem in Full. Augusta: Sprague, Owen and Nash, 1871.

Adams, Henry. *History of the United States during the Administrations of Jefferson and Madison*. Abr. with an introduction by George Dangerfield and Otey M. Scruggs. Englewood Cliffs: Prentice-Hall, 1963.

Adams, Sarah B. *Reminiscences of the Churches and Pastors of Kennebec County*. Paper read at the Kennebec Conference in Waterville, October 17, 1894. Hallowell: Register Job Print, 1894.

Allen, James. "Catholics in Maine: A Social Geography." Ph.D. dissertation, Syracuse University, 1970.

Allen, Stephen, and W. H. Pilsbury. *History of Methodism in Maine, 1793–1886*. Augusta: Charles E. Nash, 1887.

American Antislavery Society. *Proceedings of the American Antislavery Society at its Third Decade*. New York: American Antislavery Society, 1864.

American Historical Association. *Report of the American Historical Association for the Year 1908*. 2 vols. Washington: Government Printing Office, 1909.

Bangor Public Library, comp. *Bibliography of the State of Maine Compiled in the Bangor Public Library, Bangor, Maine*. Boston: G. K. Hall, 1962.

Banks, Ronald F. *Maine Becomes a State: The Movement to Separate Maine from Massachusetts, 1785–1820*. Middletown, Conn.: Wesleyan University Press, 1970.

Beedy, Helen Coffin. *Mothers of Maine*. Portland: The Thurston Print, 1895.

Benson, Lee. *The Concept of Jacksonian Democracy: New York as a Test Case*. New York: Atheneum, 1965.

Berthoff, Rowland T. *An Unsettled People: Social Order and Disorder in American History*. New York: Harper and Row, 1971.

Biographical Encyclopedia of Maine of the Nineteenth Century. Boston: Metropolitan, 1885.

Boardman, Samuel L. *Agricultural Bibliography of Maine: Biographical Sketches of Maine Writers on Agriculture, with a Catalogue of Their Works; and an Index to the Volumes on the Agriculture of Maine, from 1850 to 1892*. Augusta: the author, 1893.

———. *The Agriculture and Industry of the County of Kennebec, Maine, with Notes upon its History and Natural History*. Augusta: Kennebec Journal, 1867.

———. *A General Index to the Principal Articles and Leading Subjects in the Volumes on the Agriculture of Maine, from 1850 to 1875*. Augusta: the author, 1876.

Boorstin, Daniel J. *The Americans: The National Experience*. New York: Random House, 1965.

Bowker, Richard R., comp. *State Publications: A Provisional List of the Official Publications of the Several States of the United States from Their Organization.* New York: Publishers Weekly, 1908.

Buker, Margaret J. "The Irish in Lewiston, Maine: A Search for Security on the Urban Frontier, 1850–1880." Maine Academic Historians, Proceedings of the meeting of 1972. *Maine Historical Quarterly* 13 (1973): 3–25.

Burrage, Henry S. *History of the Baptists in Maine.* Portland: Marks Printing House, 1904.

Cathcart, William, ed. *The Baptist Encyclopedia.* Philadelphia: Louis H. Everts, 1881.

Cave, Alfred A. *Jacksonian Democracy and the Historians.* University of Florida Monographs: Social Sciences no. 22. Gainsville: University of Florida Press, 1964.

Chadbourne, Walter W. *A History of Banking in Maine, 1799–1830.* University of Maine Studies, second series, no. 37. Orono: University of Maine Press, 1936.

Chase, Edward E. *Maine Railroads: A History of the Development of the Maine Railroad System.* Portland: A. J. Huston, 1926.

Clark, Calvin M. *American Slavery and Maine Congregationalists: A Chapter in the History of the Development of Anti-Slavery Sentiment in the Protestant Churches of the North.* Bangor: the author, 1940.

———. *History of the Bangor Theological Seminary.* Boston: Pilgrim Press, 1916.

———. *History of the Congregational Churches in Maine.* Vol. 1. Portland: Southworth Press, 1926. Vol. 2. Portland: Congregational Conference of Maine, 1935.

Clark, Charles E., comp. *Maine during the Colonial Period: A Bibliographic Guide.* Portland: Maine Historical Society, 1974.

Cleaveland, Nehemiah. *History of Bowdoin College with Biographical Sketches of Its Graduates from 1806 to 1879, Inclusive.* Edited and completed by Alpheus S. Packard. Boston: James Ripley Osgood, 1882.

Clubb, Henry S. *The Maine Liquor Law: Its Origin, History, and Results, Including a Life of Hon. Neal Dow.* New York: Fowler and Wells, 1856.

Cowan, Frank I., comp. *Index to the Private and Special Laws Enacted by the Legislatures of the State of Maine from 1820 to 1944, Inclusive.* Issued as a supplement to the Biennial Report of the Attorney General. Augusta: State of Maine, 1944.

Dangerfield, George. *The Awakening of American Nationalism, 1815–1828.* New York: Harper and Row, 1965.

Day, Clarence A. *Ezekiel Holmes, Father of Maine Agriculture.* University of Maine Studies, second series, no. 86. Orono: University of Maine Press, 1968.

———. *A History of Maine Agriculture, 1604–1860.* University of Maine Studies, second series, no. 68. Orono: University of Maine Press, 1954.

de Tocqueville, Alexis. *Democracy in America.* 2 vols. Introduction by John Stuart Mill. Translated by Henry Reeve. New York: Schocken Books, 1967.

Fairbanks, Lorenzo S. *Genealogy of the Fairbanks Family in America, 1633–1897.* Boston: the author, 1897.

Fasset, Frederick G., Jr. *A History of Newspapers in the District of Maine, 1785–1820.* University of Maine Studies, second series, no. 25. Orono: University of Maine Press, 1932.

Fessenden, Samuel C. *The History of the Antislavery Cause in State and Nation.* Portland: Brown Thurston, 1886.

Fillebrown, Charles B. *The Family of Rev. John Butler.* Corrected ed. Printed for private circulation, 1908.

Finley, Raymond S. *The History of Secondary Education in Kennebec County in Maine.* University of Maine Studies, second series, no. 54. Orono: University of Maine Press, 1941.

Genealogical Society of the Church of Latter Day Saints. "Winthrop Vital Records, State of Maine." Filmed by the Genealogical Society, Salt Lake City, Utah, at Winthrop, Maine, July 2, 1953. Available in the Maine State Archives, Augusta.

Graham, Fay M. "Maine Baptists and the Antislavery Movement, 1830–1850." M.A. thesis, University of Maine, 1962.

Greenleaf, Jonathan. *Sketches of the Ecclesiastical History of the State of Maine, from the Earliest Settlement to the Present Time.* Portsmouth: Harrison Gray, 1821.

Greenleaf, Moses. *Statistical View of the District of Maine.* Boston: Cumming and Hillard, 1816.

Hall, Drew B., comp. "Maine Local History." *New York State Library Bulletin* 2 (1901): 773–920.

Hasse, Adelaide R., comp. *Index of Economic Material in Documents of the United States, Maine, 1820–1904.* Carnegie Institution of Washington, publication no. 85. Baltimore: Carnegie Institution, 1907.

Hatch, Louis C. *Maine: A History.* New York: American Historical Association, 1919.

Hazelton, Louise, comp. *Special Subject Resources in Maine, 1972.* Augusta: Maine State Library, 1972.

Kingsbury, Henry D., and Simeon L. Deyo, eds. *Illustrated History of Kennebec County, Maine, 1799–1892.* 2 vols. New York: H. W. Blake, 1892.

Little, George T., comp. *Genealogical and Family History of the State of Maine.* 4 vols. New York: Lewis Historical Pub. Co., 1909.

McLean, Ralph E. "Maine and Jackson." M. A. thesis, University of Maine, 1955.

McMurtie, Douglas C. *Maine Imprints, 1792–1820.* An open letter to R. Webb Noyes, Esq. Chicago: the author, 1935.

Maine Baptist Annual. 1857–1901.

Maine Historical Records Survey, Works Projects Administration. *Directory of Churches and Religious Organizations in Maine.* Portland: Maine Historical Records Survey Projects, 1940.

Malley, Dorothy S. "Notes on Floorcloths in New England." *Antiques* 94 (1968): 101–3.

Massachusetts Historical Records Survey, Works Projects Administration, comp. *American Portrait Inventory, American Portraits (1645–1850) Found in the State of Maine.* Preliminary vol. Boston: Historical Records Survey, 1941.

May, John W. *Inside the Bar and Other Occasional Poems.* Portland: Hoyt, Fogg and Donham, 1884.

Methodist Episcopal Church. *Annual Conference Minutes.* Maine, Providence, New York East, and New England Southern Conferences, 1867–1900.

Meyers, Marvin. *The Jacksonian Persuasion: Politics and Belief.* Stanford: Stanford University Press, 1969.

Miller, H. Clair. "History of Temple Lodge No. 25, Order of Free and Accepted Masons." Paper read at their 150th anniversary, 1967. In possession of the Office of the Grand Secretary, Maine Freemasons, Portland.

Millet, Joshua. *A History of the Baptists in Maine, Together with Brief Notices of Societies and Institutions and a Dictionary of the Labors of Each Minister.* Portland: Charles Day, 1845.

Mitchell, Nahum. *History of the Early Settlement of Bridgewater, in Plymouth County, Massachusetts, Including an Extensive Family Register.* Reprint of 1840 edition. Bridgewater: Henry T. Pratt, 1897.

Noyes, Reginald W. *A Bibliography of Maine Imprints to 1820.* Stonington: the author, 1930.

Perham, Harold C. "Reuben Wing, Senior of 'Old Winthrop,' Old Livermore's Town, Wayne and Monmouth, Maine and His Two Wives, Priscilla and Sally." Typescript, 1968. In Charles M. Bailey Public Library, Winthrop.

Pessen, Edward. *Jacksonian America: Society, Personality and Politics.* Homewood, Ill.: Dorsey, 1969.

Ring, Elizabeth, comp. *Maine Bibliographies: A Bibliographic Guide.* Portland: Maine Historical Society, 1973.

Schlesinger, Arthur M., Jr. *The Age of Jackson.* Boston: Little, Brown and Co., 1945.

Schriver, Edward O. *Go Free: The Antislavery Impulse in Maine, 1833–1855.* University of Maine Studies, no. 91. Orono: University of Maine Press, 1970.

Senior, Richard C. "New England Congregationalists and the Antislavery Movement." Ph.D. dissertation, Yale University, 1954.

Smith, Edgar C. *Maps of the State of Maine: A Bibliography of the Maps of the State of Maine.* Bangor: C. H. Glass, 1903.

Snow, Charles A. *The History of the Development of Public School Supervision in the State of Maine.* University of Maine Studies, second series, no. 46. Orono: University of Maine Press, 1939.

Stewart, I. D. *The History of the Freewill Baptists for Half a Century.* Vol. 1, *From the Year 1780 to 1830.* Dover: Freewill Baptist, 1862.

Sturtevant, Lawrence M. "Ezekiel Holmes and His Influence, 1801–1865." 2 vols. M.A. thesis, University of Maine at Orono, 1948.

Sullivan, James. *The History of the District of Maine, Illustrated by a New Correct Map of the District.* Boston: I. Thomas and E. T. Andrews, 1795.

Sydnor, Charles S. *The Development of Southern Sectionalism, 1819–1848.* Baton Rouge: Louisiana State University, 1968.

Talbot, Archie Lee. "Robbins Family, Dedham and Walpole, Mass., Winthrop and Phillips, Maine." *The Dedham Historical Register* 8 (1897): 106–22.

———. "Shaw Family. Middleborough, Mass.; Winthrop, Maine." *The New England Historical and Genealogical Register* 52 (1897): 191–95.

Thernstrom, Stephen. *Poverty and Progress: Social Mobility in a Nineteenth Century City.* New York: Atheneum, 1970.

Thernstrom, Stephen, and Richard Sennett, eds. *Nineteenth Century Cities: Essays in the New Urban History.* New Haven: Yale University Press, 1970.

Thurston, Brown, comp. *Thurston Genealogies, 1635–1892.* 2d ed. Portland: Brown Thurston, 1892.

Thurston, Samuel. "Musical Reminiscences of Seventy-five Years." Paper read before the Kotzschmar Club, 1911. In Charles M. Bailey Public Library, Winthrop.

Thurston, Stephen. *A Discourse on the Erection of a Marble Tablet in the Congregational Church of Winthrop, April 2, 1871, in Memory of Rev. David Thurston, Former Pastor of the Church.* Portland: B. Thurston, 1871.

True, Nathaniel T. "Biographical Sketch of Ezekiel Holmes, M.D." *Agriculture of Maine.* Tenth Annual Report of the Maine Board of Agriculture: 1865, pp. 207–26. Augusta: Stevens and Sayward, 1865.

Turner, Frederick Jackson. *Frontier and Section: Selected Essays of Frederick Jackson Turner.* Introduction by Ray Allen Billington. Englewood Cliffs: Prentice-Hall, 1961.

United States. Bureau of the Census. *Heads of Families at the First Census of the United States Taken in the Year 1790, Maine.* Baltimore: Genealogical Pub. Co., 1966.

Van Deusen, Glyndon G. *The Jacksonian Era, 1828–1848.* New York: Harper and Row, 1963.

Ward, John W. *Andrew Jackson —Symbol for an Age.* New York: Oxford University Press, 1966.

Wescott, Richard R. "A History of Maine Politics, 1840–1856: The Formation of the Republican Party." Ph.D. dissertation, University of Maine, 1966.

Whiting, Mabel R. "Old Inns and Taverns of Winthrop." Illustrated typescript prepared for the Patience Stanley Chapter of the Daughters of the American Revolution. In Maine State Library.

———. "Pagent of East Winthrop Presented July 26, 1932." Typescript, 1932. In Maine State Library.

Whiting, Mabel R., comp. "Cemeteries of Winthrop, Maine." Typescript, 1930. In Maine State Library.

Whittier, Charles C. "Winthrop, Maine and Her Soldiers of the American Revolution: A Complete List of Biographical Sketches." Reprinted from the *Eastern Argus,* Portland, May, June, and July, 1914. In Maine State Library.

Williams, Jean Gannett. History of *Maine Farmer* in letter to Manley Breck, November 14, 1960. In Portland Press Herald Library.

Williamson, William D. *A History of the State of Maine, from its First Discovery, A.D. 1602, to the Separation, A.D. 1820, Inclusive.* 2 vols. Hallowell: Glazier, Masters and Co., 1832.

Willis, William A. *A Descriptive Catalogue of Books and Pamphlets Relating to the History and Statistics of Maine or Portions of It.* Monisania: H. E. Dawson, 1874.

———. *History of the Law, the Courts, and the Lawyers of Maine.* Portland: Bailey and Noyes, 1863.

Wing, Henry A. *Maine's War upon the Liquor Traffic: A Series of Historical Articles.* Portland: Portland Evening Express, 1909.

Winthrop Banner. Winthrop, 1889–93.

Winthrop Budget. Winthrop, 1881–1918.

Winthrop Bulletin. Winthrop, 1867–68.

Winthrop Edition, *Turf, Farm, and Home.* Waterville, June 3, 1908.

Winthrop Gazette. Winthrop, 1866–67.

Winthrop Methodist Church. *One Hundred Fifty Years of History, 1811–1961*. Souvenir pamphlet. Winthrop: Winthrop Methodist Church, 1961.

Winthrop Weekly Budget. Winthrop, 1882.

"Winthrop's 175th Anniversary." A scrapbook collection of newspaper clippings appearing in 1946. In Maine State Library.

Wood, Richard G. "A Bibliography of Travel in Maine, 1783–1861." *New England Quarterly* 6 (1933): 426–39.

York, Robert M., comp. "A Bibliography of Religious History (Maine)." *Maine Historical Society Newsletter*, vol. 4, no. 3 (February 1965).

Index